CFEngine 3

Beginner's Guide

A step-by-step guide to setting up CFEngine and fully automating the configuration and management of your laptop, desktop, server, or mainframe

Rajneesh

[PACKT] PUBLISHING
open source
community experience distilled

BIRMINGHAM - MUMBAI

CFEngine 3

Beginner's Guide

First published: October 2011

Production Reference: 1171011

Published by Packt Publishing Ltd.
Livery Place
35 Livery Street
Birmingham B3 2PB, UK.

ISBN 978-1-84951-498-9

www.packtpub.com

Cover Image by Asher Wishkerman (a.wishkerman@mpic.de)

Credits

Author
Rajneesh

Reviewers
Nick Anderson
Clifford Pearson

Acquisition Editor
Tarun Singh

Development Editor
Neha Mallik

Technical Editor
Aaron Rosario

Project Coordinator
Kushal Bhardwaj

Proofreaders
Aaron Nash
Stephen Silk

Indexer
Tejal Daruwale

Graphics
Valentina Joseph D'silva

Production Coordinator
Melwyn D'sa

Cover Work
Melwyn D'sa

About the Author

Rajneesh works as a Senior Manager in Technical Operations at Info Edge India Ltd. He has more than seven years of experience in the IT industry. He has worked for a number of successful web hosting companies and currently leads the Technical Operations team for a few of the most visited sites in India. He studied Electronics Engineering at Shivaji University and holds a Post Graduate Diploma in Systems and Database Administration. His areas of expertise include Linux administration, configuration management, high availability systems and infrastructure architecture design. He is an avid CFEngine user and writes code to automate a lot of data center and server management tasks. In his spare time he enjoys photography.

I did not write this book on an island; it is a result of contributions from my family, colleagues, and the editorial team at various levels.

First of all, I would like to thank all of the editors who worked long and hard to make this a better and more enjoyable book. I would particularly like to thank Mary Nadar who roped me into this. I had the wonderful pleasure of working with Tarun Singh, the acquisition editor and Sneha Harkut, the project coordinator. Special thanks to the copy editors and technical editors. Their insights and corrections transformed the book to what it is.

Love and respect to Bhawna, my wife, who made sure that I got my peaceful corner to write, delicious food and fresh coffee after a hectic day or at night. Her support helped me think straight between all the hoopla.

Finally, thank you to my parents, for everything.

About the Reviewers

Nick Anderson has been a SysAdmin since 2001. He specializes in open source solutions and has has worked on traditional infrastructure, e-commerce, and HPC. Nick's core interests include configuration management, virtualization, and monitoring. He is also active in the LOPSA Mentorship Program.

Nick has been published in Linux Pro Magazine (*Right-Sizing RAID, Linux Pro Magazine, February 1, 2011*) and maintains a blog at `http://www.cmdln.org`.

Clifford Pearson is a Senior UNIX Systems Engineer at UC Santa Cruz. He has managed most types of computing and storage infrastructure within the university setting, as well as high-availability web and database servers for independent projects. Currently his focus is on Enterprise Architecture and large-scale UNIX system deployment. He particularly enjoys bringing diverse teams together to design and deliver innovative IT services.

www.PacktPub.com

Support files, eBooks, discount offers and more

You might want to visit `www.PacktPub.com` for support files and downloads related to your book.

Did you know that Packt offers eBook versions of every book published, with PDF and ePub files available? You can upgrade to the eBook version at `www.PacktPub.com` and as a print book customer, you are entitled to a discount on the eBook copy. Get in touch with us at `service@packtpub.com` for more details.

At `www.PacktPub.com`, you can also read a collection of free technical articles, sign up for a range of free newsletters and receive exclusive discounts and offers on Packt books and eBooks.

PACKTLiB®

`http://PacktLib.PacktPub.com`

Do you need instant solutions to your IT questions? PacktLib is Packt's online digital book library. Here, you can access, read and search across Packt's entire library of books.

Why Subscribe?

- Fully searchable across every book published by Packt
- Copy and paste, print and bookmark content
- On demand and accessible via web browser

Free Access for Packt account holders

If you have an account with Packt at `www.PacktPub.com`, you can use this to access PacktLib today and view nine entirely free books. Simply use your login credentials for immediate access.

For Sidhak, who creates all the magic.

Table of Contents

Preface

This book starts off with step-by-step instructions for installing and configuring the CFEngine server and clients, and then moves on to configuring systems using CFEngine scripts. The author then walks you through the policy decision flow as well as conducting system and security audits.

This is followed by detailed discussions through various examples on how you can use CFEngine to configure systems, users, networks, databases, web servers, et al. Adding to this, the book also provides a list of best practices, CFEngine policy decision flow, and how you may use the CFEngine Orion Cloud Pack. By the end of the book you should be able to write policies to automate your complex data centre tasks.

What this book covers

Chapter 1, Getting Started with CFEngine: The first chapter, as the name suggests, lets you get started with CFEngine. The chapter underlines how CFEngine may be of great help to system administrators, configuration managers, and all those who need to manage a huge number of nodes. It gives a step-by-step procedure for installing CFEngine and testing the installation. This is followed by a brief introduction to various CFEngine components. The chapter consists of some very simple examples to give you a taste of the action in store.

Chapter 2, Configuring Systems with CFEngine: The chapter deals with the architecture of CFEngine, in detail. It lists the various components of CFEngine and their functions. Step-by-step installation and configuration of CFEngine server and clients are the highlights of this chapter. In addition to this, the chapter has a number of examples which may be used to automate various system administration tasks.

Chapter 3, System Audit with CFEngine: The chapter is dedicated to auditing your systems. In this chapter we get to see a number of CFEngine "common" and "server" control promises and their usage. It also has real life, easy to understand examples proving how CFEngine may be used as a "tripwire".

Chapter 4, Scheduling Tasks with CFEngine: The chapter deals with a few more types of promises such as monitor, executor, and reporter control promises. A very important concept of CFEngine "classes" is introduced, and how this concept of "classes" may be used to execute a sequence of jobs is explained with real life, easy to understand examples, in this chapter. We will also see how CFEngine may be used as a "scheduler".

Chapter 5, Security Audit with CFEngine: The chapter outlines how CFEngine may be used to maintain a "secure" system state. It deals with the four basic concepts of security which are authorization, authentication, data protection, and application configuration. It is full of examples which showcase the prowess of CFEngine. For example, how CFEngine may be used to automate addition of rules to IPtables for access control.

Chapter 6, Logging and Reporting with CFEngine: The chapter deals with a few other aspects of CFEngine such as logging, reporting, and monitoring. CFEngine provides a very powerful logging and reporting mechanism which may be used to keep a tab on the complete system state. How these inbuilt mechanisms may be used to generate custom reports is explained with an easy to understand example.

Chapter 7, Workflows: As the name suggests, this chapter outlines how the CFEngine framework may be used to perform more complex, inter-related tasks. It also introduces the very important concept of templates in CFEngine which helps in writing generic templates which may be used for heterogeneous systems. Another extremely important concept of "Knowledge Maps" has been introduced which may be used to automate the creation and maintenance of a knowledgebase.

Chapter 8, Advanced Functions and Variables: CFEngine is a framework and it has its own very powerful set of special functions and variables. These may be used globally, they help in reducing the number of lines of promises that need to be written, and help to improve CFEngine's performance. This chapter outlines the syntax and usage of various important special functions and variables.

Chapter 9, CFEngine Best Practices: In organizations, people work in teams and hence more than one associate may be working on the CFEngine framework at any point in time. There are some 'best practices' to be followed in order to ensure that promises are written methodically, can be easily deciphered by other team members, and that they are crisp and optimal. The chapter includes a few basic considerations for writing promises and general do's and don'ts. The chapter also explains the implementation of a version control system for the promises files.

Appendix A, CFEngine Cloud Pack—Orion: The CFEngine Orion Cloud Pack is the latest offering from CFEngine which may be used to configure and maintain instances in the cloud. The chapter deals with the basic contents of the Orion Cloud Pack and a few handy hacks. It also lists a few advantages of using the Orion Cloud Pack with the enterprise CFEngine Nova.

Appendix B, Important Control Promises: The appendix describes the syntax of various CFEngine control promises. The syntax is followed by a simple example which shows the usage of the control promise. In this way, the chapter is handy when one is looking for specific promises to be used for a task or in a workflow.

Appendix C, Important Functions and Variables: CFEngine is a framework and provides inbuilt functions and variables for specific tasks. This chapter gives you an insight to these special functions and variables. The description of these special functions and variables is followed by simple examples showing their usage.

Appendix D, Functions by Usage: This appendix lists important functions by their usage. It includes functions which read strings, files, environments, classes and data. In addition, the chapter also lists functions which compare variables. These functions are frequently used while writing promises.

Who this book is for

If you are a System Administrator or Configuration Manager with a growing infrastructure and if you are looking for a dependable tool to manage your infrastructure, then this book is for you. If your infrastructure is already large with hundreds and thousands of nodes and you are looking for a secure, versatile and stable configuration management tool, you will still find this book handy. You don't need any prior experience with CFEngine to follow this book.

Conventions

In this book, you will find several headings appearing frequently.

To give clear instructions of how to complete a procedure or task, we use:

Time for action – heading

1. Action 1
2. Action 2
3. Action 3

Instructions often need some extra explanation so that they make sense, so they are followed with.

What just happened?

This heading explains the working of tasks or instructions that you have just completed.

You will also find some other learning aids in the book, including:

Pop quiz – heading

These are short multiple choice questions intended to help you test your own understanding.

Have a go hero – heading

These set practical challenges and give you ideas for experimenting with what you have learned.

You will also find a number of styles of text that distinguish between different kinds of information. Here are some examples of these styles, and an explanation of their meaning.

Code words in text are shown as follows: "We can include other contexts through the use of the `include` directive."

A block of code is set as follows:

```
body server control {
    skipverify          => { "172.16.3.*" };
    allowconnects       => { "172.16.3.*" };
    allowallconnects    => { "172.16.3.*" };
    logallconnections   => "true";
    bindtointerface     => "172.16.3.113";
    cfruncommand        => "$(sys.workdir)/bin/cf-agent";
    allowusers          => { "root" };
}
```

When we wish to draw your attention to a particular part of a code block, the relevant lines or items are set in bold:

```
body server control {
    skipverify          => { "172.16.3.*" };
    allowconnects       => { "172.16.3.*" };
    allowallconnects    => { "172.16.3.*" };
    logallconnections   => "true";
    bindtointerface     => "172.16.3.113";
    cfruncommand        => "$(sys.workdir)/bin/cf-agent";
    allowusers          => { "root" };
}
```

Any command-line input or output is written as follows:

```
root@my1.system.com# /usr/local/sbin/cf-key
```

New terms and **important words** are shown in bold. Words that you see on the screen, in menus or dialog boxes for example, appear in the text like this: "clicking the **Next** button moves you to the next screen".

> Warnings or important notes appear in a box like this.

> Tips and tricks appear like this.

Reader feedback

Feedback from our readers is always welcome. Let us know what you think about this book—what you liked or may have disliked. Reader feedback is important for us to develop titles that you really get the most out of.

To send us general feedback, simply send an e-mail to `feedback@packtpub.com`, and mention the book title via the subject of your message.

If there is a book that you need and would like to see us publish, please send us a note in the **SUGGEST A TITLE** form on `www.packtpub.com` or e-mail `suggest@packtpub.com`.

If there is a topic that you have expertise in and you are interested in either writing or contributing to a book, see our author guide on `www.packtpub.com/authors`.

Customer support

Now that you are the proud owner of a Packt book, we have a number of things to help you to get the most from your purchase.

Downloading the example code

You can download the example code files for all Packt books you have purchased from your account at `http://www.PacktPub.com`. If you purchased this book elsewhere, you can visit `http://www.PacktPub.com/support` and register to have the files e-mailed directly to you.

Errata

Although we have taken every care to ensure the accuracy of our content, mistakes do happen. If you find a mistake in one of our books—maybe a mistake in the text or the code—we would be grateful if you would report this to us. By doing so, you can save other readers from frustration and help us improve subsequent versions of this book. If you find any errata, please report them by visiting `http://www.packtpub.com/support`, selecting your book, clicking on the **errata submission form** link, and entering the details of your errata. Once your errata are verified, your submission will be accepted and the errata will be uploaded to our website, or added to any list of existing errata, under the Errata section of that title. Any existing errata can be viewed by selecting your title from `http://www.packtpub.com/support`.

Piracy

Piracy of copyright material on the Internet is an ongoing problem across all media. At Packt, we take the protection of our copyright and licenses very seriously. If you come across any illegal copies of our works, in any form, on the Internet, please provide us with the location address or website name immediately so that we can pursue a remedy.

Please contact us at `copyright@packtpub.com` with a link to the suspected pirated material.

We appreciate your help in protecting our authors, and our ability to bring you valuable content.

Questions

You can contact us at `questions@packtpub.com` if you are having a problem with any aspect of the book, and we will do our best to address it.

1

Getting Started with CFEngine

> *CFEngine is an autonomous agent and middle to high level policy language and agent for building expert systems to administrate and configure large computer networks.*
>
> —`www.cfengine.org`

The dilemma of any system administrator or data center operations group is how to manage the changes on the huge number of network entities they are managing, and how to maintain the state of similar groups of devices. This is where CFEngine comes into the picture. CFEngine is a scalable configuration-management tool. It is designed to take care of the complete system lifecycle management in any environment. It does not need reliable infrastructure; it uses very few resources and has very few software dependencies. This lack of software dependencies translates into CFEngine taking care of a heterogeneous or a homogeneous network in a breeze. In short, CFEngine is meant to make our lives easy!

Let's see what we are going to learn in this chapter:

- Why CFEngine?
- CFEngine requirements
- Installing CFEngine
- Various CFEngine components
- Writing the first promise

Why CFEngine?

With the advent of Web 2.0, more and more feature-rich applications are being developed, which has resulted in a huge demand for IT infrastructure. These applications need much more resources when compared to applications developed in the last decade. To serve these applications the data center IT infrastructure demand has grown manifolds which in turn have resulted in longer maintenance cycles of the infrastructure. Apart from maintenance cycles, security, compliance, monitoring, and patch management are a few of the other factors that put a huge pressure on the operations team.

Imagine the time it would take to just install a piece of software on hundreds of machines if we do it manually. Installing software on a single machine may be a 10 minute job but installing the same software on hundreds or thousands of machines may take months. Hence, the need for a configuration management tool which may do the same task on hundreds and thousands of machines on its own.

CFEngine is one such tool, written by Mark Burgess from Oslo University, which may complete the task(s) on as many number of servers as we want while we enjoy our coffee. As the name suggests, CFEngine is a configuration engine. It has a rich language and policy framework which may be used to monitor, maintain, and automate various system administration tasks.

CFEngine is based on the **theory of promises**. It is not a simple deployment tool that can take care of deployments or rolling them back. With CFEngine we can revise the promises in such a way so that the state of the system converges to a pre-defined 'ideal' system state.

CFEngine has been under development for years and came out with a major release of version 3 in 2010. There are a lot of changes which have been made to the original code but the basic philosophy remains the same. The major features of CFEngine 3 are as follows:

- Operating system independent language.
- All the components of CFEngine are configurable. The configuration for all components is centralized. The advantage is we do not need to maintain separate input files for servers and agents. A single configuration file may contain configurations for all parts of the system.
- Centralized policy server.
- CFEngine is decentralized in order to allow the agent to run autonomously. This allows for repairs when the policy host is unavailable. The policy host is merely a file server-agent based action where each node is responsible for itself.
- Granular access control allows role-based access control for remote activation of special promises.

- Policies, better known as promises in the CFEngine framework, are now bundled. So we have the flexibility of bundling promises into appropriately named promise bundles.
- Powerful pattern matching and expression features simplify promises. This allows consistent promises to be made from a whole set of objects according to a programmed pattern.
- Optional use of PCRE libraries for text matching.
- Improved array and list handling.
- Improved generic package management.

The following diagram shows a few things that CFEngine can take care of for us to make our lives easier:

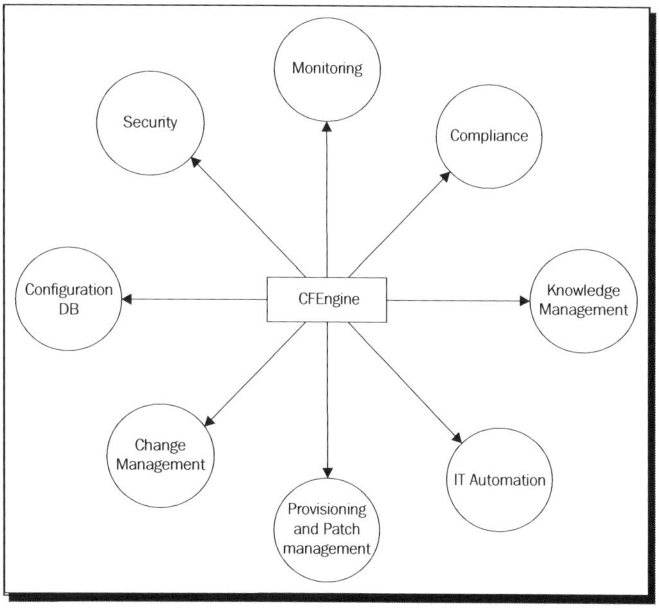

Installing CFEngine

Let's start with the installation. For installing CFEngine the following packages are required:

- **Openssl**: Open Source Secure Socket layer for encryption. The package can be downloaded from `http://www.openssl.org`.
- **Berkeley DB**: Its flat file light weight database system. The package can be downloaded from `http://www.oracle.com/technology/products/berkeley-db/index.html`.

- **Tokyocabinet DB**: May be used in place of Berkeley DB.

In addition to the above packages the following packages are strongly recommended:

- **PCRE** (Perl Compatible Regular Expression): This package can be downloaded from `http://www.pcre.org`.
- **OpenLDAP**: Client libraries for MySQL or PostgresSQL.

If you are trying to compile CFEngine from source the following packages are required to build the environment for compilation:

- **Bison**: This is a GNU parse generator which can be downloaded from `http://ftp.gnu.org/gnu/bison/`.
- **Flex**: Fast lexical analyzer is used for recognizing lexical patterns in text. It can be downloaded from `http://flex.sourceforge.net/#downloads`.

We can download the latest stable version of CFEngine from `http://www.cfengine.org/tarballs/download.php?file=cfengine-3.x.x.tar.gz`. The latest stable version of CFEngine available at the time of writing this book is 3.1.5.

The following commands install CFEngine on the server:

```
$ tar zxf cfengine-3.x.x.tar.gz
$ cd cfengine-3.x.x
$ ./configure
$ make
$ sudo make install
```

Let's take a look at various installed components of CFEngine:

- **cf-agent**: The Cfengine agent connects to a list of running instances of the `cf-serverd` service. The agent allows a user to forego the usual scheduling interval for the agent and activate `cf-agent` on a remote host. Additionally, a user can send additional classes to be defined on the remote host. Two kinds of classes may be sent: classes to decide on which hosts the agent will be started, and classes that the user requests the agent should define on execution. The latter type is regulated by `cf-serverd` role-based access control.
- **cf-execd**: The executor daemon is a scheduler and wrapper for execution of `cf-agent`. It collects the output of the agent and can e-mail it to a specified address. It can display the start time of executions across the network and work as a class-based clock for scheduling. If we execute the `cf-execd` binary without any arguments, it will go to the background and execute `cf-agent` every five

minutes, which is the default time, unless we have specified a different value in `promises.cf`. It may also send a mail if an e-mail address is configured in `promises.cf` and if the SMTP service is running on the system.

- **cf-know**: This is the knowledge modeling agent responsible for building and analyzing a semantic knowledge network.
- **cf-monitord**: The monitoring agent is a machine-learning, sampling daemon which learns the normal state of the current host and classifies new observations in terms of the patterns formed by previous ones. The data are made available to and read by `cf-agent` for classification of responses to anomalous states. The information about distributions can also be stored. The following switch may be used for histograms:

  ```
  --histograms, -H Store information about histograms/
  distributions.
  ```

- **cf-promises**: Promise validator used to verify that the promises used by other components of CFEngine are syntactically valid. A report about the configuration can also be generated using the `-r` switch.
- **cf-runagent**: Remote run agent used to run `cf-agent` on remote machines.
- **cf-serverd**: The server daemon provides two services—it acts as a file server for remote file copying and it allows an authorized `cf-runagent` to start a `cf-agent` process and set certain additional classes with role based access control. The server daemon starts at the default port 5308.
- **cf-report**: A self-knowledge extractor, which takes data stored in CFEngine's embedded databases and converts them to human readable form. The reporting agent is a merger between the older CFEngine programs cfshow and cfenvgraph. It outputs data stored in CFEngine embedded databases in human readable form. It can store information about distributions. We can generate reports in HTML or XML format, using the following switches:

  ```
  --html, -H          Prints the report in HTML.
  --XML, -X           Prints the report in XML.
  ```

- **cf-key**: Key generation tool, run once on every host to create public/private key pairs for secure communication.

All the above components may be found under the `/usr/local/sbin` directory (on a CentOS or other similar systems; for other distributions please refer to the respective distribution documentations).

Testing the installation

One of the many advantages of CFEngine is that we may test the installation without being the 'super' or 'root' user. This gives the power, to all the users new to CFEngine, to test the installation without impacting any other services or functionality on/of the system.

Let's create a user 'Kai' to test our installation. After this compile and make the software. For a normal user the work directory for CFEngine lies in the user's home directory in .cfagent:

```
kai@mysystem$ mkdir -p ~/.cfagent/inputs
kai@mysystem$ mkdir -p ~/.cfagent/bin
kai@mysystem$ cd cfengine-<version_number>
kai@mysystem$ cd src
kai@mysystem$ cp cf-* ~/.cfagent/bin
kai@mysystem$ cd ../inputs
kai@mysystem$ ls
cfengine_stdlib.cf          failsafe.cf          library.cf          site.
cf          update.cf
kai@mysystem$ cp *.cf ~/.cfagent/inputs
```

Let's test the installation:

```
kai@mysystem$ ~/.cfagent/bin/cf-promises
kai@mysystem$ ~/.cfagent/bin/cf-promises -verbose
```

If there are any mistakes in configurations the promises won't be executed. Try editing the input files under `~/.cfagent/inputs` and test the installation further.

Now we have installed and verified our installation, let's start with configuring CFEngine to fulfill our demands.

CFEngine uses a workspace for storing the executables, promises file and other configuration files. By default, CFEngine uses `/var/cfengine` directory as its workspace. The directory does not get created after the installation on its own. To create this 'work' space one may run the following command:

```
root@mysystem# cf-promises
```

This command will create a default directory structure for CFEngine workspace.

We may run the same commands as for the non-privileged user to add executables, promises files, and other configuration files:

```
root@mysystem# cd <cfengine_source_path>
root@mysystem# cp cf-* /var/cfengine/bin/
root@mysystem# cd ../inputs
root@mysystem# cp *.cf /var/cfengine/inputs/
```

CFEngine environment

You must have noticed a few more files which were created by default under the `/var/cfengine/inputs/` directory. These files set the environment for CFEngine. If there are no arguments provided to `cf-agent`, these files are read by default. Let's see how these files set the environment for CFEngine.

promises.cf

This is the first file to be read by `cf-agent` when run with no arguments. It should contain all the basic configuration settings, including a list of other files to be included. It should have a bundlesequence, at the minimum. This file may remain as it is except in cases where we want to extend the bundlesequence. For a large setup consisting of heterogeneous grouping of 'similar' hosts, we may want to have a different bundlesequence for each 'similar' class of hosts. A basic `promises.cf` file may have the following sections defining various global parameters for CFEngine; the following are a few of them which may be found in the default `promises.cf` file:

- A bundlesequence
- Other files to be included
- Sections defining various promise controls

Let's see the default `promises.cf` file created after CFEngine installation:

```
#################################################
# promises.cf
################################################
body common control     {
bundlesequence   => {
                    "update",
                    "garbage_collection",
                    "main",
                    "cfengine"
                    };
inputs           => {
                    "update.cf",
                    "site.cf",
                    "library.cf"
                    };
}
```

A common control body describes those promises which are universal to all the components of CFEngine. Hence, the common control promises impact the behavior of all the CFEngine components.

Let's see what we defined for the common control body:

- First of all we define that this is the body for the common control body.
- In the common control body we define a bundlesequence which defines the order in which the promise bundles would be executed. Here we define four bundles which are "update", "garbage_collection", "main", and "cfengine".
- If you want more files to be included you may specify with the "inputs" constraint. Here we specify four files, `update.cf`, `site.cf`, `library.cf` which come with CFEngine. These included files that have additional promises which define the default actions for CFEngine.

```
###############################################
body agent control

{
ifelapsed => "15";
}
###############################################
body monitor control      # Define a promise type
{
forgetrate => "0.7";
histograms => "true";
}
###############################################
body executor control
{
splaytime => "1";
mailto => "cfengine_mail@example.org"; # The mail id on
                                        # which you want to
                                        # get the mail after
                                        # the task is executed.
smtpserver => "localhost";
mailmaxlines => "30";
}
```

In the same promises file there are a few more control promise bodies. In the previous section we define three more control body promises, which are the agent control, monitor control, and the executor control bodies:

- An agent control body provides the details of the promises made by `cf-agent`. Here, in the agent control body we defined the `ifelapsed` constraint. By default, the value for this constraint is five minutes but there may be tasks which may run for more than five minutes and hence we set this value to 15 minutes.
- A monitor control body provides the details for the promises made, as you'll find in the file named `cf-monitord`. Here, in the monitor control body there are two constraints defined: `forgetrate` and `histograms`. The `forgetrate` constraint defines how quickly CFEngine forgets its previous history and this is expressed as fraction weighting of new values over old values in two days, average computation. The `histogram` constraint is used to enable or disable the creation of histograms by CFEngine.
- An executor control body describes the settings which define the behavior of `cf-execd`. Here, in the executor control body we define four constraints `splaytime`, `mailto`, `smtpserver`, and `mailmaxlines`:
    - `splaytime` defines the delay introduced by CFEngine while executing promises on various hosts
    - `mailto` defines the e-mail ID to which CFEngine sends mails
    - `smtpserver` defines the SMTP server to be used by CFEngine for relaying mails
    - `mailmaxlines` defines the maximum number of lines from the output of promise execution which will be mailed to the e-mail ID

> Please note that SMTPAUTH is not an option available which may be added to the executor control body, and hence the SMTP server should be open to the host for relaying mails.

```
body reporter control
{

reports => { "performance", "last_seen", "monitor_history" };
build_directory => "$(sys.workdir)/reports";
report_output => "html";
}
##################################################
body runagent control
{
hosts => {
          };
}
##################################################
```

```
body server control
{
allowconnects          => { "127.0.0.1" , "::1" };
allowallconnects       => { "127.0.0.1" , "::1" };
trustkeysfrom          => { "127.0.0.1" , "::1" };
# Make updates and runs happen in one
cfruncommand           => "$(sys.workdir)/bin/cf-agent -f failsafe.
cf && $(sys.workdir)/bin/cf-agent";
allowusers             => { "root" };
}
```

The other three control bodies in the `promises.cf` file are reporter control, runagent control, and server control:

- The reporter control defines promises for the reports that need to be generated. Here we specify the following reports: performance, last_seen, and monitor_history. In addition to this we specify the directory the reports will be written to with the help of the `build_dirctory` constraint. Finally, we also define the type of output for the reports as HTML.
- In the runagent control body we provide the name or IP address of the hosts to which CFEngine attempts to connect.
- In the server control body we define the hosts which may connect to the CFEngine server port with the help of the `allowconnects` constraint. In addition to this we also define a list of hosts which may have more than one connection to the CFEngine server port with the help of `allowallconnects`. Finally, we specify the hosts from which CFEngine may accept public keys on the basis of trust.

Other than the `promises.cf` file there are a few other files which define the default behavior of CFEngine. These files are:

- `sites.cf`: This file is used to add site-specific configuration. We may define site specific bundles. Global variables may be defined under common bundles.
- `update.cf`: This file should never change. The file defines the environment for CFEngine when it is updated. We need to ensure that the `update.cf` is readable by both the versions of CFEngine.
- `library.cf`: In this file we may define various editbundles.
- `failsafe.cf`: This file should never change. It ensures that the CFEngine system has upgraded gracefully even when there are errors. The CFEngine system, if unable to read or parse the contents in any of the above files, will failover to this failsafe configuration.
- `cfengine_stdlib.cf`: This is a standard library of definitions which can be used in building solutions with CFEngine. The library has standard tasks predefined,

contributed by the CFEngine community, which may be used while automating tasks with CFEngine. For using the standard predefined tasks we need to include the `cfengine_stdlib.cf` file while writing various CFEngine tasks. The library can be included as:

```
body common control
{
Inputs =>  { "cfengine_stdlib.cf" };
}
```

Time for action – listing open ports and associated services

We need to create promises file for CFEngine which gives us the open ports and the services running on these ports:

1. Copy and paste the following text in the promises file, which may be named as `portcheck.cf`:

```
            body common control

{
       bundlesequence => {'portcheck'};

       version => "1.1.0";

      }
################################################
      bundle agent portcheck
      {
      commands:
       "/bin/netstat"
       args => "-lnpt",
       contain => standard,
       classes => cdefine("followup","alert");
       followup::

         "/bin/ls"
         contain => standard;
    reports:
      alert::

     "What happened?";
      }
################################################
```

```
        body contain standard
        {
        exec_owner => "root";
        useshell => "true";
        }
##############################################
        body classes cdefine(class,alert)
        {
        promise_repaired => { "$(class)" };
        repair_failed => { "$(alert)" };
        }
```

The above example uses all the main features of CFEngine: promises, control, bundles, bodies, and variables

Let's verify the above example and see if we made a mistake. For this we use the new CFEngine program, `cf-promises`. Let's assume you copied the text in the file `portcheck.cf`.

```
root@mysystem# cd /var/cfengine/inputs/
root@mysystem# cf-promises -f ./portcheck.cf
```

If there is no output, congratulations we have got it all correct. Now let's run the above command to give us a verbose output.

```
root@mysystem# cf-promises -v -f ./portcheck.cf
#########
Cf3 CFEngine - autonomous configuration engine - commence self-
diagnostic prelude
cf3 ------------------------------------------------------------
---
cf3 Work directory is /var/cfengine
..
cf3 Checking integrity of the state database

cf3 Checking integrity of the module directory

cf3 Checking integrity of the PKI directory

cf3 Looking for a source of entropy in /var/cfengine/state/cf_
observations.db

cf3 couldn't find a private key (/var/cfengine/ppkeys/localhost.priv)
- use cf-key to get one

cf3  !!! System error for fopen: "No such file or directory"
```

```
..
cf3  -> Inputs are valid
############
```

> We can see in the output above that there was an error reported as below
>
> cf3 Couldn't find a private key (/var/cfengine/ppkeys/localhost.priv) - use cf-key to get one
>
> cf3 !!! System error for fopen: "No such file or directory"
>
> The error occurs because we have not generated a key file using cf-key. This has not been done because currently whatever we executing is being executed on the local machine and the keys are required for remote authentication. We'll need the keys when want to execute this same example on multiple servers.

The last line is of interest as it says, all looks good. Now we have verified the file, let's execute this and see what the output we get is. You may want to change the user with which you want to run this example.

```
root@mysystem# cf-agent -f ./portcheck.cf
```

The non verbose output of the script looks something like this:

```
[root@mysystem]# cf-agent -f ./portcheck.cf
Q: "...in/netstat -lpn": Active Internet connections (only servers)
Q: "...in/netstat -lpn": Proto Recv-Q Send-Q Local Address    Foreign
Address                State      ID/Program name
Q: "...in/netstat -lpn": tcp        0      0 172.16.3.113:80
   0.0.0.0:*                      LISTEN      2475/varnishd
Q: "...in/netstat -lpn": tcp        0      0 192.168.122.1:53
   0.0.0.0:*                      LISTEN      2463/dnsmasq
Q: "...in/netstat -lpn": tcp        0      0 :::22
   :::*                           LISTEN      2132/sshd
Q: "...in/netstat -lpn": tcp        0      0 :::5308
   :::*                           LISTEN      5676/cf-serverd
I: Last 6 QUOTed lines were generated by promiser "/bin/netstat -lpnt"
Q: ".../bin/ls": portcheck.cf
I: Last 1 QUOTed lines were generated by promiser "/bin/ls"
```

The output gives us the respective TCP ports and the services running on these ports as required.

The command can also be run with an '-r' option to generate reports. The report is generated in a text or HTML format. The generic name given to the created files are promises_output_component-type.html.

What just happened?

We defined a promise control type. Under this control promise we defined a bundlesequence, `portcheck`. Multiple bundles may be added in the order we want them to be executed, as comma-separated entries. Next we defined the attributes for this bundle agent `portcheck`, which has a command promise defined that gets the list of open ports and the services associated with them. Under the same `portcheck` bundle agent promise we defined two classes, `followup` and `alert`. The class `alert` fires alerts on the number of promises repaired and how many failed to repair. The `followup` class is defined to just get the listing of files under the directory from which the command was executed.

Once we execute the promises file with `cf-agent` we may see that in the output we get the TCP ports open on the system, the status of the port, the service associated with the open port, and the corresponding PID of the service associated with the port. The above promises may be used to audit the services and the associated ports on a host. One may use it to create a map of services running on a host or may also be used as an 'auto discovery' promise.

Time for action – creating a file under your home directory

1. Now, we'll see how to use CFEngine to create a file called "test" under your home directory `/root` and change its permissions to `-rwxr-xr--`:

2. Paste the following text in a file named `file-perms-test.cf`. We'll use the most basic promises, to keep it simple:

```
# Define a promise type
body common control

{
# Define a bundle sequence
bundlesequence => { "checkperms" };
# Include cfengine_stdlib.cf
inputs => { "cfengine_stdlib.cf" };
version => "1.0.0";
 }
bundle agent checkperms          # Define a bundle agent
{
files:
                                 # Define the file to
```

```
                                         # be created and checked
"/root/test"
create => "true",
                                         # Create the file
perms => m("754");
                                         # Set the permissions to
                                         # '-rwxr-xr--'
}
```

3. Let's verify the file:

```
root@mysystem# cd /var/cfengine/inputs
root@mysystem# cf-promise -f  file-perms-test.cf
cf3 CFEngine - autonomous configuration engine - commence
self-diagnostic prelude
cf3 -------------------------------------------------------------
------
cf3 Work directory is /var/cfengine
cf3 Checking integrity of the module directory
cf3 Checking integrity of the PKI directory
cf3 Initiate variable convergence...
cf3  -> Inputs are valid
root@mysystem#
```

The above output verifies that we got the definitions and inputs correct.

4. Now let's execute the previous example:

```
root@mysystem# cd /var/cfengine/inputs
root@mysystem# cf-agent -f file-perms-test.cf
root@mysystem# ls -lh /root
total 0
-rwxr-xr-- 1 root root 0 Oct  6 17:39 test
root@mysystem#
```

You will see that a file by the name "test" was created under `/root` with `-rwxr-xr--` permissions.

What just happened?

We defined a bundlesequence under the common control body having a single bundle named `checkperms`. Next we defined the file `CFEngine_stdlib.cf` to be included with the `inputs` promise. In the third step we defined the file which needs to be created and permissions which need to be set under the file's promise type.

While running the promise for the first time it may be a possibility that the file does not exist. We defined that if the file does not exist then CFEngine needs to create it by setting the value of the `create` constraint to `true`, in case the file does not exist. As the final step we defined the file permissions which we want the file to exit with.

Pop quiz

1. Name the core theory on which CFEngine is based.
2. Which file is read by `cf-agent`, by default, when run without an argument?
3. Name three promise types we came across in this chapter.
4. Which directory serves as the workspace for CFEngine, by default?

Time for action – deleting log files

We need to write a promises file for deleting all the log files under the directory `/var/log` which match the regex "mlog.*":

1. Paste the following lines in the promises file of your choice. Let's say the file's name is `files_log_delete.cf`, which is under the `/var/cfengine/inputs` directory.

```
body common control

   {
   bundlesequence  => {
                        "mlog_files"
                        };
   version => "1.1.1";
   }
#############################################
bundle agent mlog_files
{
files:
    "/var/log"
    delete => tidyfiles,
    file_select => mlog,
    depth_search => recurse("inf");
}
#############################################
body file_select mlog
{
leaf_name => { "mlog.*" };
file_result => "leaf_name";
```

```
}
############################################
body depth_search recurse(d)
{
depth => "$(d)";
}
#################
body delete tidyfiles
     {
     dirlinks => "delete";
     rmdirs   => "true";
     }
```

Let's see which files which need to be deleted from the/var/log directory:

```
root@mysystem# cd /var/log
root@mysystem# ls -lh mlog.*
-rw------- 1 root root 3.2K Oct  8 10:31 mlog.1
-rw------- 1 root root 2.8K Oct  8 10:31 mlog.2
-rw------- 1 root root 2.8K Oct  8 10:31 mlog.3
```

2. Let's verify the promises and inputs using `cf-promises`:

```
root@mysystem#
root@mysystem# cf-promises -f ./files_log_delete.cf
root@mysystem#
```

   As there are no errors we are good to go.

3. Execute the previous code with `cf-agent`:

```
root@mysystem# cf-agent -f ./files_log_delete
root@mysystem#
```

4. Let's check whether the files were removed:

```
root@mysystem# cd /var/log
root@mysystem# ls -lh mlog.*
ls: mlog.*: No such file or directory
root@mysystem#
```

What just happened?

We defined a common control promise. Next we defined a bundlesequence with only one bundle named `mlog_files`. To define the base directory under which the files need to be deleted we defined the `files` promise and provide the path of the base directory as '/var/log'. For selecting the files, the depth to which the files should be searched and deleting them, we define the promises 'file_select', 'delete', and 'depth_search', respectively. As the last step we define the bodies for the above three promises wherein we provide the criterion for selecting the files, the depth to which CFEngine should go to search for the files in the directory '/var/log', and finally the attributes for deleting the selected files.

Summary

Let's summarize what all we learnt in this chapter:

- Installing and testing your CFEngine installation. We also saw how cfengine may be tested without being a super user. This may be used to run tests on your CFEngine installation before you go live. Significance of cf-promises, cf-agent, cf-report, cf-execd, cf-runagent, cf-key, cf-monitord, cf-know, and cf-serverd. We also looked at how these commands may be used for verification, reporting, remote promise execution, and performing various CFEngine tasks.
- Available promise types like files, vars, commands, and others. Defining various promise types and their usage.
- How to write promise files. Verifying the promises using "cf-promises" and running our tasks with "cf-agent".

Now that we have learned how to install CFEngine, write basic promises, verify them, and execute them on a standalone system, we are ready to move to the next chapter where we will configure systems using CFEngine.

2

Configuring Systems with CFEngine

The beauty of CFEngine is that we can execute tasks on multiple systems seamlessly. In the previous chapter we saw how to write CFEngine promises; in this chapter we will see how to distribute those promises on multiple systems so that the remote systems may change their state as per the promises.

In this chapter we shall learn about:

- The CFEngine architecture
- Installing software
- Configuring users and groups
- Configuring services

As we already know, CFEngine works on the theory of promises. The promises need to be distributed to multiple systems so that the systems may change their state accordingly. Unlike conventional tools, CFEngine works on the principle of "voluntary cooperation". Rather than "pushing" the promises on remote systems CFEngine expects the remote systems to "pull" the changes from the CFEngine file server and execute the promises at their will. CFEngine, by design, cannot force its will onto other systems. At best, it can trigger a signal to remote systems and ask them to collect the changed file, at their will.

How do CFEngine components communicate?

There are three basic components involved in CFEngine communication.

- **Cf-serverd**: `Cf-serverd` is a daemon that acts as file server and also receives requests for execution of policy files on individual hosts. The execution of policy files is dependent on the access control restrictions described in the server control body and the server bundles. This is a daemon which needs to run on the policy server and acts as a distribution point for the necessary configuration files required by the clients. The policy files should be maintained on a version control system accessible by all the hosts.
- **Cf-agent**: The configuration engine's only contact with the network is through remote copy requests. It does not and cannot grant any access to a system from the network. It is only able to request access to files from the server component. The mechanism works in such a way that the updated policy files from the policy distribution server are first transferred to the individual hosts as per the promises in `failsafe.cf` and then these promises are executed at individual hosts on the basis of the `promises.cf` file. The next diagram explains this "two stage" process.
- **Cf-execd**: `Cf-execd` is a daemon which runs `cf-agent` at regular or user defined intervals. Use of `cf-execd` is the recommended way of running `cf-agent` instead of using cron to run `cf-agent`. The `cf-execd` daemon is affected by changes in common and executor control bodies.

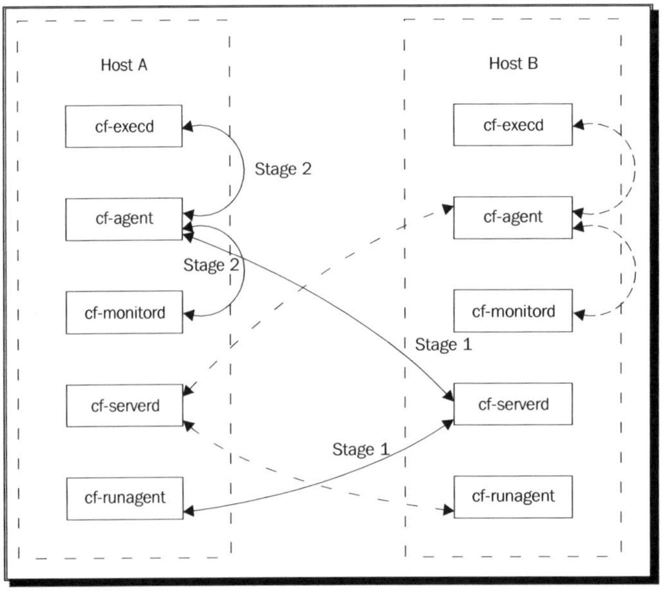

- **Cf-runagent**: This is a simple initiation program that can be used to run `cf-agent` on a number of remote hosts. It cannot be run to tell `cf-agent` what to do; it can only ask `cf-serverd` on the remote host to run `cf-agent` with its existing configuration. Privileges can be granted to users to provide a kind of Role Based Access Control to certain parts of existing policy. These three components are everything we need for effective distribution of resources for systems.

Let's see how the three components work together in tandem to make CFEngine one of the best system automation tools available. The following diagram shows policy decision flow:

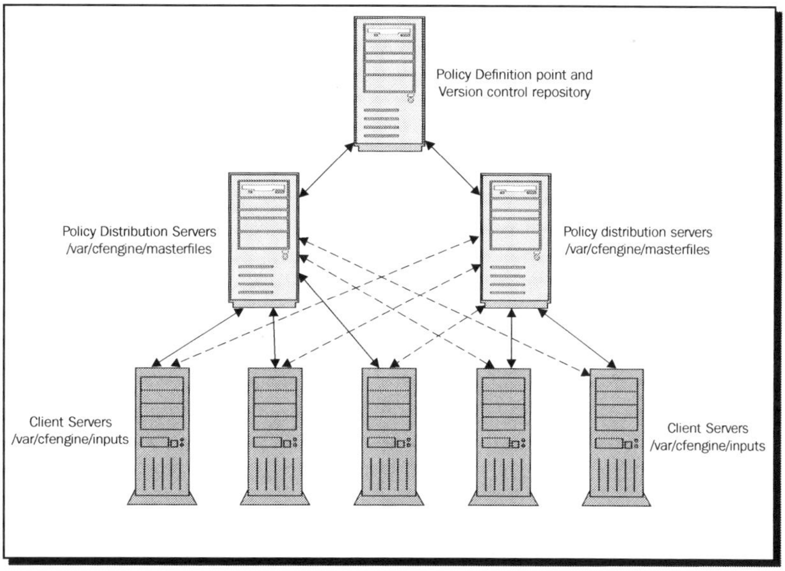

In the preceding diagram, the **Policy Distribution Servers** have the master files that need to be distributed to the remote systems. Now, to maintain consistency, the policies should first be committed to a version control system and the policy distribution servers should pull files from the version control system to distribute them to the remote hosts. You can use any of the widely available version control systems such as SVN, CVS, or GIT. The preceding diagram shows a similar process. This will also help track changes to policy files.

The number of **Policy Distribution Servers** may depend on the size of the infrastructure. If the remote servers are distributed geographically, it makes sense to have a "Policy Distribution Server" at each location, which serves the systems at that location. All the remote systems connect to the Policy Distribution Servers and download the updates.

> During this process, CFEngine verifies that the system clocks of the two hosts are reasonably synchronized. In case they are not, it does not permit copying of a file to the remote server unless the **denybadclocks** is set to false in the server control body.

Apart from verifying system clocks, CFEngine takes a step ahead and does not copy the updated file to its destination directly. The new files are copied to the remote hosts in the following manner:

CFEngine copies the new updated file from the remote Policy Distribution Server as a new file on the same file system as the destination file. The new file being copied has the suffix `.cfnew`. This transfer of policy files from the Policy Distribution Server is done on the basis of promises in `failsafe.cf`. When `cf-agent` is run it first executes `failsafe.cf` and updates the policy files from the policy distribution server to the local host. Once the file has been successfully copied to the destination file system `cfagent` makes a copy of the old file and renames the new file. This is done on the basis of promises in `promises.cf`.

In the preceding description we again come across the the "two stage" process of copying files from the policy distribution server and executing the same. CFEngine being a flexible framework, it allows merging the two stages so that both the stages may be handled by a single policy file `promises.cf, although` this approach is not recommended. By default, this is a two stage process and each process is handled by a different policy file and this is how it should be set up. This is strongly recommended so that a failure at stage 1 does not impact stage 2. As an additional precaution one should ensure that `promises.cf` only be executed once the network transfer as per `failsafe.cf` has been correctly completed. This can be done with the help of the following entry in the `cf-execd` command statement or providing a file with this entry to the `cf-execd` command as an argument:

```
#var/cfengine/bin/cf-agent -f  /var/cfengine/inputs/failsafe.cf && /var/
cfengine---------/bin/cf-agent
```

The preceding command ensures that `promises.cf` is executed only if the network transfer is completed correctly.

The above two stages are executed so as to take care of interruptions in network connections and to avoid race conditions. CFEngine also sets a timeout of a few seconds for network connections to prevent processes from hanging. One of the various advantages of using CFEngine is that no "root" or "administrator" privileges are needed for CFEngine on the local host. We just need to start the daemon as "root".

Setting up a policy server

A centralized CFEngine policy server is the core of the CFEngine framework. This helps CFEngine to scale as the changes need to be pushed only to the centralized policy server and the rest of the infrastructure is updated from there. Let's try to configure a policy server.

After installing CFEngine on the selected policy server as discussed in *Chapter 1, Getting Started with CFEngine*, we need to execute the following steps: to configure a centralized policy server.

1. Switch to root user on the policy server:

   ```
   user@my1.system.com$ su -
   ```

2. Create a source repository for the policy files:

   ```
   root@my1system.com# mkdir -p /var/cfengine/masterfiles
   ```

3. For demonstration, we will copy a few sample policy files already available with the CFEngine installation:

   ```
   root@my1.system.com# cp /usr/local/share/doc/cfengine/inputs/*.cf
   /var/cfengine/masterfiles
   ```

   ```
   root@my1system.com# cp /usr/local/share/doc/cfengine/cfengine_
   stdlib.cf /var/cfengine/masterfiles/
   ```

4. Now let's generate the public-private keys for the policy distribution server:

   ```
   root@my1.system.com# /usr/local/sbin/cf-key
   ```

   The preceding command generates a public-private key pair under `/var/cfengine/ppkeys`. Let's check that the keys were created using the following command:

   ```
   root@my1.system.com# ls /var/cfengine/ppkeys/
   localhost.priv  localhost.pub
   root@my1system.com#
   ```

   As we just saw, a pair of public-private keys were generated as well as the hashed keys for remote hosts. The CFEngine key exchange mechanism works similarly to how the key exchange mechanism of OpenSSH works, which means that it is a peer-to-peer key exchange mechanism rather than a central certificate authority model. Once you have selected and told CFEngine which keys to accept, the key exchange is handled by CFEngine. The public keys of the policy distribution server are cached by the clients so, if the keys of the policy distribution server are lost, you will have to generate the key again with `cf-key` and also purge the old cached key from the clients manually. Therefore, the key for the policy distribution server should always be backed up.

5. Now let's start CFEngine.

   To start CFEngine we need to run a `cf-serverd` daemon. The `cf-serverd` daemon reads the `promises.cf` which defines the server control and access control promises. Let's see a `promises.cf` configuration file.

```
body server control {

    skipverify          => { "172.16.3.*" };

    allowconnects       => { "172.16.3.*" };

    allowallconnects    => { "172.16.3.*" };

    logallconnections   => "true";

    bindtointerface     => "172.16.3.113";

    cfruncommand        => "$(sys.workdir)/bin/cf-agent";

    allowusers          => { "root" };

}
```

   The preceding server control promise defined the following variables:

   - `skipverify` defines a list of IP addresses for which DNS binding checks should to be skipped
   - `allowconnects` defines a list of IP addresses that are allowed to connect to the CFEngine policy distribution server
   - `allowallconnects` defines a list of IP addresses that are allowed to have more than one connection to the CFEngine policy distribution port
   - `bindtointerface` defines the network interface to which the `cf-serverd` daemon binds
   - `cfruncommand` defines the path to the `cf-agent` command
   - `allowusers` defines the user with which the clients are allowed to connect to the server port

The access control bundle defines who is allowed to access what files and directories. Shown next is an access control bundle defined in `site.cf`:

```
bundle server access_rules()
{
access:
"/var/cfengine/inputs"
```

```
admit => { "172.16.3.*" };
"/var/cfengine/masterfiles"
admit => { "172.16.3.*" };
}
```

This access control defined the following:

- `admit` defines a list of IP addresses that are allowed to access the files and directories under `/var/cfengine/inputs`.

Let's start the CFEngine server daemon with the command `cf-serverd` and see what happens.

```
root@my1.system.com# cf-serverd -v
cf3> Cfengine - autonomous configuration engine - commence self-
diagnostic prelude


…..
…..
cf3>  -> Loaded private key /var/cfengine/ppkeys/localhost.priv


cf3>  -> Loaded public key /var/cfengine/ppkeys/localhost.pub


cf3> Setting cfengine default port to 5308 = 5308


….
….
cf3> Cfengine - 3.1.5 Copyright (C) Cfengine AS 2008,2010-
….
….
cf3> SET Skip verify connections from ...


cf3> SET Allowing connections from ...


cf3> SET Allowing multiple connections from ...


cf3> SET bindtointerface = 172.16.3.113


cf3> SET cfruncommand = /var/cfengine/bin/cf-agent
```

```
cf3> SET Allowing users ...

cf3> Summarize control promises

cf3> Granted access to paths :

cf3> Path: /var/cfengine (encrypt=0)

cf3>    Admit: 172.16.3.* root=

cf3> Path: $(g.inputfiles) (encrypt=0)

cf3>    Admit: 172.16.3.* root=

cf3> Path: $(g.masterfiles) (encrypt=0)

cf3>    Admit: 172.16.3.* root=

cf3> Denied access to paths :

cf3> Path: /var/cfengine

cf3> Path: $(g.inputfiles)

cf3> Path: $(g.masterfiles)

cf3>  -> Host IPs allowed connection access :

cf3>  .... IP: 172.16.3.*

cf3> Host IPs denied connection access :

cf3> Host IPs allowed multiple connection access :

cf3>  .... IP: 172.16.3.*
```

```
cf3> Host IPs from whom we shall accept public keys on trust :

cf3> Users from whom we accept connections :

cf3>  .... USERS: root

cf3> Host IPs from NAT which we don't verify :

cf3>  .... IP: 172.16.3.*

cf3> Dynamical Host IPs (e.g. DHCP) whose bindings could vary over time :

cf3> Listening for connections ...

cf3>  -> Writing last-seen observations

cf3>  -> Keyring is empty

cf3>  -> Accepting a connection

cf3> Accepting connection from "172.16.3.178"

cf3> New connection...(from 172.16.3.178:sd 4)

cf3> Spawning new thread...

cf3> Allowing 172.16.3.178 to connect without (re)checking ID

cf3> Non-verified Host ID is my10.system.com (Using skipverify)

cf3> Non-verified User ID seems to be root (Using skipverify)

cf3>  -> Public key identity of host "172.16.3.178" is "MD5=a6d18c07c396c
fe1e74cda464493a2ec"
```

```
cf3>   -> Last saw 172.16.3.178 (-MD5=a6d18c07c396cfe1e74cda464493a2ec)
first time now

cf3>   -> Going to secondary storage for key

cf3>   -> Going to secondary storage for key

cf3> A public key was already known from my10.system.com/172.16.3.178 -
no trust required

cf3> Adding IP 172.16.3.178 to SkipVerify - no need to check this if we
have a key

cf3> Adding IP 172.16.3.178 to SkipVerify - no need to check this if we
have a key

cf3> The public key identity was confirmed as root@my10.system.com

cf3>   -> Strong authentication of client my10.system.com/172.16.3.178
achieved

cf3>   -> Receiving session key from client (size=256)...

cf3> Found a matching rule in access list (/var/cfengine/masterfiles in
/var/cfengine)

cf3> Host my10.system.com granted access to /var/cfengine/masterfiles

cf3> Found a matching rule in access list (/var/cfengine/masterfiles in
/var/cfengine)

…..
…..
```

Let's see what happened when we started the `cf-serverd` daemon. When we started the `cf-serverd` daemon it first checks the work directory `/var/cfengine`. After this it verifies the integrity of the system state database, module directory, the PKI directory, and then loads the public-private key pair from the directory `/var/cfengine/ppkeys`. Once that it is done it sets the default port to `5308`. Next, it verifies the syntax of the base configuration files. After this, CFEngine sets the grants and permissions defined in the server control body and `access_rules` bundle. It sets the IP addresses or host names of the hosts that are allowed to connect to the server, which are allowed to make multiple connections to the server and keys from which hosts should be trusted. It also sets the name of the users that are allowed to connect. The CFEngine policy distribution server is now ready to serve configuration files to the clients.

We now have a CFEngine server that can be used to distribute policy files to other hosts. Let's assume we have *m* number of systems with host name *my(n).system.com* where *n* ranges from *1* to *m*. We need to install CFEngine on all these *m* systems which may pull updates from the centralized CFEngine repository. I have deliberately kept the host name for the the central policy repository server as *my1.system.com*.

Connecting to a CFEngine server

To connect to a CFEngine server maintaining the policy repository the client hosts will need:

- An IPV4 or IPV6 address configured on the client host.
- A client program—`cf-agent`, which may connect to a CFEngine server.
- A public-private key pair—the keys may be created by running `cf-key`. The keys are stored in the directory `/var/cfengine/ppkeys`. One can check the server and key mappings as follows:

```
root@my1.system.com# cf-key -s
Direction                IP Name
 Key


Outgoing      172.16.3.178 my10.system.com        MD5=a6d18c07c396cfe
1e74cda464493a2ec
```

- Permissions to connect to the CFEngine server—the client host and key by name or IP address should be allowed to connect to the CFEngine server. This is done by granting access to the client in the server control body and with access rules. Here is a sample configuration from `promises.cf`:

```
body server control
{
port => '5308';
allowconnects          => { "127.0.0.1", "::1",  ".*\.my*\.system\.
com" };
allowallconnects       => { "127.0.0.1", "::1", ".*\.my*\.system\.
com" };
cfruncommand           => "$(sys.workdir)/bin/cf-agent -f failsafe.
cf && $(sys.workdir)/bin/cf-agent";
}
```

In this server control body, we see how various access rules have been specified for connections, multiple connections, and trustkeys.

- A trust relation between the client and the CFEngine server based on the client's and server's public keys. The host names and IP addresses for the hosts that you trust may be specified as follows:

```
body server control
{
trustkeysfrom          => { "127.0.0.1",   "::1",   ".*\.my*\.
system\.com" };
```

The username with which the clients connect to the CFEngine server port should be mentioned inside the server bundle as follows:

```
body server control
{
        allowusers               => { "root" };
         }
```

- We also need to specify the folders and directories on the policy distribution server to which the clients have access. This is defined in the server bundle within the configuration file `site.cf`. Here is a configuration snippet from `site.cf`:

```
                      bundle server access_policy
{
access:
"/var/cfengine/masterfiles"
admit => { "172.16.3.*", .....};
deny => { "10.0.0\..*"};
}
```

If all these conditions are met, a connection between the client host and the CFEngine server is established and data may be transferred between client and server. To understand how this communication between the CFEngine server and the client host takes place, let's see an example which uses a simple `copy_from` promise and copies the files from the policy distribution server to itself. We will also see in this example which configuration files play a part when the communication starts and completes.

Time for action – taking file backups

1. Let's write a configuration file for backing up important configuration files under `/etc/sysconfig` on a remote server.

2. We will use the *copy_from* promise for this. You may use the following lines in your configuration file `user_data_bkup.cf`:

```
{bundle agent backup
```

```
{
files:
"/mnt/backup"
copy_from =>  remote_cp( "/etc/sysconfig", "172.16.3.113"),
depth_search   => recurse("inf"),
}
body copy_from remote_cp(user_data,user_server)
{
source   => "$(user_data)";
servers   => "$(user_server)";
trustkey   => "true";
verify   => "true";
}
```

Now as a best practice, the file `user_data_bkup.cf` should be committed to a version control system which may be a SVN or CVS from which the policy distribution server may do a "headless" checkout and get a copy of the file.

3. Let's first check the output of `cf-serverd` on the policy distribution server. You may also start the `cf-serverd` daemon with an alternate configuration file `cf-serverd.cf` which can take care of restarting the daemon in case the server is not running. Shown next is the configuration that you could use for the same:

```
bundle agent server {

vars:

    "rc_d" string => "/usr/local/etc/rc.d";

processes:

policy_servers::

"cf-serverd"

restart_class => "start_cfserverd";

commands:

start_cfserverd::

"$(rc_d)/cf-serverd start";

}
```

Shown next is the output of `cf-serverd -v` on the CFEngine server:

```
root@my10system.com# cf-serverd -v -f /var/cfengine/inputs/cf-
serverd.cf

cf3> Cfengine - autonomous configuration engine - commence self-
diagnostic prelude

cf3> -------------------------------------------------------------
-----------

cf3> Work directory is /var/cfengine

…..

…..

cf3> Setting cfengine default port to 5308 = 5308

cf3> Reference time set to Mon Jun 20 21:01:06 2011

cf3> Cfengine - 3.1.5 Copyright (C) Cfengine AS 2008,2010-

cf3>    > Parsing file /var/cfengine/inputs/cf-serverd.cf

…..

…..

cf3> *************************************************************


cf3>  Server control promises..


cf3> *************************************************************


cf3> SET default portnumber = 5308 = 5308 = 5308


cf3> SET Allowing connections from ...


cf3> SET Allowing multiple connections from ...


cf3> SET Trust keys from ...


cf3> SET bindtointerface = 172.16.3.113


cf3> SET Skip verify connections from ...


cf3> SET denybadclocks = 0


cf3> SET cfruncommand = /var/cfengine/bin/cf-agent -f failsafe.cf
```

```
&& /var/cfengine/bin/cf-agent

cf3> SET Allowing users ...

cf3> Summarize control promises

cf3> Granted access to paths :

cf3> Denied access to paths :

cf3>  -> Host IPs allowed connection access :

cf3>  .... IP: 127.0.0.1

cf3>  .... IP: ::1

cf3>  .... IP: 172.16.3.*

cf3> Host IPs denied connection access :

cf3> Host IPs allowed multiple connection access :

cf3>  .... IP: 127.0.0.1

cf3>  .... IP: ::1

cf3>  .... IP: 172.16.3.*

cf3> Host IPs from whom we shall accept public keys on trust :

cf3>  .... IP: 127.0.0.1

cf3>  .... IP: ::1

cf3>  .... IP: 172.16.3.*
```

```
cf3> Users from whom we accept connections :

cf3>  .... USERS: root

cf3> Host IPs from NAT which we don't verify :

cf3>  .... IP: 172.16.3.*

cf3> Dynamical Host IPs (e.g. DHCP) whose bindings could vary over
time :

cf3> Listening for connections ...

cf3>  -> Writing last-seen observations
```

`cf-serverd` gets the server control parameters from `promises.cf`. Let's see the server control body from `promises.cf` for this policy distribution server:

```
body server control

{

port                    => "5308";

allowconnects           => { "127.0.0.1", "::1", "172.16.3.*" };

allowallconnects        => { "127.0.0.1", "::1", "172.16.3.*" };

trustkeysfrom           => { "127.0.0.1", "::1", "172.16.3.*" };

bindtointerface       =>   "172.16.3.113";

skipverify            =>   { "172.16.3.*" };

# Make updates and runs happen in one

cfruncommand            => "$(sys.workdir)/bin/cf-agent -f failsafe.
cf && $(sys.workdir)/bin/cf-agent";

allowusers              => { "root" };
```

```
}
```

The server control body from `promises.cf` tells the `cf-serverd` daemon to start on port `5308` of the specified interface, checks the syntax of various configuration files, and allows access to remote hosts as specified in the server control bundle.

4. Now let's execute the `cf-agent` on the client:

```
root@my10.system.com#cf-agent -v -f /var/cfengine/inputs/failsafe.
cf

cf3> Cfengine - autonomous configuration engine - commence self-
diagnostic prelude

cf3> Work directory is /var/cfenginecf3>  -> Loaded private key /
var/cfengine/ppkeys/localhost.priv

cf3>  -> Loaded public key /var/cfengine/ppkeys/localhost.pub

cf3> Setting cfengine default port to 5308 = 5308

…..

cf3> Cfengine - 3.1.5 Copyright (C) Cfengine AS 2008,2010-

cf3>  -> Input file is outside default repository, validating it

cf3>  -> Promises seem to change

cf3>  -> Input file is changed since last validation, validating
it

cf3>  -> Verifying the syntax of the inputs..

…..

…..

cf3>  -> Input file is outside default repository, validating it

cf3>  -> Promises seem to change

cf3>  -> Input file is changed since last validation, validating
it

cf3>  -> Verifying the syntax of the inputs..

…..

…..

cf3> No existing connection to 172.16.3.113 is established...

cf3> Set cfengine port number to 5308 = 5308

cf3> Set connection timeout to 10

cf3> Connect to 172.16.3.113 = 172.16.3.113, port = (5308=5308)

cf3>  -> Matched IP 172.16.3.113 to key MD5=aba77e2d0baf5ab33a464e
85cb5d37ac

cf3>  -> Going to secondary storage for key

cf3> ....................[.h.a.i.l.]...........................
```

```
....
cf3> Strong authentication of server=172.16.3.113 connection
confirmed
cf3>  -> Public key identity of host "172.16.3.113" is "MD5=aba77e
2d0baf5ab33a464e85cb5d37ac"
cf3>  -> Last saw 172.16.3.113 (+MD5=aba77e2d0baf5ab33a464e85cb5d3
7ac) first time now
cf3>  -> Going to secondary storage for key
cf3>  ->>  Entering /var/cfengine/masterfiles.....
.....
cf3>  -> File permissions on /var/cfengine/inputs/user_data_bkup.
cf as promised
cf3>  -> File /var/cfengine/inputs/user_data_bkup.cf is an up to
date copy of source
.....
.....
cf3> Performance(Copy(172.16.3.113:/var/cfengine/masterfiles > /
var/cfengine/inputs)): time=0.2074 secs, av=0.2077 +/- 0.0381
cf3> Existing connection just became free..
```

5. Now let's execute the configuration file `user_data_bkup.cf` and see what happens.

   Let's first check the contents of `/mnt`.

```
root@my10.system.com# ls -lh /mnt
total 0
root@my10.system.com#
```

   Now let's execute `user_data_bkup.cf` using `cf-agent`.

```
root@my10.system.com# cf-agent -v -f /var/cfengine/inputs/user_
data_bkup.cf
......
......
cf3>  -> Copy file /mnt/backup from /etc/sysconfig check
cf3> No existing connection to 172.16.3.113 is established...
cf3> Set cfengine port number to 5308 = 5308
cf3> Set connection timeout to 10
cf3>  -> Connect to 172.16.3.113 = 172.16.3.113 on port 5308
cf3>  -> Matched IP 172.16.3.113 to key MD5=aba77e2d0baf5ab33a464e
85cb5d37ac
```

```
cf3>  -> Going to secondary storage for key
cf3> ....................[.h.a.i.l.]............................
....
cf3> Strong authentication of server=172.16.3.113 connection
confirmed
cf3>  -> Public key identity of host "172.16.3.113" is "MD5=aba77e
2d0baf5ab33a464e85cb5d37ac"
cf3>  -> Last saw 172.16.3.113 (+MD5=aba77e2d0baf5ab33a464e85cb5d3
7ac) first time now
cf3>  -> Going to secondary storage for key
cf3>  ->>  Entering /etc/sysconfig
cf3>  -> /mnt/backup/iptables-config wasn't at destination
(copying)
cf3>  -> Copying from 172.16.3.113:/etc/sysconfig/iptables-
configcf3>  -> Copy of regular file succeeded /etc/sysconfig/
iptables-config to /mnt/backup/iptables-config.cfnew
cf3>  ?? Final verification of transmission ...
cf3>  -> New file /mnt/backup/iptables-config.cfnew transmitted
correctly - verified
cf3>  -> Updated file from 172.16.3.113:/etc/sysconfig/iptables-
config
cf3>  -> /mnt/backup/firstboot wasn't at destination (copying)
cf3>  -> Copying from 172.16.3.113:/etc/sysconfig/firstboot
cf3>  -> Copy of regular file succeeded /etc/sysconfig/firstboot
to /mnt/backup/firstboot.cfnew
cf3>  ?? Final verification of transmission ...
cf3>  -> New file /mnt/backup/firstboot.cfnew transmitted
correctly - verified
cf3>  -> Updated file from 172.16.3.113:/etc/sysconfig/firstboot
…..
…..
```

The promises seem to have executed properly; let's check the contents of `/mnt` folder.

```
root@my10.system.com# ls -lh /mnt
total 4.0K
drwxr-xr-x 9 root root 4.0K Jun 20 23:59 backup
root@my10.system.com#ls -lh /mnt/backup
total 232K
-rw------- 1 root root  646 Jun 20 23:59 auditd
-rw------- 1 root root  297 Jun 20 23:59 authconfig
```

```
-rw------- 1 root root 3.2K Jun 20 23:59 autofs
…...........
…...........
-rw------- 1 root root  391 Jun 20 23:59 wpa_supplicant
```

This output shows that a new directory `backup` was created under `/mnt` which contains a backup of all the files under `/etc/sysconfig` from the host with the IP address `172.16.3.113`.

What just happened?

We wanted to see how the `copy_from` promise works in detail. To understand it we took an example where we wanted to back up the important configuration files under `/etc/sysconfig` on the host with IP address `172.16.3.113` to a remote backup directory `/mnt/backup` on the host with IP address `172.16.3.178`. For this we need to allow access to the directory `/etc/sysconfig` on `172.16.3.113` for the remote host `172.16.3.178`. For this you would add the below lines to your `access-rules` server bundle in the configuration file `site.cf`.

```
bundle server access_rules
{

"/etc/sysconfig"

admit => { "172.16.3.*" };

}
```

Next we wrote a configuration file `user_data_bkup.cf` under `var/cfengine/masterfiles`, on the policy server, in which we used the `copy_from` promise to copy all the configuration files under `/etc/sysconfig` on `172.16.3.113` to `172.16.3.178`. We checkout the file from the master policy server to the policy distribution host under `/var/cfengine/masterfiles`. Now if we observe the execution of `failsafe.cf` on the host `172.16.3.178` we see that the host copies the new configuration files from the policy distribution server to its `/var/cfengine/inputs` directory. After the host has the updated configuration files, on running `cf-agent` on `172.16.3.178` the configuration files execute and `cf-agent` makes a connection with the host `172.16.3.113`, after a successful key exchange, and copies the files and directories under `/etc/sysconfig` to its backup folder `/mnt/backup`. Please note that the `backup` folder did not exist under `/mnt` previously. It was created upon execution of the configuration files, and all the files and directories from the remote hosts were copied into it.

Now that we are more familiar with how CFEngine network services, key exchange, and file copy works, let's go ahead and use this knowledge to automate a few important tasks.

System configuration

In the previous sections we had a detailed look at CFEngine client-server communication and the role of configuration files such as `promises.cf`, `failsafe.cf`, `update.cf`, and `site.cf`. In this next step, let's see how CFEngine can help us in configuring new systems. Once you have a system with a fresh OS and CFEngine installed, using Kickstart, there are a number of tasks that should be completed for the system to be ready to host applications and run in a production environment. A few of the common tasks are:

- Adding new users and groups
- Setting up a web service
- Setting up a database
- Setting up a network interface

Let's see how CFEngine can help us with these tasks.

Configuring users and groups

Once a fresh system is delivered, we will need to configure a number of users for the development team, DBA team or other teams who may need to work on it. We can have different groups for each team and add a user under this group for each member of the team or add users as per the organization's policy. It is always good to have a centralized user, group, and access database such as an LDAP server or Active Directory; but there may be scenarios where user authentication happens on the individual hosts. For example you may not want to store user login details of external FTP users on your internal LDAP server or active directory. The next example explains how you can add a user on the individual hosts.

Time for action – user and group configuration

1. Let's write a configuration file for adding a user and group on a client. We'll also change a few default values for this user such as his password, age, and so on. The user to be added is, say, *Clark* with complete name as *Clark Kent*, password as `superman`. This password expires after 60 days and the user starts getting a warning that the password is about to expire five days prior to the date of expiry.

   The following lines should be copied to a configuration file named `addusergroup.cf`, for instance:

```
body common control
{
bundlesequence => { 'addusergroup'};
```

```
}

bundle agent addusergroup

{
vars:
"User_name" string => "clark"
commands:

"/usr/sbin/useradd"

args => "clark",

classes => satisfied(user_created);
}

{
commands:
user_created::
"/usr/bin/chage"
args => "-M 60 -W 53 clark",
contain => standard;
}

###################
#body contain standard
###################

body contain standard
{
exec_owner => "root";
useshell => "true";
}
body classes satisfied(new_class)

{

  promise_repaired => { "$(new_class)" };

}
```

2. We can test this promise as follows:

```
root@my1.system.com# cf-promises -f addusergroup.cf
root@my1.system.com#
```

No output shows that the promise file is good. Now we need to copy this file from the centralized policy server to all the other hosts.

Let's run `cf-agent` which first copies the changes from the policy server to itself and then executes the promises as per the conditions set in its own configuration. The outputs are as follows:

```
root@my10system.com# cf-agent -v -K /var/cfengine/inputs/failsafe.
cf
cf3> Cfengine - autonomous configuration engine - commence self-
diagnostic prelude
....
cf3> Cfengine - 3.1.5 Copyright (C) Cfengine AS 2008,2010-
...
cf3> No existing connection to 172.16.3.113 is established...

cf3> Set cfengine port number to 5308 = 5308

cf3> Set connection timeout to 10

cf3> Connect to 172.16.3.113 = 172.16.3.113, port = (5308=5308)

cf3>  -> Matched IP 172.16.3.113 to key MD5=aba77e2d0baf5ab33a464e
85cb5d37ac

cf3>  -> Going to secondary storage for key

cf3> .....................[.h.a.i.l.]............................
....

cf3> Strong authentication of server=172.16.3.113 connection
confirmed

cf3>  -> Public key identity of host "172.16.3.113" is "MD5=aba77e
2d0baf5ab33a464e85cb5d37ac"
```

```
cf3>  -> Last saw 172.16.3.113 (+MD5=aba77e2d0baf5ab33a464e85cb5d3
7ac) first time now


cf3>  -> Going to secondary storage for key


cf3>  ->>  Entering /var/cfengine/masterfiles


cf3>  ->>  Entering /var/cfengine/masterfiles


cf3>  -> /var/cfengine/inputs/addusergroup.cf wasn't at
destination (copying)


cf3>  -> Copying from 172.16.3.113:/var/cfengine/masterfiles/
addusergroup.cf


cf3>  -> Copy of regular file succeeded /var/cfengine/masterfiles/
addusergroup.cf to /var/cfengine/inputs/addusergroup.cf.cfnew


cf3>  -> File permissions on /var/cfengine/inputs/addusergroup.cf
as promised


cf3>  -> Updated file from 172.16.3.113:/var/cfengine/masterfiles/
addusergroup.cf


…..
```

We can see from the output that `cf-agent` when run with the configuration file `failsafe.cf` copies the new configuration file `addusergroup.cf` from the policy distribution server with the IP address `172.16.3.113` to the client with the IP address `172.16.3.178`. Now, as the files have been copied, let's check whether the user exists:

```
root@my10system.com#cat /etc/passwd|grep clark
root@my10system.com#
```

As there is no output, the user *clark* does not currently exist on the host.

Now let's execute the configuration file and verify that the user has been created:

```
root@my10system.com# cf-agent -v -f /var/cfengine/inputs/
addusergroup.cf
cf3> Cfengine - autonomous configuration engine - commence self-
diagnostic prelude
```

```
…..
…..
cf3> Cfengine - 3.1.5 Copyright (C) Cfengine AS 2008,2010-
…..
…..
cf3>  -> Verifying the syntax of the inputs...

cf3>  -> Caching the state of validation

cf3>   > Parsing file ./addusergroup.cf

cf3> Initiate variable convergence...

cf3> Initiate variable convergence...


…..
…..
cf3>    commands in bundle addusergroup (1)

cf3>  -> Promiser string contains a valid executable (/usr/sbin/
useradd) - ok

cf3>     Promise handle:

cf3>     Promise made by: /usr/sbin/useradd

cf3>  -> Executing '/usr/sbin/useradd clark' ...(timeout=-
678,owner=-1,group=-1)

cf3>  -> (Setting umask to 77)

cf3>  -> Finished command related to promiser "/usr/sbin/useradd"
-- succeeded

cf3>  ?> defining promise result class changes

cf3> Q: "...in/useradd clar": Creating mailbox file: File exists
```

```
Q: "...in/useradd clar": useradd: warning: the home directory
already exists.

Q: "...in/useradd clar": Not copying any file from skel directory
into it.

cf3> I: Last 3 quoted lines were generated by promiser "/usr/sbin/
useradd clark"

cf3>  -> Completed execution of /usr/sbin/useradd clark

cf3>  -> Promiser string contains a valid executable (/usr/bin/
chage) - ok

cf3>     Promise handle:

cf3>     Promise made by: /usr/bin/chage

cf3>  -> Executing '/usr/bin/chage -M 60 -W 53 clark'
...(timeout=-678,owner=0,group=-1)

cf3>  -> (Setting umask to 77)

cf3>  -> Finished command related to promiser "/usr/bin/chage"
- succeeded

cf3> Q: ".../bin/chage -M 6": cf3> Changing uid to 0

cf3> I: Last 1 quoted lines were generated by promiser "/usr/bin/
chage -M 60 -W 53 clark"

cf3>  -> Completed execution of /usr/bin/chage -M 60 -W 53 clark

cf3>      +  Private classes augmented:

cf3>      -  Private classes diminished:
```

```
cf3>    commands in bundle addusergroup (2)

cf3>      +  Private classes augmented:

cf3>      -  Private classes diminished:

cf3>    commands in bundle addusergroup (3)

cf3>

cf3> Outcome of version (not specified) (agent-0): Promises
observed to be kept 0%, Promises repaired 100%, Promises not
repaired 0%

cf3> Estimated system complexity as touched objects = 0, for 2
promises
.....
root@my10system.com#
```

If we observe the output, it shows that a user was created and the appropriate password expiry was set for it. Let's see the details of the user here:

```
root@my10system.com# cat /etc/passwd|grep clark
clark:x:514:514::/home/clark:/bin/bash
root@my10system.com# chage -l clark
......
Minimum number of days between password change    : 0

Maximum number of days between password change    : 60

Number of days of warning before password expires   : 53

root@my10system.com#
```

From the output we are able to confirm that the user was created, a maximum password expiry for 60 days was set, and the number of days of warning before password expires was set to 53. Now let's execute the configuration file `addusergroup.cf` again and see what happens:

```
root@my10system.com# cf-agent -v -f /var/cfengine/inputs/
addusergroup.cf

cf3> Cfengine - autonomous configuration engine - commence
self-diagnostic prelude

…..

…..

cf3> Cfengine - 3.1.5 Copyright (C) Cfengine AS 2008,2010-

cf3>    commands in bundle addusergroup (1)


cf3>  -> Promiser string contains a valid executable (/usr/sbin/
useradd) - ok


cf3>     Promise handle:


cf3>     Promise made by: /usr/sbin/useradd


cf3>  -> Executing '/usr/sbin/useradd clark' ...(timeout=-
678,owner=-1,group=-1)


cf3>  -> (Setting umask to 77)


cf3>  !! Finished command related to promiser "/usr/sbin/useradd"
-- an error occurred (returned 9)


cf3> Q: "...in/useradd clar": useradd: user clark exists


cf3> I: Last 1 quoted lines were generated by promiser "/usr/sbin/
useradd clark"


cf3>  -> Completed execution of /usr/sbin/useradd clark


cf3> Skipping whole next promise (/usr/bin/chage), as context
changes is not relevant
```

```
.......

.......

cf3> Skipping whole next promise (/usr/bin/chage), as context
changes is not relevant


cf3> Outcome of version (not specified) (agent-0): Promises
observed to be kept 0%, Promises repaired 0%, Promises not
repaired 100%


cf3> Estimated system complexity as touched objects = 0, for 1
promises


cf3>  -> Writing last-seen observations


cf3>  -> Keyring is empty


cf3>  -> No lock purging scheduled
```

If we observe the output, we see that the command for user creation fails and hence the class `changes` was not satisfied so the next command promise was skipped.

What just happened?

We defined *common control body*. Under the common control body we defined a bundle sequence for the bundle agent `addusergroup`. Next, we defined the bundle agent `addusergroup` for creating a user and defined a commands promise for executing the command `/usr/sbin/useradd` with argument as the required username `clark`. We also set a classes promise defining how that class `change` is satisfied. Only if this class is set will the promises be executed. This was defined in the `satisfied` class body where we used the `promise_repaired` promise to set the class. When we executed the configuration file for the first time and the user did not exist on the system, the class `changes` was set and the next set of command promises for setting the password expiry and days of warning before the password expiry was set to the specified number of days. But when we executed the configuration files again, after the user was created, the commands promise for creating the user failed and hence the class `changes` was not set so further command promises were skipped. CFEngine does not provide any inbuilt if-else condition promises so all such conditional or event driven actions need to be executed using proper classes.

Time for action – setting up a web service

To set up a web service we will need a web server. We'll use Apache here. The next code snippet may be copied to a file called `webserver-config.cf`. Various methods are available for installation of packages, such as yum, apt, zipper, and so on. The method may be defined by the `package_method` attribute under the agent bundle. For example:

```
package_method  => apt
```

1. We'll use the attribute now, but in this case we will be using yum as our package method The following lines should be copied to a file:

```
#####################################################
# Apache web server installation
#####################################################

body common control

{

bundlesequence => { "webserver", "start_webserver" };

}



bundle agent webserver
{

vars:

 "match_package" slist => {

                          "apache2",

                          "apache2-mod_php5",

                          "apache2-prefork",

                          "php5"

                          };

packages:
```

```
  "$(match_package)"
     package_policy => "add",
     package_method => yum;
}


body package_method yum


{

any::

 package_changes => "bulk";
 package_list_command => "/usr/bin/yum list installed";
 package_list_name_regex    => "([^.]+).*";
 package_list_version_regex => "[^\s]\s+([^\s]+).*";
 package_list_arch_regex    => "[^.]+\.([^\s]+).*";
 package_installed_regex => ".*installed.*";
 package_name_convention => "$(name).$(arch)";


 # Use these only if not using a separate version/arch string

  package_version_regex => "2.0.55";
  package_name_regex => "apache";
  package_arch_regex => "x86_64";
  package_add_command => "/usr/bin/yum -y install";
  package_delete_command => "/bin/rpm -e";
  package_verify_command => "/bin/rpm -V";
}

bundle agent start_webserver

{

processes:


  any::


    "httpd" restart_class => "start_server";
```

```
commands:

 start_server::

  "/usr/local/apache/bin/apachectl start";

}
```

2. Let's first execute `cf-agent` with the configuration file `failsafe.cf` so that the new configuration file `webserver-config` will be copied to the individual hosts.

```
root@my10system.com#cf-agent -v -f /var/cfengine/inputs/failsafe.
cf

cf3> Cfengine - autonomous configuration engine - commence self-
diagnostic prelude

…..

…..

cf3> Cfengine - 3.1.5 Copyright (C) Cfengine AS 2008,2010-

…..

…..

cf3>  -> Copy file /var/cfengine/inputs from /var/cfengine/
masterfiles check


cf3> No existing connection to 172.16.3.113 is established...


cf3> Set cfengine port number to 5308 = 5308


cf3> Set connection timeout to 10


cf3> Connect to 172.16.3.113 = 172.16.3.113, port = (5308=5308)


cf3>  -> Matched IP 172.16.3.113 to key MD5=aba77e2d0baf5ab33a464e
85cb5d37ac


cf3>  -> Going to secondary storage for key


cf3> ....................[.h.a.i.l.]...........................
....
```

```
cf3> Strong authentication of server=172.16.3.113 connection
confirmed

cf3>  -> Public key identity of host "172.16.3.113" is "MD5=aba77e
2d0baf5ab33a464e85cb5d37ac"

cf3>  -> Last saw 172.16.3.113 (+MD5=aba77e2d0baf5ab33a464e85cb5d3
7ac) first time now

cf3>  -> Going to secondary storage for key

cf3>  ->>  Entering /var/cfengine/masterfiles

cf3>  -> /var/cfengine/inputs/webserver-config.cf wasn't at
destination (copying)

cf3>  -> Copying from 172.16.3.113:/var/cfengine/masterfiles/
webserver-config.cf

cf3>  -> Copy of regular file succeeded /var/cfengine/masterfiles/
webserver-config.cf to /var/cfengine/inputs/webserver-config.
cf.cfnew

cf3>  -> File permissions on /var/cfengine/inputs/webserver-
config.cf as promised

cf3>  -> Updated file from 172.16.3.113:/var/cfengine/masterfiles/
webserver-config.cf

…...
…...
```

This output shows that the new configuration file `webserver-config` was copied correctly from the policy distribution host with IP address `172.16.3.113` to the client host with the IP address `172.16.3.178` as per the promise in the configuration file `failsafe.cf`.

3. These promises may again be verified by running `cf-promises`.

```
root@my10system.com# cf-promises -v -f /var/cfengine/webserver-config.cf

cf3> Cfengine - autonomous configuration engine - commence self-diagnostic prelude

cf3> Cfengine - 3.1.5 Copyright (C) Cfengine AS 2008,2010-

…..

…..

cf3>  -> Input file is changed since last valiadtion, validating it


cf3>   > Parsing file ./webserver-config.cf


cf3> Initiate variable convergence...


cf3> Initiate variable convergence...


…..

…..

cf3> Initiate variable convergence...


cf3>  -> Inputs are valid

root@my10system.com#
```

The output shows that the promises were validated correctly.

4. Once the configuration file has been copied and the promises verified, let's execute the promises file to set up the HTTP web service.

```
root@my10system.com# cf-agent -f /var/cfengine/inputs/webserver-config.cf

root@my10system.com#
```

5. As there is no output, the configuration file was executed correctly and the web service was set up.

What just happened?

We had to set up a web service and for this we choose the Apache web server. We defined a bundlesequence under the common control body with two bundles named `webserver` and `start_webserver`. Under the bundle agent webserver we defined a list of required packages for apache2, php5, apache2-mod_php5, apache2-prefork. Next we defined a package addition policy and the method for adding packages. To verify, we list the installed packages, see if the required packages are there, and, if not, install the apache package and modules using *yum*. In the next bundle agent named `start_webserver` we defined a `restart_class` named `httpd`. For this class we defined a commands promise to start the web service with the command `service httpd start`.

Time for action – setting up a database service

1. For setting up a database server we'll need a database server software package. We'll use MySQL as the database server. The next code snippet should be copied to a CFEngine promises file named `mysql-install.cf`:

```
bundle agent install_mysql
{
vars:

  redhat::

    "match_package" slist => {
                               "mysql",
                               "mysql-server",
                               };
  debian::

   "match_package" slist => {
                              "mysql-server",
                              };

packages:

   "$(match_package)"

         package_policy => "add",
         package_method => generic;

processes:

  "mysqld" -> "start_mysql",

       restart_class => "start_mysql",

commands:
```

```
start_mysql::

  "/etc/init.d/mysql restart",

      handle => "start_mysql",
     comment => "Start the mysqld service";

}
```

2. Let's run `cf-agent` with the configuration file `failsafe.cf` to copy the new configuration file from the policy distribution server.

```
root@my10system.com#cf-agent -v -f /var/cfengine/inputs/failsafe.
cf

cf3> Cfengine - autonomous configuration engine - commence self-
diagnostic prelude

…..

…..

cf3> Cfengine - 3.1.5 Copyright (C) Cfengine AS 2008,2010-

…..

…..

cf3>  -> Copy file /var/cfengine/inputs from /var/cfengine/
masterfiles check


cf3> No existing connection to 172.16.3.113 is established...


cf3> Set cfengine port number to 5308 = 5308


cf3> Set connection timeout to 10


cf3> Connect to 172.16.3.113 = 172.16.3.113, port = (5308=5308)


cf3>  -> Matched IP 172.16.3.113 to key MD5=aba77e2d0baf5ab33a464e
85cb5d37ac


cf3>  -> Going to secondary storage for key


cf3> .....................[.h.a.i.l.]............................
....
```

```
cf3> Strong authentication of server=172.16.3.113 connection
confirmed

cf3>  -> Public key identity of host "172.16.3.113" is "MD5=aba77e
2d0baf5ab33a464e85cb5d37ac"

cf3>  -> Last saw 172.16.3.113 (+MD5=aba77e2d0baf5ab33a464e85cb5d3
7ac) first time now

cf3>  -> Going to secondary storage for key

cf3>  ->>  Entering /var/cfengine/masterfiles

cf3>  -> /var/cfengine/inputs/mysql-install.cf wasn't at
destination (copying)

cf3>  -> Copying from 172.16.3.113:/var/cfengine/masterfiles/
mysql-install.cf

cf3>  -> Copy of regular file succeeded /var/cfengine/masterfiles/
mysql-install.cf to /var/cfengine/inputs/mysql-install.cf.cfnew

cf3>  -> File permissions on /var/cfengine/inputs/mysql-install.cf
as promised

cf3>  -> Updated file from 172.16.3.113:/var/cfengine/masterfiles/
mysql-install.cf

…...
…...
```

3. Let's verify the promise using `cf-promises`:

   ```
   root@my1.system.com# cf-promises -f  mysql-install.cf
   root@my1.system.com#
   ```

   No output validates the promises. The file may be distributed to the servers that will act as database servers.

4. Now we may go ahead and execute the promises with `cf-agent`.

What just happened?

We defined a bundle agent `install_mysql`. Under this bundle agent we defined two classes `redhat` and `debian`. Under these two classes we defined the packages to be installed for each of the operating systems. Next, we defined promises for package installations. Finally, we defined commands to start the MySQL server after installation.

Time for action – mounting a NFS volume

For setting up a NFS shared server, the following two steps are required (besides setting up the configuration file `/etc/exports` on the NFS server).

1. Allow the IP or host name of the NFS client to connect to the NFS server in `/etc/hosts.allow` and `/etc/hosts.deny`.
2. Mounting the NFS share on the NFS client.

   Thus we'll need two CFEngine promises—one which configures the state of the NFS server and the other which mounts the NFS share on the NFS client. We presume that the host name or the IP(s) for the client host is already added to the `/etc/hosts.allow` and `/etc/hosts.deny` file as the client hosts are already part of a network.

3. Let's write a CFEngine promise file that configures the state of the NFS server first. The following lines should be copied to a file named `nfs-exports.cf`:

```
################################
# Adding lines to '/etc/exports' for an NFS server
#################################

body common control

{

any::

bundlesequence       =>      { "nfsexport" };

}

bundle agent nfsexport

{

files:
```

```
"/etc/exports"

create => "true",
edit_line => addline;

}

bundle edit_line addline

{

insert_lines:
"/data 192.168.2.0/255.255.255.0 (rw)";

}
```

4. You should copy the file from the policy distribution server to the client host by executing the `cf-agent` command with the configuration file `failsafc.cf`.

5. In case the new configuration file has been copied from the centralized policy distribution server with the IP address `172.16.3.113` to the client host with the IP address `172.16.3.178` let's verify the promise using `cf-promises`:

   ```
   root@my1.system.com# cf-promises -f nfs-exports.cf
   root@my1.system.com#
   ```

   No output validates the promises. You could also run the command in verbose mode to see how CFEngine validates the promises. CFEngine writes the validations in the file `<promises_file>.txt` and `<promises_file>.html`. If you notice, we have not included the `cfengine_stdlib.cf` in promises file here. This is because we did not use any of the predefined bundles or body.

6. Now this promises file may be put on the server which is sharing its NFS volume. This can be done by could also triggering the transfer using:

   ```
   root@my1.system.com# cf-runagent -H <IP_of_NFS_Server>
   ```

   Additionally, we need to ensure that the file is not propagated to hosts which are not to act as NFS server. For this we need to create additional access rules.

   Once we have the file system exported we need to mount the file system on the client host.

7. For this we write another configuration file `nfs-mount.cf`. The following lines should be copied to a file `nfs-mount.cf`, for instance.

> Please note: You may have to add additional access or deny rules to this file as you do not want all servers to add these lines to their `/etc/exports`. The policies should only be executed on servers which are sharing their volume.

```
##################
# Mount NFS
##################
body common control

{

bundlesequence => { "mounts" };

}



bundle agent mounts

{

storage:

  # The file system has already been exported

  "/mnt" mount  => nfs("my10.system.com","/data");

}



body mount nfs(server,source)

{

mount_type => "nfs";
mount_source => "$(source)";
mount_server => "$(server)";
edit_fstab => "true";
```

```
unmount => "true";

}
```

> Please note: You may have to add additional access or deny rules to this file as you may not want to mount the NFS volume on all hosts. The NFS volume should only be added to the required hosts.

8. The new configuration file should be copied to the client host by executing `cf-agent` with the configuration file `failsafe.cf`.

9. Once the new configuration file `nfs-mount.cf` has been copied from the policy distribution server to the client host, to validate the promises we will again use `cf-promises`.

   ```
   root@my1.system.com# cf-promises -f nfs-mount.cf
   root@my1.system.com#
   ```

   No output validates the promises.

10. Now the new configuration file `nfs-mount.cf` may be executed to mount the shared NFS volume on the client host.

What just happened?

We defined a class `any` and defined a bundlesequence for the bundle `nfsexport` under the `common control` body. Next we specified the file where we needed to add the lines. Following this we defined that the file needs to be created if it does not exist. To add a line we defined the promise `addline` for the bundle `edit_line`. Finally we defined the line to be inserted under the `edit_line` bundle using the `insert_lines` promise and provided the line that needed to be added.

In the next promise file named `nfs-mount.cf` we defined how to mount the exported file system on the host.

Time for action – setting up a network interface

This task looks a bit odd—why would one set up a network service using CFEngine when one knows that:

- Without a network service no policy files can be transferred from the central policy repository
- In almost all cases the network service would have been configured when the server was installed

But if we look around, we see that today a host does not always have only one IP address. For example:

- Virtualization—standalone hardware boxes hosting multiple virtual servers
- Multi-homed interfaces
- Load Balancers such as LVS, perlball, and so on, which need to have multiple interfaces both real and virtual
- Software routers such as Zebra, which need to have multiple interfaces

These are situations where additional interfaces might be needed, and this is where CFEngine may help in configuring interfaces on multiple multi-homed systems. Let's see how we can add additional interfaces on client hosts. We can configure the primary interface using CFEngine but let's presume that the primary interface was already configured, which will be correct in most cases.

1. The following code snippet should be copied to a CFEngine promise file named `network-interface-configure.cf`, for example.

```
##################
# Configuring network interfaces
##################

body common control

{

bundlesequence => { "niface" };

inputs    =>  {"cfengine_stdlib.cf"};

}



bundle agent niface

{



vars:
```

```
"lines" string => "DEVICE=eth1

                   BOOTPROTO=dhcp

                   HWADDR=00:07:E9:0B:59:F9

                   ONBOOT=no

                   DHCP_HOSTNAME=my15.system.com";



files:

"/etc/sysconfig/network-scripts/ifcfg-eth1"

create => "true",
empty_file_before_editing => "true"
edit_line     => append_if_no_line("$(niface.lines)");
classes => satisfied("file_updated");

commands:
file_updated::
"/sbin/ifconfig"

args  => "eth1 up",
contain => standard;


}

body contain standard
{
useshell => "true";
exec_owner => "root";
}
body classes satisfied(new_class)

{

  promise_repaired => { "$(new_class)" };

}
```

2. We should copy the new configuration file from the policy distribution server to the client host using the command `cf-agent` with the configuration file `failsafe.cf`.

3. Once the new configuration file has been copied to the client host, let's validate our configuration file with the help of `cf-promises` as follows:

   ```
   root@my1.system.com# cf-promises -f /var/cfengine/inputs/ network-interface-configure.cf
   root@my1.system.com#
   ```

   No output validates the promises. Now we may distribute the file to the respective servers.

4. Now we may execute the promises with `cf-agent`.

What just happened?

We defined a bundlesequence under the common control body with bundle `niface`. For the `niface` agent bundle we defined the string variable `lines`. We defined the name `eth1` to be given to the interface provided. To configure the interface we defined a file corresponding to the interface to be configured and appended the required network values to the file. To ensure that the file was empty we set `empty_file_before_editing` to true. To ensure that the file was edited properly we set a class `files_updated`. Further promises would only be executed once the above class was set. This ensures that if the file editing failed for some reason and the promise was not repaired, the interface was not brought up. Finally, we brought the network up by running `ifconfig <interface_name>`.

Time for action – adding a jailed user to a system

There are various instances where we moght want to `jail` a user to a specific directory. One such scenario is where in we want to create a secure FTP user *clark* who should only have secure FTP or secure cp access to the directory `/home/sftp-clark`. To achieve this we use an open source tool 'jailkit'. The latest stable version of this tool (as of this writing) can be downloaded from: `http://olivier.sessink.nl/jailkit/jailkit-2.13.tar.bz2`.

Now let's create a promise file that downloads the tool, installs it on a number of servers and then creates a `jailed` user as discussed above. As 'jailkit' is not a standard package available in all OS repositories, we will not use the standard CFEngine 'package' promises but will use `bash` commands for its installation. Alternatively, you may create an '.rpm' or '.deb' file from the source and install it using the standard CFEngine 'package' promises.

1. The following lines should be copied to a file named `installjailkit.cf`.

```
##############################################
# Installing jailkit and configuring a 'jailed' user who can only
#sftp or scp to a box
##############################################

body common control

       {

       bundlesequence  =>       { "installjailkit", "jailuser",
"linesadd" };

       inputs          =>       { "cfengine_stdlib.cf" };

       }

       bundle agent installjailkit

      {

       commands:


"/usr/bin/wget http://olivier.sessink.nl/jailkit/jailkit-2.13.tar.
bz2;/usr/bin/bunzip2 jailkit-2.13.tar.bz2;tar -xf jailkit-2.13.
tar;c
d jailkit-2.13;./configure;/usr/bin/make;/usr/bin/make install"

       contain => standard,
       classes => satisfied("jailkit_installed");


       }

      bundle agent jailuser

       {

       commands:
        jailkit_installed::

       "/usr/sbin/jk_init -v -j /home/clark sftp scp";
       "/usr/sbin/jk_init -v -j /home/clark jk_lsh" ;
       "/usr/sbin/jk_jailuser -v -j /home/clark clark" ;
       "/usr/bin/killall jk_socketd ; /usr/sbin/jk_socketd" ;
```

```
        contain => standard,
        classes => satisfied("jailkit_configured");

        }

        bundle agent linesadd

{

        vars:
        jailkit_configured::

        "lines" string => "'[clark]'

                        'paths= /usr/bin, /usr/lib/
         'executables= /usr/bin/scp, /usr/lib/sftp-server'";


   files:

        "/home/clark/etc/jailkit/jk_lsh.ini"

        create => "true",
        edit_line => append_if_no_line("$(linesadd.lines)");

}

        body contain standard

   {

   useshell => "true";
   exec_owner => "root";

   }
body classes satisfied(new_class)

     {

     promise_repaired => { "$(new_class)" };

}
```

2. You should copy the new configuration file `installjailkit.cf` by executing **`cf-agent -v -f /var/cfengine/inputs/failsafe.cf`**

3. Now that the file has been copied from the policy distribution server to the client host, let's verify the promise using `cf-promises`.

```
root@my1.system.com# cf-promises -f installjailkit.cf
root@my1.system.com#
```

4. The promises seem to be good. As the promises have been validated correctly we can go ahead and execute the configuration file with the command:

```
cf-agent -v -f /var/cfengine/inputs/installjailkit.cf
```

What just happened?

Under the common control body, we defined a bundlesequence for the two bundles `installjailkit` and `jailuser`. Next, we provided the command for downloading the tool and installing the software. In addition, to ensure that the download and install of the tool worked successfully, we set a class `jailkit_installed`. Further set of promises would only be executed if the class `jailkit_installed` is set and this will only happen if the download and install of jailkit worked. We ran `jailkit` commands to jail the user *clark* to the directory `/home/clark` and restricted him from using any commands other than `sftp` and `scp`. We again set a class `jailkit_configured` which would only be set if the commands in the bundle `jailuser` were executed correctly. Finally, we defined the bundle agent `linesadd` to append a few lines to the file `jk_lsh.ini` to provide the path for the `sftp` and `scp` binaries to the user *clark*. This would only be executed if the class `jailkit_configured` is set.

Pop quiz

In the previous sections we saw how to set up a network interface. On a multi-homed host with the following three IP addresses:

```
192.168.2.3
192.168.2.4
192.168.2.5
```

- How can you ensure that `cf-serverd` always binds only to the IP 192.168.2.3 after a restart or a reboot?
- How can you ensure that whenever the CFEngine agent process runs it sets the default Java home to `/usr/local/jdk-1.6.0_23`?
- How can you schedule a promise to be executed at 1500 Hrs on the fifteenth day of a month, if and only if the fifteenth day is a Sunday?

Have a go hero – verifying if the object is a soft link

Write a CFEngine promise file to verify whether the file object is a valid soft link.

Hint: There are various instances where we want to know whether the file object is a soft link or hard link. One such scenario is when you have created a soft link for a MySQL database pointing to an additional disk which was added separately to take care of disk space issues on a host. Here, let's assume that you have the default MySQL instance running on port `3306` and the databases are stored at `/var/lib/mysql`. Now some of the databases have been moved to `/data/mysql-data/` by your team and soft links have been created in `/var/lib/mysql/` pointing to `/data/mysql-data`. Here is an example soft link

```
lrwxrwxrwx 1 root  root    26 Jul 22  2010 db2 -> /data/mysql-data/db2/
```

Now we want to do an audit and get a list of all such existing soft links. The following lines of promises should be copied to a file named `check_soft_links.cf`.

```
body common control
{
bundlesequence => { "soft_links" };
}
bundle agent soft_links
{
vars:
"db_names" slist => { "/var/lib/mysql/db1","/var/lib/mysql/db2","/var/
lib/mysql/db3"  };
classes:
"isdir" expression => islink("$(db_names)");

reports:
isdir::
"$(db_names)Directory exists..";
!isdir::
"$(db_names) Directory does not exist..";

}
```

Summary

The chapter is loaded with CFEngine promises for performing various tasks. The highlights of this chapter are:

- Distribution of promises file to remote hosts from a centralized policy server.
- How to configure the CFEngine clients and servers to transfer files between themselves on the basis of the keys, access rules, number of connections and so on.
- How to configure a host using CFEngine and a PXE boot server. In addition to this, we learned how to define the packages that we want to install after the installation of the operating system.
- How to set up web and database services.
- Configuring Apache as a web server, MySQL as a database server, and configuring a jailed user who has permissions only for SFTP or SCP to the host. This is needed when you want to allow third-party users to access your server securely and get or put files on this host.
- Editing or appending lines in various configuration files using CFEngine.
- This automation chapter dealt with most system configuration issues. In the next chapter we'll deal with auditing already installed systems.

3
System Audit with CFEngine

We made a number of CFEngine promises in the previous two chapters for various tasks. Let's look at a bit of the theory behind these promises.

In this chapter we shall:

- Learn about CFEngine classes
- Learn about a few control promises
- Learn the syntax for writing these promises
- Use CFEngine for system audits

The modus operandi of individual CFEngine promises is fixed and defined in the code. We may configure the details of the behavior using the control promise bodies, though. Promises can be made about all kinds of different aspects of a system: from file attributes, access control decisions, command executions, to creating knowledge relationships. These are classes, vars, and report promises. Also, we may write a combination of these promises in a file to achieve the desired result and hence we may say that the final behavior is 'user defined'.

Classes

Classes in CFEngine are Boolean classifiers that can be used to describe context. While all promise types used are specific to a particular interpretation, they need a "bundle type" interpreter. There are promises which may be defined in any kind of bundle and these promises are of a generic input or output. These are used to classify the properties of an environment or context in which CFEngine runs. There are two types of classes:

1. Hard classes—These are classes which are discovered on CFEngine invocation
2. Soft classes—These are user-defined classes

These two types of classes may be a global class or a local class that depends on the bundle type that the classes are defined under. Classes defined under the "common" bundle type are global classes, whereas classes defined under all other bundle types are local classes. Lets see how we can define CFEngine classes:

```
body common control
{
bundlesequence => { "example", "example_classA", "example_classB" };
}
bundle common example
{
"class_A" expression => "test";
}
bundle agent example_classA
{
classes:
"class_B" expression => "test";
}
bundle agent example_classB
{
"class_C" expression => "test";

reports:
class_A.class_B.class_C::
"Failure";

}
```

In the given example `class_A` is global because it is defined inside the `bundle` global, whereas `class_B` and `class_C` are local classes because they are defined under bundle `agent` and are local to their local bundles. The report result is a `Failure` because for the bundle agent `example_classB`, only `class_A` (a global class) and `class_C` (a local class) are in scope. `class_B` lies outside the scope of bundle agent `example_classB`. Lets see a few promise attributes for classes:

- **or**
    - Type: clist
    - Allowed input range: [a-zA-Z0-9_!&@$|.()]+
    - The given attribute combines class sources with an inclusive OR. This can be defined as shown next:

```
classes:
"test_class"
```

- or => { classmatch("Apache-2.0.63"), "Nginx" };

In the given example, the LHS is true if any one or more of the RHS class expressions are true.

- **and**
  - Type: clist
  - Allowed input range: [a-zA-Z0-9_!&@$|.()]+
  - The given attribute is used to combine class sources with AND. This can be defined as shown next:

    ```
    classes:
    "test_class" and => { classmatch("linux_x86_64_2_6_18.*"),
    ```

  - "Apache-2.0.55" };

In the given example, the LHS is defined if and only if all the RHS class expressions match.

- **xor**
  - Type: clist
  - Allowed input range: [a-zA-Z0-9_!&@$|.()]+
  - The given attribute is used to define combine class sources with XOR. This can be defined as shown next:

    ```
    classes:
    ```

  - "test_class" xor => { "Linux", "solaris", "AIX"};

In the given example, the class on the LHS is defined if any one of the class expressions in the RHS matches.

- **dist**
  - Type: rlist
  - Allowed input range: -9.99999E100,9.99999E100
  - The given attribute is used to generate a probabilistic class distribution. This can be defined as given next:

    ```
    classes:
    "test_class"
    ```

  - dist => { "10", "30", "90" };

In the given example, the sum of 10+30+90 equals 130, and CFEngine, while generating a distribution, picks a number between 1 to 130. The following classes will be generated:

```
test_class_10 (10/130 of the time)
test_class_30 (30/130 of the time)
```

- test_class_90 (90/130 of the time)

- **expression**
  - Type: class
  - Allowed input range: [a-zA-Z0-9_!&@$|.()]+
  - The given attribute is used in evaluating string expression of classes in a normal form. This can be defined as shown next:

    ```
    classes:
    ```

  - "test_class" expression => "apache|nginx";

- **not**
  - Type: class
  - Allowed input range: [a-zA-Z0-9_!&@$|.()]+
  - The given class is used to evaluate the negation of string expressions in normal form. This can be defined as shown next:

    ```
    classes:
    ```

  - "test_class" not => "Windows|AIX";

  In the given example the class on the LHS will only be defined if the class expression on RHS is false.

We just saw how classes may be defined; lets move ahead and see more about the common, agent, and server control promise types.

Control promises

There are promises provided by CFEngine which control the behavior of the components. The control promises are the promises used by all CFEngine components. For example, the "inputs" promise which describes the additional configuration files to be included or the "bundlesequence" promise defining the sequence of bundles to be executed. Although the promises are hard-coded within the code, one can still control the behavior by altering the control body for each of these. When we talk about the behavior of the promises it means that we can alter the default behavior of the hard-coded promises. For example, the "mailmaxlines" promise, by default, sends the 30 lines of output in the e-mail which can then be changed to the desired number of lines that will be sent in the e-mail as follows:

```
body executor control
{
mailmaxlines => "50";
}
```

Let's now see a few control promises in `detail`-Common Control promises.

A common control promise body refers to those promises which are hard-coded in all the components of CFEngine and therefore affect the behavior of all the components. Let's look at a few control parameters for different components:

- bundlesequence
    - Type: slist
    - Allowed input range: .*

    Since CFEngine 3, there is a clearer separation between internal control parameters and user definitions. User defined behaviors require a promise and therefore should be defined in a bundle type. The *bundlesequence* control parameter specifies a list of promise bundles to verify in order. As it is a list of promise bundles, the parameter is of *vars* promise type **slist**. As it is a list of bundle names there is no default value but not specifying a *bundlesequence* may result in a compilation error. Now bundles act as characteristics of a system and hence for different group of servers you may specify a different *bundlesequence*. The example below sets different *bundlesequences* for different groups of servers, which have been put in two different categories using classes.

    Here's an example:

    ```
    body common control
    {
    mailservers::
    bundlesequence => { "sendmail", "pop_config" };
    webservers::
    bundlesequence => { "apache", "log_rotate" }
    ```

    - }
- 3.1.2.
- inputs
    - Type: slist
    - Allowed input range: .*

This control parameter can be used to add filenames to parse for the promises. As the parameter specifies a list of files the parameter is a *vars* promise type **slist**. It has no default values. If no files are specified, no other filenames will be included during compilation. It assumes the filenames to be present in the same directory as the file which references it. The next example shows us the usage of this control parameter:

```
body common control
{
inputs => { "update.cf", "cfengine_stdlib.cf" };
```

- }

Here we have included two additional files, `update.cf` and `cfengine_stdlib.cf`, which will be parsed with the files that reference them.

> We cannot use regular expressions for file names here. We should specify file names that exist.

Agent control promises

The agent control promise defines the promises made by cf-agent. Let's look at a few important agent control promises:

- **bindtointerface**
    - Type: string
    - Allowed input range: .*

  This control promise is used to specify the interface which may be used by the server and the client on multi-homed hosts. We need to specify the IP address of the interface and not the name of the interface:

    - bindtointerface => 192.168.2.1

- **expireafter**
    - Type: int
    - Allowed input range: 0, 9999999999
    - Default value: 1 min

  The expireafter promise specifies the locking time after which CFEngine will kill and restart its attempt to keep a promise. This locking time may be specified as follows:

    - expireafter => "60";   #1 hour

- **ifelapsed**
  - Type: int
  - Allowed input range: 0, 9999999999
  - Default value: 1 minutes

  This control promise is used for specifying the global default time that must elapse before promise will be rechecked. This is used to protect promises which may take longer to verify. This may be used to override the global settings. The next example shows how this can be specified:

```
body agent control
{
  ifelapsed => "240";      #4 hours
```

  - }

- **hostnamekeys**
  - Type: (menu options)
  - Allowed input range: true, false, yes, no, on, off
  - Default value: false

  This control promise is an important one in context to the CFEngine server client communications. This specifies whether the pppkeys should be labeled by host names or IP. If this is set as 'true' the pppkeys will be labeled by host name. The next example shows how to use this:

```
hostnamekeys => "true";
```

- **maxconnections**
  - Type: int
  - Allowed input range: 0, 9999999999
  - Default value: 30 remote queries

  This control promise defines the maximum number of allowed outgoing connections to `cf-serverd`. While specifying the maximum number of connections please note that this value should not breach the kernel limit on total open file descriptors. The promise can set the value for both the client machine and the server machine. This value can be specified as follows:

```
# For client host
body agent control
{
maxconnections => "300";
}
```

```
# For server host
body server control
{
maxconnections => "300";
}
```

Please note that for the client host it will be an agent control promise and for the server host it will be a server control promise.

- **suspiciousnames**
    - Type: slist
    - Allowed input range: string

The given promise is used to specify a list of file names which if found during a file search an alert flag should be raised. This list supports regular expressions. The list of files may be specified as follows:

```
body agent control
{
suspiciousnames => { "suspect", "*.lkm", "rootkithunter" }
}
```

Time for action – file and directory permissions audit

1. We are already aware that a file system has specific permissions for a few important files and directories, by default. These permissions are set keeping in mind the access each user needs on these files and directories, which in turn builds a layer of security. Lets see the default permissions of a few important files and directories:

```
root@my1.system.com# ls -lh /etc/passwd
-rw-r--r-- 1 root root 1.5K 2010-08-26 14:54 /etc/passwd
root@my1.system.com# ls -lh /etc/shadow
-rw-r----- 1 root shadow 1.1K 2010-08-20 11:05 /etc/shadow
root@my1.system.com# ls  -lh /etc/sysctl.conf
-rw-r--r-- 1 root root 2.3K 2009-03-19 03:47 /etc/sysctl.conf
```

```
[root@teche ~]# ls -lh /
total 168K
drwxr-xr-x   2 root root 4.0K Apr  8  2010 bin
drwxr-xr-x   4 root root 3.0K Apr  7  2010 boot
drwxr-xr-x   3 root root 4.0K Jan 31  2010 data
drwxr-xr-x  12 root root 3.9K Jun 24 12:48 dev
drwxr-xr-x 109 root root  12K Jun 26 04:02 etc
drwxr-xr-x   6 root root 4.0K Nov 23  2010 home
drwxr-xr-x  11 root root 4.0K Apr  6  2010 lib
drwxr-xr-x   7 root root 4.0K Jun  2  2010 lib64
drwx------   2 root root  16K Jan  6  2010 lost+found
drwxr-xr-x   2 root root 4.0K Mar 11  2009 media
drwxr-xr-x   2 root root 4.0K Sep  4  2009 misc
drwxr-xr-x   2 root root 4.0K Mar 11  2009 mnt
drwxr-xr-x  16 root root 4.0K Jun 20 14:27 opt
dr-xr-xr-x 101 root root    0 May  8 19:46 proc
drwxr-x---  12 root root 4.0K Jun 19 14:38 root
drwxr-xr-x   2 root root  12K Apr  8  2010 sbin
drwxr-xr-x   2 root root 4.0K Jan  6  2010 selinux
drwxr-xr-x   2 root root 4.0K Mar 11  2009 srv
drwxr-xr-x  11 root root    0 May  8 19:46 sys
drwxrwxrwt   5 root root 4.0K Jun 26 15:48 tmp
drwxr-xr-x  15 root root 4.0K Jan 30  2010 usr
drwxr-xr-x  23 root root 4.0K Nov  1  2010 var
[root@teche ~]#
```

2. As we see in the previous screenshot, these are the default permissions assigned to important files and directories by the operating system. Now these and a few more permissions should be maintained 'as is' unless there are special needs where we want to alter these default permissions. To keep a tab on any changes in this default setup we need to audit the permissions for the above and a few more directories.

3. Let's see how we can do this using CFEngine. You may save the following code snippet in the file `check_permissions.cf`:

```
body common control

{

bundlesequence => { "checkpermissions" };

inputs => { "cfengine_stdlib.cf" };

}

bundle agent checkpermissions

{
```

```
vars:

"dirlist" slist => {

                    "/bin", "/boot", "dev", "/etc", "/home", "/
lib", "/media", "/mnt", "/opt", "/sbin", "/selinux", "/srv", "/
sys", "/usr", "/var"

                        };

files:
"/etc/passwd"
perms => mog("644","root","root");
"/etc/shadow"
perms => mog("400","root","shadow");
"/etc/sysctl.conf"
perms => mog("644","root",root);
"$(dirlist)"
perms => mog("755","root","root");
"/root" perms => mog("750","root","root");
"/tmp" perms => mog("1777","root","root");
"/lost+found" perms => mog("0700","root","root");

"/proc" perms => mog("555","root","root");
}
```

4. Let's verify the promises:

```
root@my.system.com# cf-promises -f /var/cfengine/inputs/check-
permissions.cf
root@my.system.com#
```

No output means we are good with the promises. If you want to see a more verbose output you may use the **-v** switch with the command.

5. Now let's execute the promises and see what happens:

```
root@my.system.com# cf-agent -v -f /var/cfengine/inputs/check-
permissions.cf


..
..
=============================================================


cf3    files in bundle checkpermissions (1)
```

```
cf3   ============================================================
cf3
cf3 Verifying SQL table promises is only available with Cfengine
Nova or above
cf3
cf3     .........................................................
cf3     Promise handle:
cf3     Promise made by: /etc/passwd
cf3     .........................................................
cf3
cf3  -> Using literal pathtype for /etc/passwd
cf3  -> Handling file existence constraints on /etc/passwd
cf3  -> File permissions on /etc/passwd as promised
cf3  -> Handling file existence constraints on /etc/passwd
cf3  -> File permissions on /etc/passwd as promised
cf3
cf3     .........................................................
cf3     Promise handle:
cf3     Promise made by: /etc/shadow
cf3     .........................................................
cf3
cf3  -> Using literal pathtype for /etc/shadow
cf3 Unknown group 'shadow'
cf3 Promise (version not specified) belongs to bundle
'checkpermissions' in file '/var/cfengine/inputs/check_
permissions.cf' near line 19
cf3  -> Handling file existence constraints on /etc/shadow
cf3  -> File permissions on /etc/shadow as promised
cf3  -> Handling file existence constraints on /etc/shadow
cf3  -> File permissions on /etc/shadow as promised
cf3
cf3     .........................................................
cf3     Promise handle:
cf3     Promise made by: /etc/sysctl.conf
cf3     .........................................................
cf3
cf3  -> Using literal pathtype for /etc/sysctl.conf
```

```
cf3  -> Handling file existence constraints on /etc/sysctl.conf
cf3  -> File permissions on /etc/sysctl.conf as promised
cf3  -> Handling file existence constraints on /etc/sysctl.conf
cf3  -> File permissions on /etc/sysctl.conf as promised
..
..
cf3    ==========================================================
cf3    files in bundle checkpermissions (3)
cf3    ==========================================================
cf3
cf3 Verifying SQL table promises is only available with Cfengine
Nova or above
cf3 Outcome of version (not specified) (agent-0): Promises
observed to be kept 100%, Promises repaired 0%, Promises not
repaired 0%
cf3 Estimated system complexity as touched objects = 22, for 25
promises

root@my.system.com#
```

6. Now if you see the previous output you may note that CFEngine gives a warning about a non-existent user shadow. If there are files or directories which do not have the permissions as specified in the promise file, the permissions for the corresponding files and directories will be changed.

7. The default permissions for the `/tmp` directory is as given in the previous snippet. Let's change the permissions of this directory and try to execute the same promises again:

```
root@my.system.com# chmod 1775 /tmp
root@my.system.com# ls  -lh /
..
..
drwxrwxr-t   5 root root 4.0K Nov 15 04:02 tmp
..

root@my.system.com# cf-agent -v -f /var/cfengine/inputs/check-
permissions.cf
..
..
```

```
........................................................
cf3     Promise handle:
cf3     Promise made by: /tmp
cf3     ........................................................
cf3
cf3  -> Using literal pathtype for /tmp
cf3  -> Handling file existence constraints on /tmp
cf3  -> Object /tmp had permission 1775, changed it to 1777
cf3  -> Handling file existence constraints on /tmp
cf3  -> File permissions on /tmp as promised
..
..
```

8. Note that in the previous output the permission for the `/tmp` directory was changed from '1775' to '1777' as specified in the promises file.

The given promises may be used to audit and fix permissions for files and directories as required.

What just happened?

The objective for the bundle of promises we just discussed was to audit and fix the permissions of files and directories. A list of files, directories, and corresponding permissions is already available with the user, I presume. Here we defined a bundlesequence. There is only one promise bundle and we name it as 'checkpermissions'. After this we defined the list of files and directories under for the agent bundle. Next, we defined the mode, owner, and group for the various files and directories. Please note that all directories that have similar permissions have been grouped and are defined by variable `dirlist`. We can also group files that have similar permissions and define a single promise for them. The promisee `perms` is already defined in the `cfengine_stdlib.cf` file which we have already included.

Time for action – user and group audit

1. Let's look at another example where we perform a user and group audit. We need to check if specific user groups exist and also that there are no new users or groups added. The following code snippet may be copied to a file `user-group-audit.cf`:

```
body common control

{
bundlesequence  => { "user_group_check", "detect_file_change" };
}
```

```
bundle agent user_group_check

{
classes:
  "userOK1" expression => userexists("root");

  "userOK2" expression => userexists("clark");

  "userOK3" expression => userexists("peter");

  "groupOK1" expression => groupexists("root");

  "groupOK2" expression => groupexists("clark");

  "groupOK3" expression => groupexists("peter");

reports:

 userOK1::

    "User root exists";

 !userOK1::

    "User root does not exist";

 userOK2::

     "User clark exists";

!userOK2::

     "User clark does not exist";

..
..

body agent control

{
agentaccess => { "bruce", "root" };
}
bundle agent detect_file_change
```

```
{
files:
  "/etc/passwd"
       changes      => baseline,
       action       => background;
  "/etc/groups"
       changes      => baseline;
}

body changes baseline
{
hash           => "md5";
report_changes => "content";
update_hashes  => "true";
}

body action background
{
background => "true";
}
```

2. Let's check our promises:

```
root@my.system.com# cf-promises -f /var/cfengine/inputs/user-group-audit.cf
root@my.system.com#
```

No output shows that we are good with the promises.

3. Let's execute the promise and see what the output is:

```
root@my.system.com# cf-agent -v -f /var/cfengine/inputs/user-group-audit.cf


R: User root exists


R: User clark exists


R: User peter does not exist


R: Group root exists


R: Group clark exists
```

```
R: Group peter does not exist


root@my.system.com#
```

We get to know which user and group exists and which user and group does not exist. We also get to know that the `/etc/passwd` and `/etc/shadow` has not changed. Now let's alter these two files and execute the promises again to see what happens if the files altered. The following commands will alter the two files:

```
root@my.system.com# useradd test
root@my.system.com# passwd test
Enter new UNIX password:
Retype new UNIX password:
passwd: password updated successfully
root@my.system.com#
```

By adding the user `test` we have altered the file `/etc/passwd` and by setting the passwd of user 'test' we have altered the file `/etc/shadow`. Now let's run our promises and see what happens:

```
root@my.system.com# cf-agent -f /var/cfengine/inputs/user-group-audit.cf
R: User root exists


R: User clark exists


R: User peter does not exist


R: Group root exists


R: Group clark exists


R: Group peter does not exist


!!!!!!!!!!!!!!!!!!!!!!!!!!!!!!!!!!!!!!!!!!!!!


ALERT: Hash (md5) for /etc/passwd changed!


!!!!!!!!!!!!!!!!!!!!!!!!!!!!!!!!!!!!!!!!!!!!!
```

```
!!!!!!!!!!!!!!!!!!!!!!!!!!!!!!!!!!!!!!!!!!!!!!!!!!

ALERT: Hash (md5) for /etc/shadow changed!

!!!!!!!!!!!!!!!!!!!!!!!!!!!!!!!!!!!!!!!!!!!!!!!!!!
```

CFEngine raised a flag that the files have changed, which is exactly what we wanted.

What just happened?

The objective of the promises was to check if the given users exist on the system and whether there have been any user related changes that have been made. Any user related changes will affect the two files: `/etc/passwd` and `/etc/shadow`, and we audit for any changes in any of the files by comparing the md5 sum of these files with the md5 sum of the base reference file, which means that CFEngine saves the md5 sum of the files when we execute the promise for the first time, and any changes to these files will be compared to this md5 sum. Here we have two specific tasks—check whether the listed users and groups exist, and check whether there were any changes in the files `/etc/passwd` and `/etc/shadow`.

We defined a bundlesequence giving names of the two bundles `user_group_check` and `detect_file_change`, as well as the order in which they need to be executed. After this, we want to check for the existence of three users and groups which are `root`, `clark`, and `peter`. In addition to this, we also need to check if there are any changes in the files `/etc/passwd` and `/etc/shadow`. For verifying the existence of the users we use a CFEngine built-in function called `userexists` and for verifying the existence of the groups we use a CFEngine built-in function group `exists`. We also defined a few classes which reports the existence or non existence of users. So the following promise can be interpreted as "for class `userOK1` check whether the user root exists"; and report whether the user exists:

```
"userOK1" expression => userexists("root");
```

If the user does not exist, then report that the user does not exist. For the `detect_file_change` bundle, we define a promise `change` with the promisee `baseline`. The body for the baseline is defined such that the md5 sum is calculated for the content and is compared with the md5 sum of the base file. If there are any changes in the contents of the file a note is made while executing the promise. You'll also see that we have defined an `action` which tells the CFEngine to verify the md5 checksum in the background.

Server control promises

Server control promises define the fixed behavioral promises made by `cf-serverd`. It specifically describes the access policy for the connections made to the server itself. Additionally, we need to provide the access to specific files.

Let's look at a few server control promises and their syntax:

- **cfruncommand**
  - Type: string
  - Allowed input range: "?(([a-zA-Z]:\\.*)|(/.*))

  The cfruncommand server control promise is used for providing the path of the **cf-agent** command or the **cf-execd** command for remote execution. The path may be specified as follows:

  ```
  body server control
  {
  cfruncommand => "/var/cfengine/bin/cf-agent";
  }
  ```

- **denybadclocks**
  - Type: (menu option)
  - Allowed input range: true, false, yes, no, on, off
  - Default value: true

  This server control promise is used to allow or deny connections from hosts which have their clocks out of sync. Currently, a server's clock is said to be 'out of sync' when the clock has drifted by an hour. The control helps in raising a warning flag if the clocks are not synchronized beyond the acceptable limits and preventing Denial Of Service attacks based on clock corruption. The option can be disabled as follows:

  ```
  body server control
  {
    denybadclocks => "false";
  }
  ```

- **allowconnects**
  - Type: slist
  - Allowed input range: (arbitrary string)

The `allowconnects` server control promise specifies the list of IP addresses or host names which are allowed to connect to the CFEngine server port. The list of IP addresses or host names may be specified as follows:

```
body server control
{
allowconnects => { "127.0.0.1", "::1", "192\.168\.2\..*",
  "my[0-9]+\.system\.com" }
}
```

- **denyconnects**
    - Type: slist
    - Allowed input range: (arbitrary string)

This promise specifies a list of IP addresses and host names which are **not** allowed to connect to the CFEngine server port. The IP addresses and host names which are not allowed to connect can be specified as follows:

```
body server control
{
denyconnects => { "192\.168\.8\..*", "test[0-9]*\.system\.com" }
}
```

- **allowallconnects**
    - Type: slist
    - Allowed input range: (arbitrary string)

This server control promise is used for specifying a list of IP addresses and host names which can have more than one connection to the CFEngine server port. Hosts that are not listed in this list must wait for the `TCP_FIN_WAIT` timeout before they can attempt a reconnection. The list of such hosts may again be specified as in **allowconnects**.

- **trustkeysfrom**
    - Type: slist
    - Allowed input range: (arbitrary string)

This allows us to accept public keys from the IP addresses or host names listed here at runtime. CFEngine gives an option to say 'yes' or 'no' at the time of accepting the keys at runtime for hosts whose public keys have not already been trusted. You can specify the list of IP addresses and host names as follows:

```
body server control
{
trustkeysfrom => {"10\.240\.0\..*"};
}
```

- **allowusers**
  - Type: slist
  - Allowed input range: (arbitrary string)

  This server control promise specifies a list of users who may execute requests from this server. The users may be specified as follows:

```
body server control
{
allowusers => { "cfengine", "root", "clark" };
}
```

After going through few of the control promise types let's write promises for a few more tasks.

Time for action – log rotation using CFEngine

1. Log management is one task that needs to be performed on all servers at regular intervals. The logs may be web server logs, mail logs, application logs, or user access logs, and they need to be rotated or archived regularly on the basis of size or when they were modified. Let's see how this can be done using CFEngine; you may copy the following code snippet to a file `rotate-logs.cf`:

```
body common control

{

bundlesequence => { "log_rotate" };

inputs => { "cfengine_stdlib.cf" };

}

bundle agent log_rotate

{

files:

"/var/log/httpd/access_log*"
```

```
rename => rotate("10");

"/var/log/httpd/error_log*"

rename => rotate("10");

"/var/log/maillog*"

rename => rotate("15");

commands:

"/usr/local/apache-2.0.63/bin/httpd -k restart";
}
```

2. Let's verify the promises written in our file `rotate-logs.cf`:

```
root@my.system.com# cf-promises -f /var/cfengine/inputs/rotate-logs.cf
root@my.system.com#
```

No output means our promises are good.

3. Now let's first note the listing of the logs that already exist on the paths that we specified in the promises file:

```
root@my.system.com# ls /var/log/httpd/access_log*
/var/log/httpd/access_log    /var/log/httpd/access_log.1 /var/log/httpd/access_log.2  /var/log/httpd/access_log.3

root@my.system.com# ls /var/log/httpd/error_log*
/var/log/httpd/error_log /var/log/httpd/error_log.1  /var/log/httpd/error_log.2 /var/log/httpd/error_log.3

root@my.system.com# ls /var/log/maillog*
/var/log/maillog /var/log/maillog.1 /var/log/maillog.2 /var/log/maillog.3 /var/log/maillog.4 /var/log/maillog.5
```

4. Now let's execute the promises and see what happens:

```
root@my.system.com# cf-agent -v -f /var/cfengine/inputs/rotate-
logs.cf

...

...

cf3 -> Bundlesequence =>  {'log_rotate'}

cf3*****************************************************************
**

cf3 BUNDLE log_rotate

cf3*****************************************************************
**

cf3      +  Private classes augmented:

cf3      -  Private classes diminished:

cf3    =========================================================

cf3    files in bundle log_rotate (1)

cf3    =========================================================

cf3

cf3 Verifying SQL table promises is only available with Cfengine
Nova or above

cf3

cf3     .........................................................

cf3     Promise handle:

cf3     Promise made by: /var/log/httpd/access_log*

cf3     .........................................................

cf3

cf3  -> Using regex pathtype for /var/log/httpd/access_log* (see
pathtype)

cf3  -> Using expanded file base path /var/log/httpd/access_log

cf3  -> Handling file existence constraints on /var/log/httpd/
access_log

cf3  -> Rotating files /var/log/httpd/access_log in 10 fifo

cf3  -> Handling file existence constraints on /var/log/httpd/
access_log

cf3  -> Rotating files /var/log/httpd/access_log in 10 fifo

cf3

cf3     .........................................................

cf3     Promise handle:
```

```
cf3     Promise made by: /var/log/httpd/error_log*
cf3     ..........................................................
cf3
cf3   -> Using regex pathtype for /var/log/httpd/error_log* (see
pathtype)
cf3   -> Using expanded file base path /var/log/httpd/error_log
cf3   -> Handling file existence constraints on /var/log/httpd/
error_log
cf3   -> Rotating files /var/log/httpd/error_log in 10 fifo
cf3   -> Handling file existence constraints on /var/log/httpd/
error_log
cf3   -> Rotating files /var/log/httpd/error_log in 10 fifo
cf3
cf3     ..........................................................
cf3     Promise handle:
cf3     Promise made by: /var/log/maillog*
cf3     ..........................................................
cf3
cf3   -> Using regex pathtype for /var/log/maillog* (see pathtype)
cf3   -> Using expanded file base path /var/log/maillog
cf3   -> Handling file existence constraints on /var/log/maillog
cf3   -> Rotating files /var/log/maillog in 15 fifo
cf3   -> Handling file existence constraints on /var/log/maillog
cf3   -> Rotating files /var/log/maillog in 15 fifo
cf3>   -> Promiser string contains a valid executable (/usr/local/
apache-2.0.63/bin/httpd) - ok


cf3>


cf3>     ..........................................................


cf3>     Promise handle:


cf3>     Promise made by: /usr/local/apache-2.0.63/bin/httpd -k
restart


cf3>     ..........................................................
```

```
cf3>

cf3>  -> Executing '/usr/local/apache-2.0.63/bin/httpd -k start'
...(timeout=-678,owner=-1,group=-1)

cf3>  -> (Setting umask to 77)

cf3>  -> Finished command related to promiser "/usr/local/apache-
2.0.63/bin/httpd -k restart" -- succeeded

..
..
cf3 Outcome of version (not specified) (agent-0): Promises
observed to be kept 14%, Promises repaired 86%, Promises not
repaired 0%
cf3 Estimated system complexity as touched objects = 3, for 3
promises
root@my.system.com#
```

5. Let's check the list of files specified on the paths in the promises file:

```
root@my.system.com# ls /var/log/httpd/accesss_log*
/var/log/httpd/access_log    /var/log/httpd/access_log.1 /var/log/
httpd/access_log.2  /var/log/httpd/access_log.3 /var/log/httpd/
access_log.4

root@my.system.com# ls /var/log/httpd/error_log*
/var/log/httpd/error_log /var/log/httpd/error_log.1  /var/log/
httpd/error_log.2 /var/log/httpd/error_log.3 /var/log/httpd/error_
log.4

root@my.system.com# ls /var/log/maillog*
/var/log/maillog /var/log/maillog.1 /var/log/maillog.2 /var/log/
maillog.3 /var/log/maillog.4 /var/log/maillog.5 /var/log/maillog.6
```

What just happened?

In the given example, we wanted to rotate the apache webserver access logs and mail logs and keep only the last ten files. This also requires that the log file be rotated and renamed. For example, a log file with the name `/var/log/access_log.(n)` needs to be renamed to `/var/log/access_log.(n+1)`. For this we defined a bundlesequence with a single bundle `log_rotate`. After this we defined the files to be considered, so a regular expression `/var/log/access_log.*` is used to define all the apache web server access logs. Here we use the `rotate` option for the promise rename. Now because we have to always keep the 10 files always we supply the number 10 to the `rotate` option. Once the logs were rotated we started the webserver by executing the command `/usr/local/apache-2.0.63/bin/httpd`. Let's look at the `rename` promise and the other options available for it in detail:

- **rename** (compound body)
    - Type: ext body
    - Options: 'disable'
    - Type: (menu option)
    - Allowed input range: True, False, yes, no, on, off
    - Default value: False

  The given option (if set to true) automatically renames and removes permissions.

    - 'disable_mode'
    - Type: string
    - Allowed input range: [0-7augorwxst,+-]+

  The given option is used to define the permissions to set when a file is disabled.

    - 'disable_suffix'
    - Type: string
    - Allowed input range: (arbitrary string)

  The given option is used to add a suffix to the files that are being disabled.

    - 'newname'
    - Type: string
    - Allowed input range: (arbitrary string)

  The given option is used to define the name for the current file.

    - 'rotate'
    - Type: int
    - Allowed input range: 0, 99

The given option is used to define the maximum number of file rotations to keep.

From the given output, we see that the files have been rotated by one level.

Access control using CFEngine

Access control using an access control list (acl) may be used to defined access for various users on specific files and directories. This is an agent control promise. This is available only in CFEngine Nova or above. Let's see the syntax for setting ACLs:

- **acl** (compound body)
  - Type: ext body
  - 'aces' Type: slist
  - Allowed input range: ((user|group):[^:]+:[-=+,rwx()dtTabBpcoD]*(:
  - (allow|deny))?)|((all|mask) =+,rwx()]*(:(allow|deny))?)

  The 'aces' constraint type defines the native settings for access control lists.

- **'acl_directory_inherit'**
  - Type: (menu option)
  - Allowed input range: nochange, parent, specify, clear

  A directory has default ACLs associated with them but in addition to this the ACLs may be inherited by the directories of files created under them. The constraint acl_directory_inherit gives control over the default ACL of this directory. This can be left unchanged (nochange), explicitly specified (specify) and empty (clear). Additionally, the files and directories under the parent directory may inherit the ACL of the parent directory if we specify the 'parent' option.

- **'acl_method'**
  - Type: (menu option)
  - Allowed input range: append, overwrite

  While defining ACLs, we may use this as the starting point or use an existing ACL and append a new rule to it. If we want to use the ACL as the starting point and want only the specified entries to exist, we may use the menu option 'overwrite'. If we want to use an existing ACL and want to append a new entry to it we may use the 'append' menu option.

- **'acl_type'**
  - Type: (menu option)
  - Allowed input range: generic, posix, ntfs

  ACLs on different platforms support different permission flags. For instance the POSIX permission flags are not supported on a Windows file system. The given constraint may be used to specify the platform of the affected file system.

- **'specify_inherit_aces'**
  - Type: slist
  - Allowed input range: ((user|group):[^:]+:[-=+,rwx()dtTabBpcoD]*(:
  - (allow|deny))?)|((all|mask)=+,rwx()]*(:(allow|deny))?)

  This constraint specifies a list of access control entries that are set on child objects. This is only applicable if **acl_directory_inherit** is set to **specify**. It is parsed from left to right and allows multiple entries with the same entity type and id. Here's a sample code snippet for such an ACL:

```
body common control

{

bundlesequence => { "acls" };

}

#########################################

bundle agent acls

{

files:

  "/var/opt/acl/test"

    depth_search => include_base,

    acl => acl_test;

}

#########################################
```

```
body acl acl_test

{

acl_method => "overwrite";

acl_type => "posix";

acl_directory_inherit => "parent";

aces => { "user:*:rwx:allow", "group:*:+rw:allow",
  "all:r"};

}

body depth_search include_base

{

include_basedir => "true";

}
```

What just happened?

We defined a bundlesequence for the common control promise. We define a single bundle `acls` in this sequence. Next, we defined the ACL file under the `files` promise. The path is `/var/opt/test/acl`. After this we defined two promises `depth_search` and `acl`. We also defined the body for promise `acl` and promisee `test`. The `acl_method` constraint is defined as `overwrite`. Therefore, the entry will overwrite the existing ACLs and add a single new entry. The `acl_type` constraint is defined as "posix", which defines the platform for the ACL. The `acl_directory_inherit` constraint is defined as `parent`, hence the parent directory's default ACL will be inherited. We define the native access control list settings with the constraint `aces`. The native settings are defined as follows:

- "user:*:rwx:allow"—Any user has read, write, and execute access. If you want to specify this for a specific user you will have to put the user id for that user in place of `*`.
- "group:*:+rw:allow"—We add the read and write permissions for any user to the default ACL. If you want to do this for a specific group, use `all:r`.
- "all:r"—Everybody has read permissions.

We also define that while doing depth search, the base directory is included.

Pop quiz

1. We wrote a promise for rotating files in one of the sections above. Now, if we want to rotate the file's basis size, which other constraint should be used?
2. Which promise constraint may be used for checking if any of the attributes of a file are changed?

OSSEC and CFEngine—a robust security system

OSSEC is a host based **Intrusion Detection System** (**IDS**). It performs rootkit detection, file integrity checking, log analysis, policy monitoring, real time alerting, and active response. Although CFEngine is good at performing quite a few of these tasks, a few tasks, that is, Rootkit detection and real time alerting, are OSSEC's strong point. Hence, a combination of OSSEC and CFEngine may provide a complete open source security solution for your IT infrastructure. Here are a few pointers on how CFEngine may compliment OSSEC:

- Automated OSSEC installation on new hosts being added to your infrastructure.
- Making changes to a group of hosts on the basis of flags raised on a single host. For example, one of your web servers is being bogged down by a DOS attack; OSSEC may detect it on this host and may make changes to the system to block the traffic but it may not be able to do so on all the other hosts in the web server group. This is where CFEngine may jump in and make the changes to all the other hosts in the web server group so that your web server infrastructure is safe from DOS attacks.
- Making changes to the application configuration file basis alerts generated by OSSEC.

Lets see how this can be achieved to build a more robust open source security solution for your IT infrastructure.

Time for action – installing OSSEC

1. We need to install OSSEC on all our hosts—for this you may copy the following code snippet to a configuration file named `ossec_install.cf`:

```
bundle agent ossec_install
{
commands:
"/usr/bin/wget http://www.ossec.net/files/ossec-hids-2.5.1.tar.gz
-P /opt/"
class => satisfy("downloaded");


        commands:
      downloaded::
```

```
        "/bin/tar"
         args => "-zxvf  /opt/ossec-hids-2.5.1.tar.gz",
        class => ("uncompressed");

        commands:
        uncompressed::
        "/opt/ossec-hids-2.5.1/./install.sh"
         contain => standard;
}
body contain standard

{

exec_owner => "root";

useshell => "true";

}

body classes satisfied(new_class)

{

  promise_repaired => { "$(new_class)" };
}
```

The given configuration file can be used to install OSSEC on all your hosts. After getting OSSEC installed on all your hosts you may proceed with configuring your OSSEC system. The complete OSSEC configuration is beyond the scope of this book and we'll cover only a few important scenarios. You may refer to the manual at `http://www.ossec.net/doc/manual/` for more information.

Making changes to configuration files on the basis of alerts generated by OSSEC

Let's assume that you get the following alerts from OSSEC:

```
OSSEC HIDS Notification.
2010 Aug 09 17:04:21

Received From: xx->/var/log/httpd/access_log
Rule: 31151 fired (level 10) -> "Multiple web server 400 error codes
from same source ip."
Portion of the log(s):
```

```
x.x.x.x - - [09/Aug/2010:17:04:21 -0300] "GET /phpMyChat-0.24.6//chat/
messagesL.php3 HTTP/1.1" 404 298 "-" "Mozilla/4.0 (compatible; MSIE
6.0; Windows 98)"
x.x.x.x - - [09/Aug/2010:17:04:20 -0300] "GET /phpMyChat//chat/
messagesL.php3 HTTP/1.1" 404 291 "-" "Mozilla/4.0 (compatible; MSIE
6.0; Windows 98)"
x.x.x.x - - [09/Aug/2010:17:04:20 -0300] "GET /phpMyChat-0.24.4//chat/
messagesL.php3 HTTP/1.1" 404 298 "-" "Mozilla/4.0 (compatible; MSIE
6.0; Windows 98)"
x.x.x.x - - [09/Aug/2010:17:04:20 -0300] "GET /phpMyChat-0.24.3//chat/
messagesL.php3 HTTP/1.1" 404 298 "-" "Mozilla/4.0 (compatible; MSIE
6.0; Windows 98)"
x.x.x.x - - [09/Aug/2010:17:04:20 -0300] "GET /php/phpmychat//chat/
messagesL.php3 HTTP/1.1" 404 295 "-" "Mozilla/4.0 (compatible; MSIE
6.0; Windows 98)"
x.x.x.x - - [09/Aug/2010:17:04:18 -0300] "GET /forum//chat/messagesL.
php3 HTTP/1.1" 404 287 "-" "Mozilla/4.0 (compatible; MSIE 6.0; Windows
98)"
x.x.x.x - - [09/Aug/2010:17:04:18 -0300] "GET /chats//chat/messagesL.
php3 HTTP/1.1" 404 287 "-" "Mozilla/4.0 (compatible; MSIE 6.0; Windows
98)"
x.x.x.x - - [09/Aug/2010:17:04:18 -0300] "GET /chatroom//chat/
messagesL.php3 HTTP/1.1" 404 290 "-" "Mozilla/4.0 (compatible; MSIE
6.0; Windows 98)"
x.x.x.x - - [09/Aug/2010:17:04:18 -0300] "GET /PhpMyChat//chat/
messagesL.php3 HTTP/1.1" 404 291 "-" "Mozilla/4.0 (compatible; MSIE
6.0; Windows 98)"
x.x.x.x - - [09/Aug/2010:17:04:19 -0300] "GET /phpchat//chat/
messagesL.php3 HTTP/1.1" 404 289 "-" "Mozilla/4.0 (compatible; MSIE
6.0; Windows 98)"
```

These logs show that your web server is receiving a large number of HTTP requests from the IP `x.x.x.x` for files it is not intended to serve. Now we need to block this IP. This can be done in two ways:

1. You add an IP tables rule.
2. You add the IP to your web server configuration file's blacklist.

Time for action – auditing the system with CFEngine and OSSEC

1. Let's see how this can be done for the second scenario using CFEngine. You may copy the following code snippet in a file `web_blacklist`:

```
body common control

{

bundlesequence  => { "web_blacklist", "web_restart" };

}

bundle agent web_blacklist
{
files:

  "/etc/httpd/conf/httpd.conf"
       create    => "true",
       edit_line => AppendIfNoLine("Deny","from ");

}
bundle edit_line AppendIfNoLine(parameter,two)
  {
  vars:

    "list"        slist => { "192.168.2.1", "192.168.2.2",
  "192.168.2.3"};

  insert_lines:
   "$(parameter) $(two) $(list)" select_region => MySection("New
Section");
"# New IP added to deny list" select_region => MySection("New
section");

select_region => MySection("New section");

}
body select_region MySection(x)
{
select_start => "Allow from all";
select_end => "</Directory>";
}
bundle agent web_restart
```

```
{
commands:
"/usr/local/apache-2.0.63/bin/httpd -k restart";
```

- }

2. Let's verify these promises:

```
root@my.system.com# cf-promises -f /var/cfengine/inputs/web_
blacklist.cf
root@my.system,com#
```

A blank output means there are no issues with the promises.

3. Now let's execute the promises:

```
root@my.system.com# cf-agent -v -f /var/cfengine/inputs/web_
blacklist.cf
..
..
cf3 Initiate variable convergence...
cf3  -> Immunizing against parental death
cf3 -> Bundlesequence =>  {'web_blacklist'}
cf3
cf3*****************************************************************
**
cf3 BUNDLE web_blacklist
cf3*****************************************************************
**
cf3
cf3
cf3      +  Private classes augmented:
cf3
cf3      -  Private classes diminished:
cf3
cf3
cf3
cf3    =========================================================
cf3    files in bundle web_blacklist (1)
```

```
cf3    ==========================================================
==
cf3
cf3 Verifying SQL table promises is only available with Cfengine
Nova or above
cf3
cf3     .........................................................
cf3     Promise handle:
cf3     Promise made by: /etc/httpd/conf/httpd.conf
cf3     .........................................................
cf3
cf3   -> Using literal pathtype for /etc/httpd/conf/httpd.conf
cf3   -> File "/etc/httpd/conf/httpd.conf" exists as promised
cf3   -> Handling file existence constraints on /etc/httpd/conf/
httpd.conf
cf3   -> Handling file edits in edit_line bundle AppendIfNoLine
cf3
cf3* * * * * * * * * * * * * * * * * * * * * * * * * * * * * * *
*
cf3       BUNDLE AppendIfNoLine( {'Deny','from '} )
cf3* * * * * * * * * * * * * * * * * * * * * * * * * * * * * * *
*
cf3
cf3     ? Augment scope AppendIfNoLine with parameter
cf3     ? Augment scope AppendIfNoLine with two
cf3
cf3       = = = = = = = = = = = = = = = = = = = = = = = = = = = = =
cf3       vars in bundle AppendIfNoLine
cf3       = = = = = = = = = = = = = = = = = = = = = = = = = = = = =
cf3
cf3
cf3     .........................................................
cf3     Promise handle:
cf3     Promise made by: list
cf3     .........................................................
cf3
cf3      ??  Private class context
```

```
cf3
cf3
cf3      = = = = = = = = = = = = = = = = = = = = = = = = = = = =
cf3      insert_lines in bundle AppendIfNoLine
cf3      = = = = = = = = = = = = = = = = = = = = = = = = = = = =
cf3
cf3
cf3    .........................................................
cf3    Promise handle:
cf3    Promise made by: Deny from  192.168.2.1
cf3    .........................................................
cf3
cf3  -> Inserting the promised line "Deny from  192.168.2.1" into
/etc/httpd/conf/httpd.conf after locater
..
..
..
cf3    files in bundle web_blacklist (3)
cf3    cf3>    commands in bundle web_restart (1)

cf3>    =========================================================

cf3>

cf3>  -> Promiser string contains a valid executable (/usr/local/
apache-2.0.63/bin/httpd) - ok

cf3>

cf3>     .........................................................

cf3>     Promise handle:

cf3>     Promise made by: /usr/local/apache-2.0.63/bin/httpd -k
restart
```

```
cf3>    ...............................................................


cf3>


cf3>  -> Executing '/usr/local/apache-2.0.63/bin/httpd -k restart'
...(timeout=-678,owner=-1,group=-1)


cf3>  -> (Setting umask to 77)


cf3>  -> Finished command related to promiser "/usr/local/apache-
2.0.63/bin/httpd -k restart" -- succeeded

cf3

cf3 Verifying SQL table promises is only available with Cfengine
Nova or above

cf3 Outcome of version (not specified) (agent-0): Promises
observed to be kept 75%, Promises repaired 25%, Promises not
repaired 0%

cf3 Estimated system complexity as touched objects = 1, for 1
promises
```

From the output we can see that the required lines for blacklisting IP(s) using the apache web server configuration were added to the apache configuration file `httpd.conf`.

What just happened?

The objective of the given promises was to add the IP(s), for which OSSEC has raised an alert, to the web server configuration file so that the access from the same IP is denied. Here, we defined the bundlesequence under the common control body. The bundle sequence has a single bundle by the name of `web_blacklist`. Next, we defined the file which needs to be edited, which is `/etc/httpd/conf/httpd.conf`. After this we defined the `edit_line` promise, which also specifies a list of IP addresses that need to be added to the `blac006B` list. We defined a region `MySection` to which the lines should be appended. Finally, we defined the start of the section and end of the section. The lines to be added will be added in between the start of the section and end of the section. In the last step we restarted apache so that the changes come into effect.

Have a go hero – verifying the web server configuration files after changes

In the previous example, we added a few access and deny rules to the Apache web server configuration file and restarted the web server. What happens if the changes had a syntax error and the web server failed to restart? To handle this we need to check for any syntax errors in the web server configuration file. How can this be done using CFEngine ?

> **Hint**: You may use a native apache/web server command for this.

Pop quiz

1. We added a few IP addresses to the web server black list and now we want to remove a few of them because we don't consider them suspicious—which `edit_line` promise should you use?
   a. delete_select
   b. insert_select
   c. edit_field
   d. replace_with
2. We rotated a log file in one of the previous sections. If we want to create a compressed backup of the log files, which file promise can be used?
   a. touch
   b. rename
   c. transformer
   d. file_select

Have a go hero – removing hashes for lines matching a string

We wrote a few promises in previous sections wherein we edited a few of the files. Now there are various instances where we want to enable functionality or modules for an application. We do it by removing the comments on the corresponding line or lines in the application configuration file. How can we use CFEngine to do this task to uncomment all lines starting "#   Error Document"?

Answer: You may copy the following code to a file `apache-unhash.cf.`:

```
body common control
{
version => "1.0.0";
bundlesequence  => { "Apache-unhash", "web_restart" };
}
```

```
bundle agent Apache-unhash

{

files:


  "/usr/local/apache-2.0.63/conf/httpd.conf"


        create    => "true",

        edit_line => uncomment_lines_matching("ErrorDocument","#");


}

bundle edit_line uncomment_lines_matching(regex,comment)

{

replace_patterns:

 "#$(regex)" replace_with => uncomment;

}

body replace_with uncomment

{

replace_value => "ErrorDocument";

occurrences => "all";

}
bundle agent web_restart
{
commands:
"/usr/local/apache-2.0.63/bin/httpd restart";
}
```

Summary

In this chapter we learned the following points in detail:

- Very important common control promises, such as bundle sequence, which are used in almost all promises to define the sequence and other important definitions for the complete promise
- Agent control promises—which define the behavior of promises made by `cf-agent`
- Server control promises—which define various controls for the communication between the CFEngine server and client
- We learned how to audit the users on the system and check the files and directory permissions using CFEngine
- We learned how to build a robust open source security infrastructure using CFEngine and OSSEC, as well as how to run audits using OSSEC and change the rules for accessing an application on the fly

Armed with this newly attained knowledge let's see how we can schedule more complex tasks using CFEngine.

4
Scheduling Tasks with CFEngine

CFEngine can be used to schedule recurring tasks on a large number of hosts. In the previous few chapters we learned how to use CFEngine for system audits. Let's see how CFEngine can be used to monitor systems and processes in this chapter. We will also see a few more control promises. :

In this chapter, we shall

- Learn about some monitor control promises
- Learn about some runagent control promises
- Learn about some executor control promises
- Learn about reporter control promises
- Learn about how CFEngine interprets classes and takes policy decisions
- Learn about how CFEngine can be used as a monitoring tool
- Learn about how to generate reports

When we add the knowledge of control promises that we are going to learn to what we have already learned about them, we can see that CFEngine can control the complete life cycle of a host or device and this was what we intended to do from the start.

Let's see the other control promises that CFEngine has to offer, and their usage. Given next is a small example that exhibits a few of these promises types and their usage. In this example we'll try to disable all xinetd services on a system. You may use the following lines of code in a configuration file:

```
body executor control
{
splaytime => "5";
mailto => "techops@system.com";
```

```
smtpserver => "localhost";
mailmaxlines => "50";
schedule => Hr01Min59;
}
bundle agent disable_services
{
services slist => { "ipop2", "ipop3", "pop3s", "klogin", "imap",
"imaps" };
methods:
"any" usebundle => disable_xinetd("$(services)");
processes:
"$services"
signals => { "kill" };
}
bundle agent disable_xinetd(name_service)
{
vars:
"xinetd_services_status" => execresult("/sbin/chkconfig -list $(name_
service)", "useshell");
classes:
"running" expression => regcmp(".*on.*". "$(xinetd_service_status)");
commands:
running::
"/sbin/chkconfig "$(name)" off";
reports:
on::
"disabled service $name";
}
```

Let's try to validate the given configuration file:

```
root@my10.system.com# cf-promises -f /var/cfengine/inputs/disable_
services.cf
```

The new configuration file may be copied from the policy distribution service by executing `cf-agent` with the file `failsafe.cf`. Once the file has been copied we can execute the configuration file using `cf-agent`. Let's look at the output when we execute the configuration file:

```
root@my10.system.com# cf-agent -v -f /var/cfengine/inputs/disable_
services.cf

cf3> Cfengine - autonomous configuration engine - commence self-
diagnostic prelude

cf3> Cfengine - 3.1.5 Copyright (C) Cfengine AS 2008,2010-

......
```

```
…...
cf3>  -> Verifying the syntax of the inputs...

cf3>  -> Caching the state of validation

cf3>   > Parsing file ./disable_services.cf

cf3> Initiate variable convergence...

cf3> Initiate variable convergence.
cf3> BUNDLE disable_services
cf3>    commands in bundle disable_xinetd (1)

cf3>  -> Promiser string contains a valid executable (/sbin/chkconfig) -
ok

cf3>     Promise handle:

cf3>     Promise made by: /sbin/chkconfig ipop2 off

cf3>  -> Executing '/sbin/chkconfig ipop2 off' ...(timeout=-678,owner=-
1,group=-1)

cf3> -> Would execute script /sbin/chkconfig ipop2 off

…...
cf3> Skipping whole next promise (disabled service ipop2), as context on
is not relevant
cf3>    processes in bundle disable_services (1)

cf3> Observe process table with /bin/ps -eo user,pid,ppid,pgid,pcpu,pmem,
vsz,pri,rss,nlwp,stime,time,args

cf3>     Promise handle:

cf3>     Promise made by: ipop2
```

```
cf3>  -> No restart promised for ipop2


cf3>     Promise handle:

cf3>     Promise made by: portmap

cf3>     ..........................................................

cf3>

cf3>  ->  Found matching pid 1747

    (rpc       1747     1  1747  0.0  0.0   1812  14   528    1 Jun22
00:00:00 portmap)

cf3>  -> Need to keep signal promise 'kill' in process entry 1747

cf3>  -> No restart promised for portmap

cf3>
```

From the output, we see that the following actions were performed:

- Services that were not running but were marked as enabled in the `/sbin/chkconfig` output—were disabled
- No action was taken for services that were not running and which were not enabled
- Services that were running, and enabled and running, were disabled and terminated

The given example used various control promises. Let's see the control promises and constraints that they offer in more detail.

Monitor control promises

The monitor control promise settings describe the fixed behavior of promises made by `cf-monitord`. The various constraints for this type of control promise are as follows:

- **forgetrate**
    - Type: real
    - Allowed input range: 0,1
    - Default value: 0.6

This constraint defines the settings for the machine learning algorithm which monitors system behavior. The value is a decimal fraction [0,1] weighting of new values over old in 2d-average computation. This value determines (in combination with the monitoring rate) how quickly CFEngine forgets its previous history. The settings may be defined as follows:

```
body monitor control
{
forgetrate => "0.6";
}
```

- **monitorfacility**
    - Type: Menu option
    - Allowed input range: LOG_USER, LOG_DAEMON, LOG_LOCAL0, LOG_LOCAL1, LOG_LOCAL2, LOG_LOCAL3, LOG_LOCAL4, LOG_LOCAL5, LOG_LOCAL6, LOG_LOCAL7
    - Default value: LOG_USER

This constraint defines the setting of the log level for the syslog facility. The settings for this constraint may be defined as follows:

```
body monitor control
{
monitorfacility => LOG_LOCAL3;
}
```

- **histograms**
    - Type: Menu option
    - Allowed input range: true, false, yes, no, on off
    - Default value: true

This constraint is used to enable or disable the storing of signal histogram data by CFEngine. The value can be defined as follows:

```
body monitor control
{
histograms => "false";
}
```

- **tcpdump**
  - Type: Menu option
  - Allowed input range: true, false, yes, no, on, off
  - Default value: false

  This constraint can be used to enable or disable the packet dump for an interface. The following example shows how we can enable `tcpdump`:

```
body monitor control
{
tcpdump => "true";
}
```

- **tcpdumpcommand**
  - Type: string
  - Allowed input range: "?(([a-zA-Z]:\\.*)|(/.*))

  This constraint describes the path of the `tcpdump` command to be used on this system. We can specify the switches available for the `tcpdump` command and also the interface name as the arguments. The next example shows how we can specify the value for this constraint:

```
body monitor control
{
tcpdumpcommand => "/usr/sbin/tcpdump -i eth0";
}
```

Runagent control promises

The runagent control promises settings describe the behavior of promises made by `cf-runagent`. It is a utility that talks to `cf-serverd` and requests `cf-serverd` to execute `cf-agent` on the host. Therefore, it can be use to "push" changes to the hosts. This does not mean that the new updates are pushed to the clients; `cf-runagent` only requests `cf-serverd` to execute `cf-agent` on the client hosts, which in turn are configured to "pull" updates from the policy distribution server. Out of all the constraints for this promise, the most important is the list of hosts that `cf-runagent` will poll for connecting to `cf-serverd`. Given next are the various constraints available for this promise type:

- **hosts**
  - Type: slist
  - Allowed input type: (arbitrary string)

This constraint defines a list of hosts identified by host names or IP addresses which will be polled by CFEngine for connection. We may also specify a port number different from the default CFEngine port number by adding a suffix ':' and a port number to the host name or IP address. If the number of hosts is large, CFEngine can also read the list from a file. It is a good practice to ensure that the file list is readable by CFEngine at all times and is not dependent on network connectivity or any other environment variable. The next example shows how a list of hosts may be provided to CFEngine:

```
body runagent control
{
webserver::

hosts => { "my100.system.com", "my101.system.com", my102.system.
com };

Dbserver::

hosts => { "192.168.1.100", "192.168.2.200:4000", "192.168.3.103"
};

}
```

- **port**
  - Type: int
  - Allowed input range: 1024, 99999

This parameter is used to specify the default port for CFEngine server. The default CFEngine server port is 5308. We may change this using this constraint. The next example shows how this can be done:

```
body runagent control
{
port => "2200";
}
```

> Changing the default port number is not a recommended practice. You should change it only when you have good reason to do so.

- **force_ipv4**
  - Type: Menu option
  - Allowed input range: true, false, yes, no, on off
  - Default value: false

This constraint is used to force the use of ipv4 connection. By default it is disabled and can be enabled as follows:

```
body test example
{
force_ipv4 => "true";
}
```

- **trustkey**
    - Type: Menu option
    - Allowed input range: true, false, yes, no, on, off
    - Default value: false

The constraint is used to enable or disable the automatic acceptance of any keys, on trust, from servers. This is when the server's key has not been trusted already. If you have already exchanged the public keys for any two hosts the trust option has no effect. If any two hosts have built a trust relationship it will exist unless the keys are manually revoked. As a security precaution this should always be set to the default value 'false' to avoid key exchanges between hosts one is not sure about. The option can be enabled as follows:

```
body test example
{
trustkey => "true";
}
```

- **encrypt**
    - Type: Menu option
    - Allowed input range: true, false, yes, no, on, off
    - Default value: false

This constraint is used to enable or disable the encryption of connections with the servers. When enabled the client connections are encrypted using a blowfish randomly generated session key. The initial handshake between the client and server is encrypted using the private/public keys. The option can be enabled as follows:

```
body test example
{
servers => { "my100.system.com" };
encrypt => "true";
}
```

- **background_children**
  - Type: Menu option
  - Allowed input range: true, false, yes, no, on, off
  - Default value: false

The constraint is used for enabling or disabling parallel connections to servers by runagent. The option can be enabled as follows:

```
body runagent control
{
background_children => "true";
}
```

- **max_children**
  - Type: int
  - Allowed input range: 0, 9999999999
  - Default value: 1 concurrent agent promise

This constraint may be used to define the maximum number of concurrent connections that may be attempted. The value should be set to a number so that the system resources are not hogged. The value can be set as follows:

```
body runagent control
{
max_children => "3";
}
```

- **output_to_file**
  - Type: Menu option
  - Allowed input range: true, false, yes, no, on, off
  - Default value: false

The constraint can be used to send the collected output to file(s). We need not specify a file name as the file names are automatically chosen and written under `WORKDIR/outputs/hostname_runagent.out`. The option can be enabled as follows:

```
body runagent control
{
output_to_file => "true";
}
```

Executor control promises

The executor control promises define the behavior of promises made by `cf-execd` including the scheduling times, output capture to `WORKDIR/outputs`, and relay through e-mail. Let's see what constraints CFEngine has for us under these control promises:

- **splaytime**
  - Type: int
  - Allowed input range: 0, 9999999999
  - Default value: 0

  This constraint is used to insert a delay in execution of the promises on various hosts. This is required so that the CFEngine is not overloaded by executing promises on a large number of hosts at the same time. We are well aware that `cf-execd` can schedule an execution of `cf-agent`. The actual execution is delayed by an 'integer' number of seconds between 0 and the splaytime value in minutes. The exact amount of delay for a particular host is based on the hash for the host name of the particular host. Thus a collection of hosts will all execute the promise at a different time and hence surges in network traffic and resource utilization can be avoided. To decide on a value of splaytime, the following thumb rule may be used:

  `splaytime = 1 + number of clients/50`

  The `splaytime` can be set as follows:

  ```
  body executor control
  {
  splaytime => "2";
  }
  ```

- **mailfrom**
  - Type: string
  - Allowed input range: *.*

  This particular constraint is used for specifying the e-mail address CFEngine mails appear to come from. The e-mail address may be specified as follows:

  ```
  body executor control
  {
  mailfrom => "sysad@system.com"
  }
  ```

- **mailto**
  - Type: string
  - Allowed input range: *.*

This particular constraint is used for specifying the e-mail address that the CFEngine mails are sent to. If there are multiple persons who need to receive the mail it is better to configure a mail group. The e-mail address may be specified as follows:

```
body executor control
{
mailto => "techops@system.com";
}
```

- **smtpserver**
  - Type: string
  - Allowed input range: .*

This constraint is used for specifying the host name or IP address of the host, which will act as a SMTP relay for the CFEngine e-mails. This should point to the standard SMTP port 25 of the relaying server, without encryption. The SMTP server may be specified as follows:

```
body executor control
{
smtpserver => "smtpenterprise.system.com";
}
```

> Please note: The `smtpserver` executor control promise does not support SMTPAUTH, SSL encryption, or TLS encryption. Hence, one needs to ensure that this controller points to the standard SMTP port 25 without encryption.

- **mailmaxlines**
  - Type: int
  - Allowed input range: 0, 1000
  - Default value: 30

This particular constraint can be used to limit the number of output lines in the e-mails generated by CFEngine so that the receiver's mail box is not clogged with unusually large outputs. The complete original output is anyway stored under `WORKDIR/outputs/` and can be viewed on demand. The maximum number of lines in the e-mailed output may be set as follows:

```
body executor control

{
mailmaxlines => "60";
}
```

- **schedule**
  - Type: slist
  - Allowed input range: (arbitrary string)
  - Default value:
    schedule => { "Min00", "Min05", "Min10", "Min15", "Min20", "Min25", "Min30", "Min35", "Min40", "Min45", "Min50", "Min55" };

This constraint is used to specify the class schedule used by `cf-execd` to invoke `cf-agent`. The list should have the class expression comprising of classes which are known to `cf-execd`. Any defined class expression will trigger `cf-execd` to schedule the execution of `cf-agent`. The classes listed are date or time based.

> The actual execution of `cf-agent` may be delayed by the splaytime, it will be deferred due to the promise cache and value of `IfElapsed`

The schedule may be specified as follows:

```
body executor control
{
schedule => { "Min00", "Min05", "(Evening|Night).Min15_20",
  "Min30", "(Evening|Night).Min45_50" };
}
```

- **executorfacility**
  - Type: Menu option
  - Allowed input range: LOG_USER, LOG_DAEMON, LOG_LOCAL0, LOG_LOCAL1, LOG_LOCAL2, LOG_LOCAL3, LOG_LOCAL4, LOG_LOCAL5, LOG_LOCAL6, LOG_LOCAL7
  - Default value: LOG_USER

This particular constraint is used to specify the log level to the syslog facility. The log level may be specified as follows:

```
body executor control
{
executorfacility => "LOG_DAEMON"
}
```

- **exec_command**
  - Type: string
  - Allowed input range: "?(([a-zA-Z]:\\.*)|(/.*))

This particular constraint can be used to specify the full path and the command to the executable run by default. The following example shows how this can be done:

```
body executor control
{
exec_command => "$(sys.workdir)/bin/cf-agent -f failsafe.cf &&
$(sys.workdir)/bin/cf-agent";
}
```

> If you notice, we have used the ampersand in the command. This is fine because the command is run in a shell encapsulation and so shell symbols may be used.

Reporter control promises

The reporter control promises define a list of reports to write into the build directory. The format of the reports may be:

- Text
- HTML
- XML

Let's see what constraints CFEngine provides for this promise type:

- **4.6.1 aggregation_point**
  - Type: string
  - Allowed input range: "?(([a-zA-Z]:\\.*)|(/.*))

  This constraint is used to specify the root directory of the data cache where reports for multiple hosts are to be aggregated. In order to make the reports browse-able the directory should be somewhere under the document root of the web server. The directory of configuration management for the database may be specified as follows:

```
body reporter control
{
aggregation_point => "/var/www/html/reports";
}
```

> This feature is only used in enterprise versions of CFEngine.

- **auto_scaling**
    - Type: Menu option
    - Allowed input range: true, false, yes, no, on, off
    - Default value: true

  This constraint is used for enabling or disabling auto-scale graph output to optimize use of space. This can be disabled as shown in the following example:

```
body reporter control
{
auto_scaling => "false";
}
```

- **cvs2xml**
    - Type: slist
    - Allowed input range: (arbitrary string)

  The constraint is used to specify a list of comma separated files in the build directory to be converted to XML. The feature is helpful as it is easier to generate CSV files with individual CFEngine promise logging functions whereas it is easier to upload or display the output on the Web in XML. The schema of XML file is similar to:

```
<output>
<line> <one>...</one> <two>...</two> ... </line>
<line> <one>...</one> <two>...</two> ... </line>
</output>
```

  The list of CSV files may be specified as follows:

```
body reporter control
{
cvs2xml => { "reprt1.csv", "report2.csv", "report3.csv" };
}
```

- **error_bars**
    - Type: Menu option
    - Allowed input range: true, false, yes, no, on, off
    - Default value: true

  By default, CFEngine generates error bars from its machine learning data. This makes it easier to detect anomalies in the state of the system. The constraint may be used to enable or disable the generation of `error_bars`. This can be disabled as shown in the following example:

```
body reporter control
```

```
{
error_bars => "true";
}
```

- **reports**
  - Type: Menu option
  - Allowed input range: all, audit, performance, all_locks, active_locks, hashes, classes, last_seen, monitor_now, monitor_history, monitor_summary, compliance, setuid, file_changes, installed_software, software_patches, value, variables
  - Default value: none

CFEngine can generate various types of reports as given in the allowed input range. The type of report to be generated may be specified as shown in the following example:

```
body reporter control
{
reports => { "audit", "performance" };
}
```

> The report types compliance, setuid, file_changes, installed_software, software_patches, value, and variables are only available in enterprise versions of CFEngine.

- **report_output**
  - Type: Menu option
  - Allowed input range: CSV, HTML, Text, XML
  - Default value: none

We can specify the format for the output report. This feature may be used to set the output format for embedded database reports. The output format may be specified as shown in the next example:

```
body reporter control
{
report_output => "xml";
}
```

- **time_stamps**
  - Type: Menu option
  - Allowed input range: true, false, yes, no, on, off
  - Default value: false

This constraint enables or disables the addition of timestamps to the output directory names. This may be useful if you want to keep the time tagged snapshots of system state data. CFEngine tends to forget the historical data at a predetermined rate. This can be enabled as shown in the following example:

```
body reporter control
{
time_stamps => "true";
}
```

Let's write promises for a few more tasks using the knowledge we have gained up to now.

Time for action – monitoring a web server

1. The promise file given next may be used to monitor a web server; you may save the following code snippet in the file `webmonitor.cf`:

```
body common control
{
bundlesequence => { "web_monitor" };
inputs => { "cfengine_stdlib.cf" };
}
bundle agent web_monitor
{

vars:
comment => "This is used to store the response of the HTTP request
in a variable",
"mywebserver" string => readtcp("myweb3.system.com","80","GET /
index.txt HTTP/1.1");

classes:
comment => "compare the response of the HTTP request to a
successful response",
"webserver_ok" expression => regcmp("test successful","$(mywebser
ver)");

reports:

webserver_ok::
comment => "Action if the above comparison returns TRUE",
"Web server myweb3.system.com is working";

!webserver_ok::
comment => "Action if the above comparison returns FALSE",
```

```
"Web server myweb3.system.com is not responding, please check";

}

body agent control
{
default_timeout => "30";
}
```

2. Let's verify the given promises file:

```
root@my.system.com# cf-promises -f /var/cfengine/inputs/
webmonitor.cf
root@my.system.com#
```

No output verifies that the promises are valid.

3. Now let's execute the given promises and see what happens:

```
root@my.system.com# cf-agent -f /var/cfengine/inputs/webmonitor.cf
cf3 Cfengine - autonomous configuration engine - commence self-
diagnostic prelude
..
..
cf3   > Parsing file /var/cfengine/inputs/webmonitor.cf
cf3 Initiate variable convergence...
cf3 Set cfengine port number to 80 = 80
cf3  -> Connect to myweb3.system.com = 192.168.2.113 on port 80
cf3 LastSaw host myweb3.system.com now
..
..
cf3  -> Immunizing against parental death
cf3 SET timeout = 30
cf3 -> Bundlesequence =>  {'web_monitor'}
cf3
cf3 ****************************************************************
**
cf3 BUNDLE web_monitor
cf3 ****************************************************************
**
..
..
```

```
cf3     Promise handle:
cf3     Promise made by: Web server myweb3.system.com is working
cf3     .........................................................
cf3
cf3 Reporting about this...
cf3 R: Web server myweb3.system.com is working
cf3
cf3 . . . . . . . . . . . . . . . . . . . . . . . . . . . . .
cf3 Skipping whole next promise (Web server myweb3.system.com is
not responding, please check), as context !webserver_ok is not
relevant
..
..
cf3 Skipping whole next promise (Web server myweb3.system.com is
not responding, please check), as context !webserver_ok is not
relevant
..
cf3 Outcome of version (not specified) (agent-0): Promises
observed to be kept 50%, Promises repaired 50%, Promises not
repaired 0%
cf3 Estimated system complexity as touched objects = 0, for 7
promises
root@my.system.com#
```

The output proves that our web server is working fine. If we check the output, CFEngine first verified the promises file. After this it tried to get response for the HTTP request and compares the response with the string "test successful" and returns TRUE if the strings match, or returns FALSE if they do not. There were two scenarios, one when the web server is working and one when the web server is not working. In the previous case, since the web server is working the context `!webserver_ok` is skipped, and you see the output "Promises observed to be kept 50%".

What just happened?

A web server is an integral part of any network infrastructure, whether it is for viewing reports, checking your e-mail on a web interface, managing a Wiki server, or applying for your leave. There are various web servers available today. Let's assume we are running an Apache web server. The port this HTTP service runs is port 80 by default. Now we need to monitor the HTTP service availability. We'll use a special function, readtcp, which returns a string which can be compared against a regex for verification. Let's learn about the readtcp function in detail:

Function : readtcp

Syntax : readtcp(arg0,arg1,arg2,arg3)

Return Type: string

- arg0: Host name or IP address of the socket in the range .*
- arg1: Port number in the range 0, 9999999999
- arg2: Protocol query string in the range .*
- arg3: Maximum number of bytes to read 0, 9999999999

To test the HTTP service, let's download a file `heartbeat.txt` from the remote server `myweb3.system` on which we want to check the HTTP service availability. On the host `myweb3.system.com` let's create a file `heartbeat.txt` under the document root of the web server with the text "test successful". We will also match the output of `heartbeat.txt` using the function `regcmp`. Given next is the synopsis for the function `regcmp`:

Function: regcmp

Syntax : regcmp(arg0,arg1)

Return Type: class

- arg0: Regular expression in the range .*
- arg1: Match string in the range .*

The function returns true if `arg0` is a regular expression matching string arg1.

As we saw in the previous example, CFEngine reported that the web server on the host `myweb3.system.com` is working fine. Here we defined a common control promise under which we defined a bundlesequence. The bundlesequence has only one bundle by the name of **web_monitor**. We then defined the bundle agent `web_monitor`. For the bundle `web_monitor` we define a string variable 'mywebserver', which stores the output of the function `readtcp` and provided the arguments to the function `readtcp`. After this we defined a class `webserver_ok`, which is true if the output of the function `regcmp` is true. We also defined the variable `reports`, which echoes the relevant message depending on whether the `webserver_ok` class is true or false. Now, the HTTP connections to the remote servers may hang, depending on the HTTP timeout values. To take care of this we defined an agent control body wherein we increased the value of the constraint `default_timeout` to 30 seconds. The default value for the constraint `default_timeout` is 10 seconds. Now let's say we want to log the state of web server for reporting purposes and generate an HTML report in the following format:

```
Timestamp:<System_Time>
Web Server status is: <Status of web server>
```

The following lines may be added to the promises file `webmonitor.cf`:

```
..
..
reports:
webserver_ok::
"
<html>
Time: $(sys.date)<br>
Web Server status is: Web server myweb3.system.com is working<br>
</html>
"
report_to_file => "/var/www/html/cf3-reports/web_report.html";

!webserver_ok::
"
<html>
Time: $(sys.date)<br>
Web Server status is: Web server myweb3.system.com is not responding,
please check<br>
</html>

"
report_to_file => "/var/www/html/cf3-reports/web_report.html";
}
..
..
```

So we create an HTML report `web_report.html` under the document root of the web server. We also tell CFEngine to add the time stamp and the status for the web server below it. After executing the promises file using `cf-agent`, let's verify the report:

```
root@my.system.com# cat /var/www/html/cf3-reports/web_report.html"
<html>

Time: Wed Apr 15 13:31:32 2010<br>

Web Server status is: Web server myweb3.system.com is working<br>

</html>
```

Similar lines, giving the state of the web server, with the timestamps, will be logged to the file on successive cf-agent runs. Now you may also open the report file `web_report.html` in the browser of your choice.

This same promises file may be extended to monitor a number of web servers.

Time for action – generating an average load report for a host

Unix or Linux systems provide a very useful means to assess the performance of a system, called load average. This is the average of the total number of processes waiting for CPU time over a period of time. I will not go into the details of how load average is calculated; it is beyond the scope of this book. Unix or Linux provide a number of utilities such as 'top', 'w', and so on for checking the load average. Here we'll use a special variable `mon.value_loadavg` provided by CFEngine. In addition to this, whenever the `loadavg` breaches the threshold we also need to record the CPU utilization at that instance.

1. What we actually want is to log the load averages in a file and then analyze them or generate reports from this data. You may copy the next code snippet to the file `load-report.cf`:

```
body common control

{

bundlesequence => { "mload" };

inputs => { "cfengine_stdlib.cf" };

}

bundle agent mload

{

vars:

"kload" int => $(mon.value_loadavg);

classes:

"load_ok" expression => isgreaterthan("$(kload)", "1");

reports:

load_ok::

"

<html>
```

```
Time: $(sys.date)<br>

Host loadavg greater than 1<br>

Host CPU 1 utilization: $(mon.av_cpu1)<br>

Host CPU 2 utilization: $(mon.av_cpu2)<br>

Host CPU 3 utilization: $(mon.av_cpu3)<br>
</html>

"

report_to_file => "/var/cfengine/reports/load_report.html";

}
```

2. Let's verify the promises using `cf-promises`:

```
root@my.system.com# cf-promises -f /var/cfengine/inputs/load-report.cf
root@my.system.com#
```

   No output justifies our promises.

3. Let's execute our promises using `cf-agent` and see what happens:

```
root@my.system.com# cf-agent -f /var/cfengine/inputs/load-report.cf
root@my.system.com#
```

   No output means the promises were executed without any issues. Now let's check the `load_report.html` file:

```
root@my.system.com# cat /var/cfengine/reports/load_report.html
cf3

<html>

Time: Wed Dec 15 18:22:43 2010<br>

Host my.system.com loadavg greater than 1<br>

Host CPU 1 utilization: 15.00<br>
```

```
Host CPU 2 utilization:  3.00<br>

Host CPU 3 utilization:  9.00<br>

</html>
```

The report shows that the load was greater than the threshold of '1' and when CFEngine found this it also noted the CPU utilizations.

What just happened?

We defined a bundlesequence under the common control body. The bundlesequence has just one bundle by the name `mload`. After this we defined the agent bundle for `mload`. Next, we defined a variable `kload` using a special variable `mon.value_loadavg`. We also defined a class `load_ok`, which returns `true` if the expression `isgreaterthan("$(kload)","1")` returns true. This means if the value of variable `kload` is greater than 1, the class `load_ok` returns `true`. In addition to this, we defined a `reports` promise. The `reports` promise generates an HTML report wherein it also notes the percentage of CPU utilizations in case the load average is greater than '1'. Lastly, we defined that the HTML output should be reported to the file `/var/cfengine/reports/load_report.html`.

Scheduling tasks with CFEngine

On Linux or Unix systems we can schedule recurring tasks with the help of **cron**. It is one of the most important features, with the help of which you may run unmanned programs. The limitation of cron is that it is limited to a single server. Therefore to alter a single cron job we either need to log on to each server and make the changes, or use a configuration management tool such as CFEngine to edit the cron job on each individual server. If there were a centralized cron server, imagine how easy life would be; we would only need to make changes on a central server and it would be propagated to all the servers. Seems like CFEngine fits the bill? Yes, CFEngine can be configured as a replacement for cron. What we get is a centralized scheduling server where it is easier to keep a track of what scheduled jobs are running on the system. In addition to this we get all the features of Cfengine and what we need to do is define groups and user-defined classes which clearly describe which host should run what. Let's see how this can be done.

To implement the suggested idea we need to do the following:

1. Schedule a regular cron job that invokes `cf-agent` at regular intervals on all servers. This means that all hosts will have the same cron job in their `crontab` file. This can be done as follows:

   ```
   */10 * * * * /usr/local/sbin/cf-agent -F
   ```

Now each time `cf-agent` is invoked it evaluates time-classes and runs the commands given in its configuration file.

We can make do without this cron job with the use of `cf-execd` in daemon mode, which would invoke `cf-agent` at regular intervals. Just to gain confidence however, let's not do away with the cron completely, but instead limit it to just a single cron job. Once we are confident enough that the system will work fine, we can do away with cron completely.

2. Define groups and user-defined classes that clearly describe which hosts run what command. This is one thing which you would have already done while performing other tasks. You would have grouped servers running Apache under the web server group and servers running MySQL under the `dbserver` group.

3. The third major action item is to build flexible time classes.

Point 1 is easy to implement and depends on how you want to go about it. Point 2 is something you may have already done. Let's look at point 3, which is building flexible time classes.

Building flexible time classes

CFEngine defines classes based on the system time and date each time it is started. The purpose of building flexible time classes is to define classes that refer to arbitrary intervals and which may be combined to define a precise start time. For this, we need to use the group or classes to create an alias for a group of time values. Here are a few examples:

```
"Workdays"          expression => !(Saturday|Sunday);
"LunchandTea"       expression => (Workdays).(Hr10|Hr12|Hr15);
"AfternoonShift"  or => { "Hr14Min05", "Hr15Min05", "Hr16Min05",
              "Hr17Min05", "Hr18Min05", "Hr19Min05",
              "Hr20", "Hr21", "Hr22" };
"DeploymentDays"  or => { "Day15", "Day30"};
"TimeSlices"        or =>  { "Min01", "Min02", "Min03",
               "Min10_15", "Min33", "Min34", "Min35" };
```

The use of 'OR' in the last three examples ensures that if any of the classes on the right-hand side are defined, the classes on the left-hand side get defined.

Let's see how we can use these time classes. Given next is a generic format in which the classes may be used:

```
promise-type:
    time-based classes::
        Promise
```

Let's see a few practical implementations using the time-based classes that we just defined:

- So, if you want to execute a script every hour during the afternoon shift:

  ```
  bundle agent example
  {
  scripts:
  Afternoonshift::
  "/path/script.pl";
  }
  ```

  This promise gets executed every 1405 hrs, 1505 hrs...1905 hrs.

- If you want to execute a command between 1010 and 1015 hrs on all workdays:

  ```
  body agent test
  {
  commands:
  WorkDays.Hr10.Min10_15::
  "/path/command -arg1 -arg2";
  }
  ```

- If you want to execute a script every Saturday and Sunday:

  ```
  body agent test
  {
  scripts:
  !WorkDays::
  "/path/script.sh";
  }
  ```

Once we have defined appropriate time-based classes depending on how granular we want them to be, we just need to define a scheduling interval and CFEngine will take care of executing the tasks at those scheduled intervals. In previous chapters we have already seen that CFEngine has a very effective set of locking and timeout policies that take care of any hanging commands from previous tasks.

Defining a sequence of jobs

We have already seen how to schedule individual jobs. Now there are instances where individual job scheduling may not work because we want to execute a task on the basis of success or failure of another task. With CFEngine you may define a sequence of jobs. This can be done using classes. To define a job sequence you may simply set a class that returns 'true' if the previous job is completed and predicate the antecedent on that class. Let's see a generic example of how this can be done:

```
body agent jobs_sequence
{
commands:
Monday.Hr01.Min10_15::
"/path/scripts/job_first" classes => if_else("success","failure");
success::
"/path/scripts/job_next";
failure::
"/path/scripts/display_error_condition";

}
```

A point worth considering while defining a sequence of jobs is that each link in the sequence introduces a level of potential failure. The outcome of a sequence of jobs should be achievable after execution of `cf-agent` a sufficient number of times and should be achievable repeatedly. CFEngine, in general, executes `cf-agent` up to three times to determine all the classes and dependencies. This makes the job sequence highly non-convergent. Therefore, it is generally not recommended to create flows with a long sequence of jobs.

Logging execution of promises

CFEngine provides a number of flexible ways to log events that may get executed while executing a complete task. Let's see a generic example:

```
bundle agent example
{
commands:
"/usr/local/mysql/bin/mysqld_safe &"
action => task_logging(task);
}
body action task_logging(x)
{
log_repaired => "/var/log/my_$x.log";
log_string => "$(sys.date) $x job executed"
}
```

If we check the file `/var/log/my_$x.log` it will have the following line:

```
Tue Apr 15 15:10:00 2010 myjob executed
```

Triggering a schedule

Any event which may be measured can trigger a response from `cf-agent`. Let's take the previous example where we checked the HTTP service for a host. Now apart from just appending the response to the report, we can actually trigger another event. The following lines may be added to the file `webmonitor.cf`:

```
commands:
!webserver_ok::
"/usr/sbin/service restart";
```

Defining a calendar using CFEngine

Another interesting task will be defining a calendar with CFEngine. We may define more time-based classes as we did previously in the chapter and define holidays, weekly offs, or other important dates. Let's see an example:

```
"holidays" or => { "April.Day15",
                   "December.Day25",
                   "January.Day1"
                 }
```

Have a go hero – scheduling load average reports

Given next is a small task based on the previous task of monitoring load average of a host.

Schedule the previous promise file `load-report.cf` to run every five minutes so that we may monitor the load every five minutes.

Iterations in CFEngine

Iterations are about repeating tasks in a list. In terms of CFEngine it is to make a number of related promises based on the elements of a list. Given next is a small example of how iterations may be used in CFEngine:

```
bundle agent example
{
reports:
cf3::
"mon.value_diskfree is $(mon.value_diskfree)";
"mon.value_smtp_in is $(mon.value_smtp_in)";
"mon.value.loadavg is $(mon.value.loadavg)";
```

```
"mon.value_cpu1 is $(mon.value_cpu1)";
"mon.value_cpu2 is $(mon.value_cpu2)";
"mon.value_cpu3 is $(mon.value_cpu3)";
}
```

Here we are creating six distinct reports where each report shows the variable that it's reporting and the actual value of the monitor variable. The previous method does have a few disadvantages:

- If we have more monitor variables to add, we have to add another promise
- If we have to change the report format, we have to make the change in all the six promises

This is where CFEngine iterations may be used. Let's look at the following promises:

```
bundle agent example
{
vars:
"monvars" slist =>  { "diskfree","smtp_in","loadavg","cpu1","cpu2","c
pu3" };

reports:
cf3::
"mon.value_$(monvars) is $(mon.value_$(monvars))";
}
```

This example generates the exact same report as the previous one. So we have defined a list variable `monvars` and iterated over the elements in the list by referencing the list variable as scalar. In this way we have removed the two disadvantages.

In the previous section, we saw how CFEngine iterates a single variable list. However, CFEngine can also iterate multiple lists. Let's see an example:

```
bundle agent example
{
vars:
"stats"   slist => { "value", "av", "dev" };
"monvars" slist => { "diskfree","smtp_in","loadavg","cpu1","cpu2","cp
u3" };
reports:
cf3::
"mon.$(stats)_$(monvars) is $(mon.$(stats)_$(monvars))";
}
```

CFEngine provides the average and standard deviation values for the monitor variables. We now create another list providing the three values for the previous monitor variables.

CFEngine now iterates the two lists to get the name of the exact monitor variable. Use of multiple lists should be done carefully because whenever a promise contains an iteration it is successively re-stated with successive values from the list.

Intelligent use of iterations may cut down the maintenance burden by a huge margin.

Pop quiz

Given next is an example of using multiple lists for iteration. Will this work?

Please provide reasons for success or failure.

```
bundle agent example
{
vars:
"stats" slist =>  { "value", "av", "dev" };
"inout" slist => { "in", "out" };
"monvars" slist => {"rootprocs",
                    "otherprocs",
                    "diskfree",
                    "loadavg",
                    "smtp_$(inout)",
                    "www_$(inout)",
                    "wwws_$(inout)";
reports:
cf3::
"mon.$(stats)_$(monvars) is $(mon.$(stats)_$(monvars))";
}
```

Time for action – disk housekeeping

All hosts running some or other applications generate logs that occupy disk space. To ensure that enough disk space is available for the application to work, regular disk cleanups are a must. Let's try to write promises which perform this housekeeping task if the available disk space is less than 15%. The following tasks should be performed:

1. Check for free disk space.
2. If free disk space is less than 15%, check the following directories:
    - Apache logs directory—`/var/log/httpd`
    - Mail logs files—`/var/log/maillog.*`
3. Delete any files of size greater than 200 MB in these directories.

4. Report the names of files deleted and the available disk space after this operation.
5. These promises should be executed every six hours each day.

   Let's see how this can be done. The following code snippet may be used in a configuration file; let's call it `housekeeping.cf`:

```
bundle agent housekeeping
{
vars:
"free_disk" int => diskfree("/");
classes:
"df_ok" expression =>  islessthan($(free_disk),"15000000" );
df_ok::
files:
"/var/log/httpd/access_log*"
file_select => apache_log_size(".*","200000","inf"),
depth_search => recurse("1"),
transformer => "/bin/rm -f ($this.promiser)";
"/var/log/maillog.*"
file_select => maillog_log_size(".*","200000","inf"),
depth_search => recurse("1"),
transformer => "/bin/rm -f ($this.promiser)";
}
body file_select apache_log_size(a,b,c)
{
leaf_name => { "$(a)" };
search_size => irange("$(b)", "$(c)");
file_result => "leaf_name";
}
body file_select maillog_log_size(a,b,c)
{
leaf_name => { "$(a)" };
search_size => irange("$(b)", "$(c)");
file_result => "leaf_name";
}
…...
…...

body executor control
{
schedule => { "Hr00", "Hr06", "Hr12", "Hr18" };
}
```

6. Let's verify the promise:

```
root@my.system.com# cf-promises -f /var/cfengine/inputs/
housekeeping.cf
root@my.system.com#
```

No output justifies the promises.

7. Now let's execute the promises using `cf-agent`:

```
root@my.system.com# cf-agent -f /var/cfengine/inputs/housekeeping.
cf
root@my.system.com#
```

No output means the promises were executed successfully.

What just happened?

In the given promises file, we defined a bundlesequence under the common control body. The bundlesequence has only one bundle, `housekeeping`. After this, we moved ahead and defined the promises for the `housekeeping` bundle. We used the function special `diskfree` which gives the free space (in KB) available on the directory's current partition. The value returned by this function was stored in a variable `free_disk` with data type integer. Next, we defined the class `df_ok` which returns true if the value of `free_disk` is less than 15 GB. Now if the value returned is true we need to delete all the apache logs under `/var/log/httpd`, and the mail logs under the directory `/var/log` that are bigger than 200 MB. For this, we defined two file promises: the first one provides the file names for the apache access logs, and the second one provides the file names for the mail logs. From these files we select files that are bigger than 200 MB. For this we use the `search_size` constraint for the `file_select` file promise. Once we get the name of files which are bigger than 200 MB, we remove them using the `transformer` file promise.

The following flowchart explains the complete process:

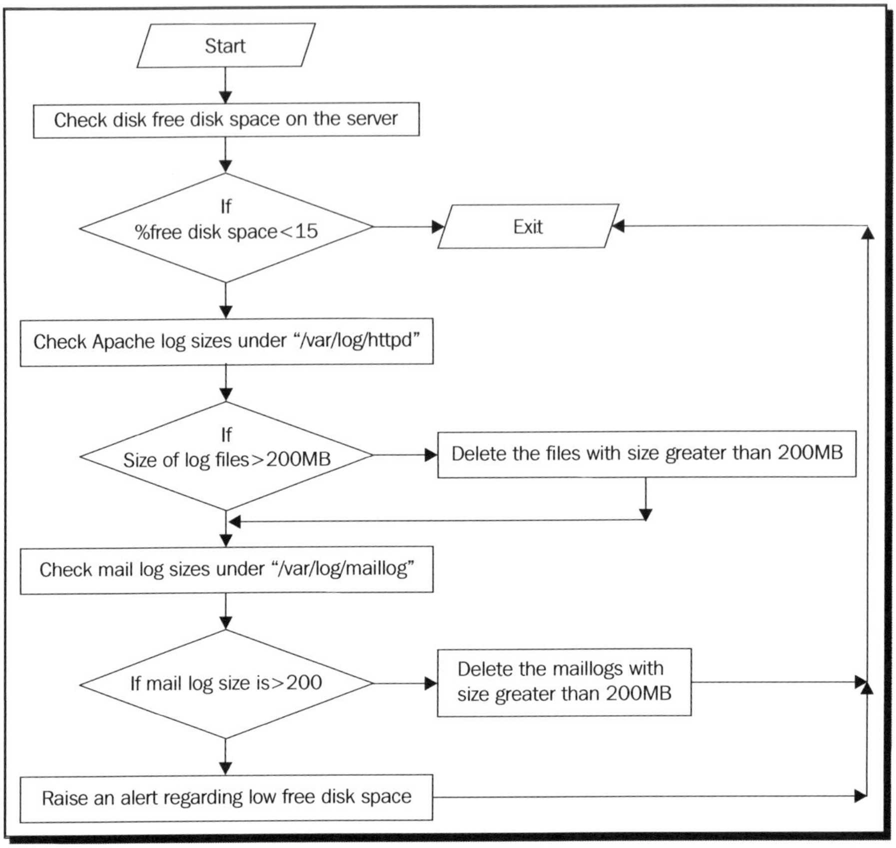

Time for action – restarting a process that's not running

In the previous sections, we learned how to monitor a service. However, we only made an entry in the logs regarding the availability or non availability of the service or process—we did not take any corrective action. CFEngine can be told to take corrective action in these scenarios. Up next, we observe a scenario where we want to start the services `cf-monitord`, `cf-serverd`, `cf-execd`, `cf-know`, and `httpd` if they are not running. For starting the services, we use a predefined promise under the agent control promises `restart_class`. Here's a brief on the `restart_class` promise:

- **restart_class**
  - Type: string
  - Allowed input range: [a-zA-Z0-9_$()\[\].]+

A `restart_class` promise needs to be defined globally if a process is not running so that a command rule may be defined to start the service.

Let's see how we can use this promise in our scenario.

1. You may copy the following promises to a file, `services_check.cf`:

```
body common control
{
bundlesequence => { "selfheal" };
inputs => { "cfengine_stdlib.cf" };
}
bundle agent selfheal
{
vars:
"services" slist => { "cf-monitord", "cf-serverd", "cf-execd" };
"new_service" slist => { "cf-know", @(services) };
"web_services" slist => { "httpd" };
processes:
"$(services)" restart_class => canonify("start_$(services)");
"web_services" restart_class => canonify("start_web_services");
commands:
"/bin/echo /var/cfengine/bin/$(component)";
"/bin/echo service httpd start";
}
```

2. Let us verify these promises with `cf-promises`:

```
root@my.system.com# cf-promises -f /var/cfengine/inputs/services_
check.cf
root@my.system.com#
```

No output means that we are good to execute the promises.

3. Let's execute the promises with `cf-agent` and see what happens:

```
root@my.system.com# cf-agent -v -f /var/cfengine/inputs/services_
check.cf
cf3 Cfengine - autonomous configuration engine - commence self-
diagnostic prelude
..
..
cf3 BUNDLE selfheal
..
..
cf3 Observe process table with /bin/ps auxw
cf3
```

```
cf3     ..........................................................
cf3     Promise handle:
cf3     Promise made by: cf-serverd
cf3     ..........................................................
cf3   -> No signals to send for cf-serverd
cf3   -- Matches in range for cf-serverd - process count promise
kept
cf3     ..........................................................
cf3     Promise handle:
cf3     Promise made by: cf-execd
cf3     ..........................................................
cf3   -> Making a one-time restart promise for cf-execd
cf3     ..........................................................
cf3     Promise handle:
cf3     Promise made by: web_services
cf3     ..........................................................
cf3   -> Making a one-time restart promise for web_services
cf3    commands in bundle selfheal (1)
cf3   -> Promiser string contains a valid executable (/bin/echo) -
ok
cf3     ..........................................................
cf3     Promise handle:
cf3     Promise made by: /bin/echo /var/cfengine/bin/$(component)
cf3     ..........................................................
cf3
cf3   -> Executing '/bin/echo /var/cfengine/bin/$(component)'
...(timeout=-678,owner=-1,group=-1)
cf3   -> (Setting umask to 77)
cf3   -> Finished script - succeeded /bin/echo /var/cfengine/bin/
$(component)
cf3 Q: ".../bin/echo /var/": /var/cfengine/bin/$(component)
cf3 I: Last 1 QUOTed lines were generated by promiser "/bin/echo
/var/cfengine/bin/$(component)"
cf3   -> Completed execution of /bin/echo /var/cfengine/bin/
$(component)
cf3   -> Promiser string contains a valid executable (/bin/echo) -
ok
cf3
cf3     ..........................................................
cf3     Promise handle:
cf3     Promise made by: /bin/echo service httpd start
cf3     ..........................................................
cf3
```

```
cf3   -> Executing '/bin/echo service httpd start' ...(timeout=-
678,owner=-1,group=-1)


cf3   -> Finished script - succeeded /bin/echo service httpd start
cf3 Q: ".../bin/echo servi": service httpd start
cf3 I: Last 1 QUOTed lines were generated by promiser "/bin/echo
service httpd start"
cf3   -> Completed execution of /bin/echo service httpd start
..
..
cf3      +  Private classes augmented:
cf3      +        start_cf_execd
cf3      +        start_web_services
..
```

If we see the output of cf-agent here, we get to know that the the services `cf-serverd` and `cf-monitord` were running and hence were not sent a restart signal, whereas the other services which were not running were sent a restart signal on execution of the commands promises that we had specified.

What just happened?

We defined a bundlesequence under the common control body having just a single bundle by the name of `selfheal`. We defined a list variable `services` which provides the list of services to be checked to CFEngine. The list of services that need to be checked are `cf-monitord`, `cf-serverd`, and `cf-execd`. Similar to the definition of `services`, we also defined two more variables: `new_services` and `web_services`—which provide CFEngine with a list of services that need to be checked. The services `cf-know` and all the services in the list variable `services` are listed under the variable `new_services`. The `HTTPD` service is listed under the list variable `web_services`. We do this just to segregate the types of services; we could have specified all services under the variable `services` itself. We passed the complete list `services` to a new list variable `new_services` using `@(services)`. Next, we defined the `processes` promises under the agent control bundle. Here we use the `restart_class` promise under the `processes` promise for agent control. The `restart_class` takes the list elements defined under the variables `services`, `new_services`, and `web_services` as arguments. We defined the `commands` promises, which are commands to be executed to start the services, if they are found not running. On execution, CFEngine runs the command `ps auxw` to get a list of processes and then matches this list to the list of elements that we provided to verify which services are running and which are not, and then starts the services as per the commands that we have provided for services not running.

Reading log files

We generated a lot of logs and reports in the previous sections. Other than logs or reports generated by CFEngine, there are system logs or application logs that we may need to read on a regular basis and generate reports from. One such log is the web server access log. To keep track of what kind of HTTP requests and where they are coming from we generally need to parse the web server access logs and then generate presentable reports. So let's take the Apache web server (as it is the most widely used) and check its access logs. You may now specify different formats for an Apache Access log. I'll take a sample access log in the following format:

```
192.168.8.102  [17/Dec/2010:17:07:08 +0530] "GET / HTTP/1.1" 200 324
"Mozilla/5.0 (X11; U; Linux i686; en-US) AppleWebKit/534.7 (KHTML, like
Gecko) Chrome/7.0.517.44 Safari/534.7"
```

In this access log line we have the IP, a time stamp, request URL, Apache status return code, and web browser information. Now we need to get the number of hits on the home page—we may tell CFEngine to parse the log file and match all lines having the request URL as **GET / HTTP 1.1**. This can be done as shown in the next example. You may copy the code snippet to a file named `apache_stats.cf`:

```
..
..
body monitor apache_logs
{
measurements:
"/var/log/httpd/access_log"
handle => "line_count";
stream_type => "file";
data_type => "counter";
match_value => scan_log("GET / HTTP/1.1");
history_type => "log";
action => sample_rate(0);
}
body match_value(x)
{
select_line_matching => "$(x)";
track_growing_file => "true";

}
 body action sample_rate(x)
{
ifelapsed => "$(x)";
expireafter => "15";
}
```

```
..
..
```

Given here was a small snippet of code for getting the number of hits on the home page of our domain. Let's see what the code does:

1. We defined the file that needed to be parsed under the monitor control promise.
2. We defined a handle `line_count`, which is a unique string for referring to this as a promisee elsewhere.
3. Next, we defined a file `stream_type` which defines how CFEngine treats all inputs as a file.
4. Then we defined a `data_type` as `counter`.
5. We then defined a `regex`, which should match the lines as per the need.
6. We defined a history type as `log` so that the measured value is logged as an infinite time series in `WOKDIR/state`.
7. We then defined a sample rate so that the log file is parsed in real time.
8. Next, we defined the `expireafter` promise so that if the parsing of new lines in the log file takes more than 15 seconds, CFEngine should kill the process.
9. Setting the `track_growing_file` constraint as `true` makes CFEngine assume this file is an ever growing file, and it then only reads the new entries after the previous sampling time on each invocation.

Here is a small brief on all the unique promises we have just used:

- **handle**
  - Type: string
  - Allowed input range: [a-zA-Z0-9_$()\[\].]+

  With this promise type, you may define a unique tag which may be used as a promisee somewhere else.

- **stream_type**
  - Type: Menu option
  - Allowed input range: pipe, file

  This promise type defines the interface to which the data is being collected. CFEngine may take the input from a file or directly from the `stdout` of a command using `pipe`.

- **data_type**
  - Type: Menu option
  - Allowed input range: counter, int, real, string, slist

  The `data_type` promise defines the data type being collected.

- **history_type**
  - Type: Menu option
  - Allowed input range: weekly, scalar, static, log

  This promise type defines whether the data can be seen as a time-series or as an isolated value.

  weekly—A standard CFEngine two-dimensional time average (over a weekly period) is retained.

  scalar—A single value. The value of the data is not expected to change much during the life time of the daemon.

  static—This is the same as the 'static'.

  log—The measured value is logged as an infinite time-series in WORKDIR/state.

Distributed scheduling

In previous sections, we saw how to schedule jobs using CFEngine on individual hosts. We also learned how to define a sequence of jobs, that is, defining your next job on the basis of the 'success' or 'failure' of the previous job on individual machines. Distributed scheduling is the next step, wherein jobs are chained on a network of hosts. There are scenarios where you may want to process jobs on host1 as well as host2, and when these are completed successfully, a third job on host3 needs to be executed. CFEngine facilitates such scenarios and it is called distributed scheduling. Now there may be two methods of scheduling jobs spanning a network of hosts:

- A centralized system, where a single host acts as a 'commander' and all the other hosts report the status of their jobs to this 'commander'. The commander decides on what to do next.
- A decentralized system, where each host sends a signal on completion or failure of its job to its peers, and they decide on what do do next.

Now there are advantages and disadvantages to both the systems. A centralized system is easy to manage but may cause bottlenecks at the 'commander'. The 'commander' has to process all the status signals sent by peers and then decide on what signal should be passed on to the other peers that are next in the line of action. A decentralized system on the other hand utilizes fewer resources. Each host executes its job and signals other peers of its status, and the peers decide on the execution of individual jobs based on the signal received. It's up to you to decide which architecture you would like to set up.

Let's see a generic example describing the two architectures.

We want to schedule a job on `Host1` every Monday at 1100 hrs and another job on `Host2` every Monday at 1120 hrs. This complete sequence of jobs may be defined for a centralized architecture and also with a decentralized architecture, as follows:

- **Centralized architecture**

```
bundle agent centralized
{
methods:
        Host1.Mon.Hr11.Min00_05::
"any" usebundle => my_job;

commands:
Host2:Mon.Hr11.Min20_25::
"/usr/sbin/job.pl"
}
```

In this method, `Host1` executes its jobs every Monday, it starts at 1100 hrs, and continues till 1105 hrs. `Host2` runs the job every Monday, it starts at 1120 hrs, and continues till 1125 hrs. Now there is no direct communication between `Host1` and `Host2` but the problem is that the 'commander' needs to know how long the jobs need to run. `Host2` does not know whether `Host1` has completed its job or not, and hence it may result in `Host2` processing no data.

The outline for this architecture can be summarized in the following diagram:

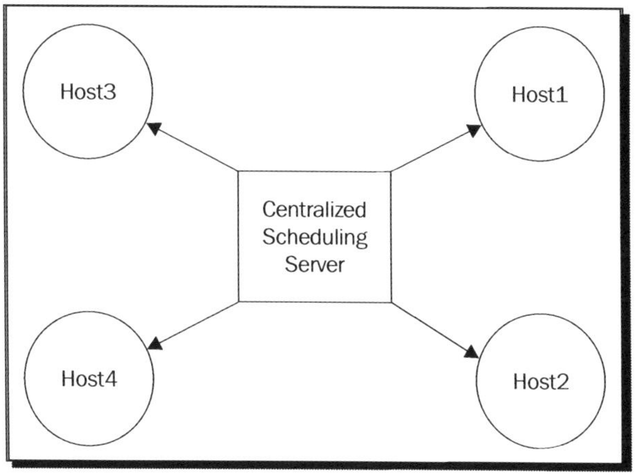

- **Decentralized architecture**

  In a decentralized architecture `Host1` sends a signal to `Host2` after it completes its jobs successfully, and `Host2` starts the execution of its jobs once it gets a 'success' signal from `Host1`. Now the hosts are communicating amongst themselves. Given next is a code snippet showing how we can achieve this:

```
body agent decentralized
{
classes:
Host1::
"success" expression => remoteclassesmatching(
                                                  "true.*",
                                                  "false",
                                                  "Host1",
                                                );

methods:
Host1.success
"any" usebundle => my_job;

commands:
Host2.Mon.Hr11.Min00_05::
"/usr/sbin/job.pl",
classes => state_repaired("success");

}
```

  In this decentralized architecture, the `methods` promise runs on `Host1` and the `commands` promise runs on `Host2`. Now, `Host1` sets a signal class 'success' which is collected by `Host2` after contacting `cf-serverd` on `Host1`. We need to ensure that `Host2` is able to connect to `Host1`. The advantage of this architecture is that jobs on `Host2` will start only when jobs on `Host1` are successfully completed. So we need not be concerned about how long it takes to complete jobs on `Host1`. Thus distributed scheduling may be used to create a longer chain of jobs on multiple hosts. The next diagram summarizes this:

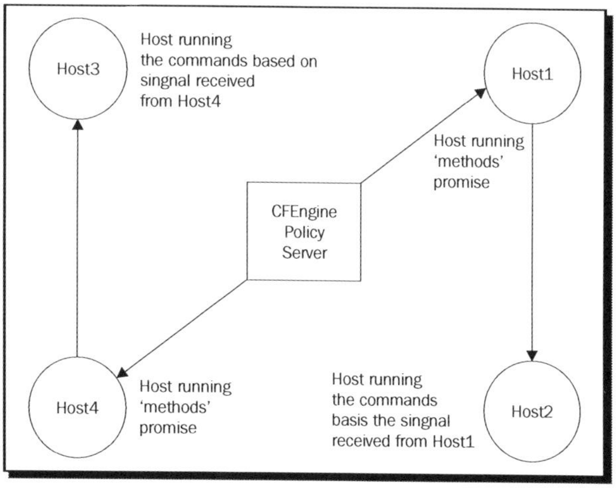

Pop quiz

Have a look at the following time class:

```
MorningShift or => { "Hr08", "Hr09", "Hr10", "Hr11", "Hr12",
  "Hr13" };
```

If there is no "splaytime" defined and `cf-agent` executes every five minutes, when will `cf-agent` execute the file?

- Once every hour at the start of the hour
- Once every hour at the end of the hour
- Every five minutes, starting from 0805 hrs, to 1205 hrs
- Once during the morning shift

Summary

In this chapter we learned about the details and the usage of the monitor, runagent, executor, and reporter control promises. We also learned how to schedule tasks, generate logs, and create reports using these promises. In addition to this, we saw in detail how iterations and loops can be handled in CFEngine. Through various examples we saw how a complex sequence of jobs may be defined within CFEngine. Apart from scheduling jobs on individual hosts we also saw how the execution of jobs can be handled on a span of networked machines using distributed scheduling. In distributed scheduling we learned about the two available types: centralized distributed scheduling and decentralized distributed scheduling.

With this newly acquired knowledge, let's move on to performing a complete security audit in the next chapter.

5
Security Audit with CFEngine

The security policy of an organization is based on the organization's need to protect its information resources. This policy is of practical value in preventing security compromises only if it is implemented reliably and the state of a system adheres to the changes in this policy. Discussions on securing the organization's resources are generally more focused on how to configure the systems as per the security policy, but they say little on how to ensure that the system will maintain configuration or how a change in the security policy will be implemented on all the systems. Once again, CFEngine saves the day—it can be configured to audit systems and make changes in case it finds an anomaly so that all the systems have a defined 'secure' state as per the organization's security policy.

A security policy takes care of the four important areas:

- Authorization
- Authentication
- Data protection
- Application configuration

Defining a security policy is beyond the scope of this book. We'll see how to automate regular security audits so that the systems maintain the 'secure' state as per the security policy implemented.

> For guidance on design and implementation of a robust IT security policy, one may choose a training course from http://www.sans.org/security-training/courses.php#management. Besides that, LOPSA has a mentorship program, details of which may be found at https://lopsa.org/mentor/.

In this chapter we shall learn about:

- Auditing access controls
- Auditing authentication controls
- Auditing data protection measures
- Auditing application configurations

Configuring and auditing access controls

Let's see a few examples of how CFEngine can help us with configuring and auditing the access controls for a host.

Time for action – managing access control with TCP wrapper

TCP wrapper is a host-based networking access control system that may be used to filter network access-basis IP addresses, names, and/or indent query replies. Let's see how SSH access control can be done using TCP wrapper. A Linux-like operating system provides us with two files, /etc/hosts.allow and /etc/hosts.deny, which may be used to specify a list of IP addresses and host names for filtering the access to network services. For allowing an IP to access SSH service we may add the following line to /etc/hosts.allow:

```
SSHD:<IP_address_to_be_allowed>
```

For denying an IP to access SSH service we may add the following line to /etc/hosts.deny:

```
SSHD:<IP_address_to_be_denied>
```

To configure a SSH access control mechanism we will need:

- A trusted centralized host that may be used for maintaining the pair of master files we just mentioned, and
- To distribute these master files to each host whenever there is a change

So let's say we start maintaining the two files, hosts.allow and hosts.deny, on a trusted host under /var/cfengine/repo_policy/.

1. Let's see the contents of the files `hosts.allow` and `hosts.deny` on the master host `my1.system.com` and on the client host `my.system.com`:

```
root@my1.system.com# cat /var/cfengine/repo-policy/hosts.allow

# hosts.allow This file describes the names of the hosts which are
#    allowed to use the local INET services, as decided
#    by the '/usr/sbin/tcpd' server.
#

ALL:172.16.0.
ALL:172.16.1.
ALL:172.16.2.
ALL:172.16.3.
ALL:172.16.7.
sshd:192.168.2.224
root@my1.system.com#

root@my1.system.com# cat /var/cfengine/repo-policy/hosts.deny

# hosts.deny This file describes the names of the hosts which are
#    *not* allowed to use the local INET services, as decided
#    by the '/usr/sbin/tcpd' server.

# The portmap line is redundant, but it is left to remind you that
# the new secure portmap uses hosts.deny and hosts.allow.  In
particular
# you should know that NFS uses portmap!
sshd:ALL
root@my1.system.com#

root@my.system.com# cat /etc/hosts.allow

# hosts.allow This file describes the names of the hosts which are
```

```
#    allowed to use the local INET services, as decided
#    by the '/usr/sbin/tcpd' server.
#



root@my.system.com#
root@my.system.com# cat /etc/hosts.deny


#
# hosts.deny This file describes the names of the hosts which are
#    *not* allowed to use the local INET services, as decided
#    by the '/usr/sbin/tcpd' server.
#
# The portmap line is redundant, but it is left to remind you that
# the new secure portmap uses hosts.deny and hosts.allow.  In
particular
# you should know that NFS uses portmap!



root@my.system.com#
```

2. Let's write a promises file that will distribute these files to each host. We need to ensure that the client hosts or network is allowed to access the files from the repository on the master policy distribution server. The following lines may be copied to a file named `tcpwrapper_policy.cf`:

```
body common control
{
bundlesequence => { "ssh_access_policy" };
inputs => { "cfengine_stdlib.cf" };
version => "1.1.1";
}
bundle agent ssh_access_policy
{
files:
"/etc/hosts.allow"
"/etc/hosts.deny"
vars:
"hosts_files" string => { "/var/cfengine/repo-policy/hosts.allow",
"/var/cfengine/repo-policy/hosts.deny" };
```

```
copy_from => secure_cp("$(hosts_files)","my1.system.com");");
}
```

3. Let's verify the promises file using `cf-promises`:

```
root@my.system.com# cf-promises -f /var/cfengine/inputs/tcpwrapper
_policy.cf
root@my.system.com#
```

No output indicates that the promises are good to be executed.

4. Let's execute the promises using `cf-agent` and check the output:

```
root@my.system.com# cf-agent -f /var/cfengine/inputs/tcpwrapper_
policy.cf
root@my.system.com#
```

No output indicates that the promises have been executed without any errors.

5. Now let's check the two files on the client host `my.system.com` and verify if the files were copied correctly:

```
root@my.system.com# cat /etc/hosts.allow

# hosts.allow This file describes the names of the hosts which are

.....
ALL:172.16.0.
ALL:172.16.1.
ALL:172.16.2.
ALL:172.16.3.
ALL:172.16.7.
sshd:192.168.2.224
root@my.system.com#


root@my.system.com# cat /etc/hosts.deny

# hosts.deny This file describes the names of the hosts which are

......
sshd:ALL
root@my.system.com#
```

As we see here, the files from the master CFEngine repository were copied correctly to the client host.

What just happened?

In the promises file `tcpwrapper_policy.cf`, we defined a bundlesequence having a single bundle `ssh_access_policy` under the common control body. Additionally, we defined that the file `cfengine_stdlib.cf` should be included. We also defined the version number for this file. In the bundle agent body we defined the files which need to be updated under the "files" promise type, the source files are defined by the variable `hosts_files` under the "vars" promise type. In addition to the source and destination paths we also define the server from where the files need to be copied and the mode of copying as "secure_cp". We need not define the body for the promisee "secure_cp" as it is already defined in the files `cfengine_stdlib.cf` which we had included.

Time for action – auditing SSHD log files for break-in attempts

1. The SSH daemon logs a message whenever a script kiddie tries to gain access to your system and is denied access due to the tcpwrapper rules you have already put. The message appears in the files '/var/log/secure' by default. The message is similar to the one given below

   ```
   Jan  2 15:33:09 sshd[32128]: refused connect from <IP_Address>
   ```

   Now we may ask CFEngine to scan the file and log such IP addresses. These IP addresses may further be fed to your firewall rules or any other applications for detailed analysis.

2. Let's write a promise file that scans the logs and prepares a list of rogue IP addresses which are trying to connect to your system. You may copy the following code snippet to a file `ssh_deny.cf`:

   ```
   body common control

   {

   bundlesequence => { "check_breakin_attempts" };

   version => "1.0.0";

   }

   bundle agent check_breakin_attempts

   {
   ```

```
vars:

"my_value" string => execresult("/bin/cat /var/log/secure | grep
'refused connect from' | gawk '{print $10}'", "useshell");

reports:

linux::

"$(my_value)"

report_to_file => "/var/cfengine/outputs/IP_breakin_attempt";

}
```

3. Let's verify the promises file with `cf-promises`:

```
root@my.system.com# cf-promises -f /var/cfengine/inputs/ssh_deny.
cf
root@my.system.com#
```

No output indicates that the promises file is good to be executed.

4. Before executing the promises and with the help of `cf-agent`, let's check the contents of the file, if it exists.

```
root@my.system.com# cat /var/cfengine/outputs/IP_breakin_attempt
cat: /var/cfengine/outputs/IP_breakin_attempt: No such file or
directory
root@my.system.com#
```

5. Let's execute the promises using cf-agent and check the results:

```
root@my.system.com# cf-agent -f /var/cfengine/inputs/ssh_deny.cf
cf3 Cfengine - autonomous configuration engine - commence self-
diagnostic prelude

cf3 ------------------------------------------------------------

cf3 Work directory is /var/cfengine
..
..
cf3 ************************************************************
```

```
cf3 BUNDLE check_breakin_attempts

cf3 ****************************************************************
..
..
cf3     Promise handle:

cf3     Promise made by: 208.2.135.10

208.2.135.11

208.2.135.12

208.2.135.13

208.2.135.14

208.2.135.15

208.2.135.16

208.2.135.17

..
..
```

Let's check the contents of the file `/var/cfengine/outputs/IP_breakin_attempt` again:

```
root@my.system.com# cat /var/cfengine/outputs/IP_breakin_attempt
208.2.135.10

208.2.135.11

208.2.135.12

208.2.135.13
```

```
208.2.135.14

208.2.135.15

208.2.135.16

208.2.135.17
root@my.system.com#
```

Now we have the list of IP addresses that tried to gain unauthenticated SSH access to your host. You can run this script at a pre defined frequency and feed the output to your firewall so that the connections are dropped at the firewall level itself.

What just happened?

In this task, we wanted to get a list of IP addresses that were trying to connect to your host but were not allowed. We used the file `/var/log/secure`, which stores the status of SSH connections. We defined a bundlesequence under the common control body having a single bundle with the name `check_breakin_attempts`. We defined the version for this promises file as `1.0.0` using the `version` promise. Under the body of the `check_breakin_attempts` bundle agent we defined a variable `my_value` under the `vars` promise type. The data type for this variable was defined as `string` and it stores the result of the execution of the command, returning the IP addresses that were refused connection by SSH due to the tcpwrapper policy. After this, under the `reports` promise type we defined a class `linux`, which defined that the IP addresses should we written to the file `/var/cfengine/outputs/IP_breakin_attempt`. On executing the promises the command gives the IP addresses, which were refused connection by the SSH daemon, addresses that are stored as `string` in the variable `my_value`.

Configuring a firewall

We just saw how to use the TCPWrapper library for SSH access control. Now there are services that may not actually be using the TCPWrapper library but we might still like to have access control defined for such services or daemons. All operating systems provide one or the other utility or programs which may be used to filter access to a service without using the TCPWrapper library. Now all such utilities or programs work with a set of firewall rules which need to be altered on a regular basis, depending on the incoming and outgoing traffic on your network. Altering these rules manually on a regular basis may be a daunting task and Cfengine is there to help. Cfengine is capable of making changes to the configuration of a system. Let's see how Cfengine can help us in configuring a firewall on a GNU/Linux based operating systems. All GNU/Linux based operating systems provide one such program called Iptables, which is an application program with which one may specify rules for filtering traffic destined for a specific IP address or port. Now you may need to write tens of rules for controlling access to a number of services on your system using the command 'iptables'. IP tables provides a handy command, "iptables-save", for saving the filter rules which you may have written to a file "/<your_path>/iptables_rules". This file is again used by the iptables init script to reload the rules written in the file. Now we can manage IPtables with Cfengine if we write a promises file which can edit the file "/<your_path/iptables_rules>".

Time for action – managing iptables with CFEngine

1. You would already be using Iptables to filter access to various services, ports, and so on. One of the common filtering rules is allowing or restricting access to your web server server basis host IP addresses. The rules may look similar to the following:

```
-A INPUT -s 152.168.2.0/24 -m state -state NEW -m tcp -p tcp -
dport 80 -j ACCEPT
-A INPUT -s 152.168.4.0/24 -m state -state NEW -m tcp -p tcp -
dport 80 -j ACCEPT
-A INPUT -s 220.1.4.0/24 -m state -state NEW -m tcp -p tcp -dport
80 -j ACCEPT
-A INPUT -s 220.2.4.0/24 -m state -state NEW -m tcp -p tcp -dport
80 -j ACCEPT
-A INPUT -s 15.3.5.0/24 -m state -state NEW -m tcp -p tcp -dport
80 -j ACCEPT
-A INPUT -s 15.3.6.0/24 -m state -state NEW -m tcp -p tcp -dport
80 -j ACCEPT
```

   These rules can either be added to the file `/<your_path>/iptables_rules` or may be added using the the command `iptables`. Here we'll use the first method of adding the rules to the file `/etc/sysconfig/iptables` and then reload the iptables rule. Let's write a promise file that can be used to add these rules on a number of web servers existing in your IT infrastructure. You may copy the following code snippet to the file `ip_tables_config.cf`:

```
body common control
{
bundlesequence => { "iptables_config" };
inputs => { "cfengine_stdlib.cf" };
version => "1.1.1.";
}
bundle agent iptables_config
{
files:
"/etc/sysconfig/iptables"
create => "true";
edit_line => add_rules;
restart_class => "iptables_reload";

commands:
iptables_reload::
"/etc/init.d/iptables restart",
comment => "start the iptables service";
}

bundle edit_line add_rules
insert_lines:
{
"-A INPUT -s 152.168.2.0/24 -m state -state NEW -m tcp -p tcp -
dport 80 -j ACCEPT
-A INPUT -s 152.168.4.0/24 -m state -state NEW -m tcp -p tcp -
dport 80 -j ACCEPT
-A INPUT -s 220.1.4.0/24 -m state -state NEW -m tcp -p tcp -dport
80 -j ACCEPT
-A INPUT -s 220.2.4.0/24 -m state -state NEW -m tcp -p tcp -dport
80 -j ACCEPT
-A INPUT -s 15.3.5.0/24 -m state -state NEW -m tcp -p tcp -dport
80 -j ACCEPT
-A INPUT -s 15.3.6.0/24 -m state -state NEW -m tcp -p tcp -dport
80 -j ACCEPT
-A INPUT -m state -state NEW -m tcp -p tcp -dport 80 -j DROP
";
}
```

2. Let's verify this promises file using `cf-promises`:

```
root@my.system.com# cf-promises -f /var/cfengine/inputs/ip_tables_
config.cf
root@my.system.com#
```

No error output justifies the promises.

3. Let's execute the promises file using `cf-agent`:

```
root@my.system.com# cf-agent -f /var/cfengine/inputs/ip_tables_
config.cf
root@my.system.com#
```

No errors or output indicate that the promises were successfully executed.

4. Let's check the contents of the file `/etc/sysconfig/iptables`:

```
root@my.system.com# cat /etc/sysconfig/iptables
-A INPUT -s 152.168.2.0/24 -m state -state NEW -m tcp -p tcp -
dport 80 -j ACCEPT
-A INPUT -s 152.168.4.0/24 -m state -state NEW -m tcp -p tcp -
dport 80 -j ACCEPT
-A INPUT -s 220.1.4.0/24 -m state -state NEW -m tcp -p tcp -dport
80 -j ACCEPT
-A INPUT -s 220.2.4.0/24 -m state -state NEW -m tcp -p tcp -dport
80 -j ACCEPT
-A INPUT -s 15.3.5.0/24 -m state -state NEW -m tcp -p tcp -dport
80 -j ACCEPT
-A INPUT -s 15.3.6.0/24 -m state -state NEW -m tcp -p tcp -dport
80 -j ACCEPT
root@my.system.com#
```

As we just saw, the rules were added to the file that would get reloaded when iptables restarts.

What just happened?

We needed to define a mechanism to update iptables on all the hosts running a web server. We are going to add the first rules to the file provided at the beginning of the task, we need to add to the file `/etc/sysconfig/iptables` We define a bundlesequence under the common control body, which currently has a single bundle by the name of `iptables_config`. We then include the file `cfengine_stdlib.cf` with the `inputs` promise type. We also define a version number for this promises file and this version number is `1.1.1`. To define the bundle agent `iptables_config` we first provide the name of the file to which the rules need to be added with the `files` promise type. We also set the value of the constraint `create` as `true` so that if the file does not exist, it should be created. After this we define the `edit_line` promise and the `restart_class` promise. For the `edit_line` promise, we provide the rules that need to be added in the body of the promise. For the `restart_class` promise we provide the command for restarting the `iptables` service after the changes have been saved to the file `/etc/sysconfig/iptables`.

From these steps, we have our basic `iptable` rules file ready that may be copied to the other hosts with a `copy_from` promise. Now we may need to keep adding rules to this file as we may need to allow or deny more IP addresses or networks to the HTTP service. Let's see how we can update this rules file on a regular basis. For this you may have two files; `http.allow`, which has a list of rules for IP addresses that need to be allowed (separated by a new line), and the other file `http.deny` with a list of rules for IP addresses that need to be denied access (again, separated by a new line). These files may be updated regularly based on various criterion such as all the IP addresses sending more than a 100 requests in a minute, all the IP addresses on a public network trying to access the admin URL which is otherwise only accessible from the LAN, and so on. Suppose we already have a mechanism for updating the `http.allow` and `http.deny` files, you may use other shell scripts, log analysis tools, or write another CFEngine promise file which may append or delete IP addresses to the `http.allow` and `http.deny` files. Once such a mechanism is in place you may use the CFEngine special function **readstringlist** to read the two files and get the rules added to `ip_tables_config.cf`.

Auditing the file system

As part of the organization's security policy, one should conduct a file-system audit for all critical systems on a regular basis. Let's see a few examples on how CFEngine may help us in conducting such audits.

Time for action – looking out for suspicious file names

As part of routine security audits, CFEngine may be used to keep an eye on suspicious files names in important directories. For example, there need not be an HTML or JPG file under the `/etc` directory:

1. Let's write a promises file to audit important directories and raise an alert if it finds a file with a name listed as a suspicious name. You may copy the following promises to a file named `shouldnotexist.cf`:

```
body common control
{
bundlesequence => "suspicious_files";
inputs => { "cfengine_stdlib.cf" };
version => "1.0.0"
}
bundle agent suspicious_files
{
files:
"dir_list" slist => {"/etc","/var/spool/mail","/bin","/usr/bin","/
sbin"};
```

```
file_select => suspicious
}
body file_select suspicious
{
suspiciousnames => {"$dir_list/*.JPG","$dir_list/*.html","$dir_
list/*gif","$dir_list/*.lkm"};

reports:
<html>
Time: $(sys.date)<br>
Alert ! The file $file_result exists.<br>
</html>

}
```

2. Let's verify the promises using `cf-promises`:

   ```
   root@my.system.com# cf-promises -f /var/cfengine/inputs/
   shouldnotexist.cf
   root@my.system.com#
   ```

   No output indicates that the promises are good to be executed.

3. Let's execute the promises with `cf-agent` and verify whether the promises written by us are able to point to suspicious files:

   ```
   root@my.system.com# cf-agent -f /var/cfengine/inputs/
   shouldnotexist.cf
   root@my.system.com#
   ```

   No error output indicates that the promises are correct.

What just happened?

We wanted to get the names of suspicious files under the important directories, `/etc`, `/var/spool/mail`, `/bin`, `/usr/bin` and `/sbin`. For this we defined a bundlesequence `suspicious_files` under the common control body in the promises file `shouldnotexist.cf`. We also included the file `cfengine_stdlib.cf` using the `inputs` promise. We also defined the version for the promises file. Next, we defined a variable `dir_list` under the `files` promise type, which is a list of directories that need to be searched for suspicious files. We then defined the `file_select` promise. For the `file_select` promise we defined the promiser `suspiciousnames`, which has the regular expressions that will be expanded by CFEngine to match the list of file names in the respective directories and hence print a list of suspicious files. Besides this, we may also define the deletion of these suspicious files.

Time for action – verifying the sudoers file

Unix or Linux-like operating systems provide a facility wherein unprivileged system users may work as privileged 'root' users to perform certain tasks which can only be performed by the super user 'root'. The tasks these unprivileged users may perform are predefined, in the form of commands or scripts, by the super user in the file `/etc/sudoers`. Apart from defining the tasks, an unprivileged user may also define whether they will have to supply a password while executing the commands. As part of the security audit, we need to verify that the file remains in a 'secure' state, which means that only super-users are allowed to perform super-user tasks, as per the policy of an organization. Therefore, we need to compare the `/etc/sudoers` file on each host with the master sudoers file on the CFEngine server. Let's say the master sudoers file for a group of similar hosts is maintained at `/var/cfengine/master-files/sudoers` on the CFEngine server:

1. Now let's write a promise file `check_sudoers.cf`, which should exist on the client hosts and should compare the `/etc/sudoers` on the host with the master sudoers file existing on the master CFEngine server:

```
body common control
{
bundlesequence => { "verify_sudoers" };
version => "1.0.0";
}
bundle agent verify_sudoers
{
vars:
sudoers_file string => { "/var/cfengine/master-files/sudoers" };

files:
"/etc/sudoers"
perms => m("440");
perms => og("root","root");
copy_from => secure_cp("$(sudoers_file)","my1.system.com");
}
body copy_from secure_cp(from,server)
{
source => "$(from)";
servers => { "$(server)" };
compare => "digest";
encrypt => "true";
verify => "true";
}
```

2. Let's verify the promises using `cf-promises`:

   ```
   root@my1# cf-promises -f /var/cfengine/inputs/check_sudoers.cf
   root@my1#
   ```

   No output indicates we are good with the above promises.

3. Let's execute the promises using `cf-agent`:

   ```
   root@my1# cf-agent -f /var/cfengine/inputs/check_sudoers.cf
   root@my1#
   ```

   No error output indicates the promises were executed without any issues.

What just happened?

We needed do an audit of the `/etc/sudoers`, and if there is a difference between the file on the client and on the CFEngine server, the correct file should be copied from the CFEngine server repository to the client's path. For this we defined a bundlesequence under the common control body with a single bundle named `verify_sudoers`. We also set the version for this file. We define the variable `sudoers_file` which has the value `/var/cfengine/master-files/sudoers`. We also defined the destination file `/etc/sudoers` under the `files` promise type. Next, we define the checks for the permissions, owner, and group. We defined the `copy_from` promise that copies the file from CFEngine's master files repository to the host if there is change in the content of the host's file. We set the constraint `compare` under the body for `copy_from` promise to `digest`. Additionally, we set the `encrypt` and `verify` constraints to transfer the file securely and to ensure that the file has been correctly transferred.

Agent control promise – auditing

In the previous example we checked the file permissions for the `sudoers` file. Apart from just checking the permissions, CFEngine can also maintain an audit database recording the details for verification of the current promise. Let's see the `auditing` agent control promise in more detail:

- **auditing**
  - Type: (menu option)
  - Allowed input range: true, false, yes, no, on, off
  - Default value: false

This agent control promise may be set to TRUE for activating the `cf-agent` audit log.

For generating the audit database, let's add the following lines to the previous configuration file check_sudoers.cf:

```
body agent control
{
auditing => "true";
}
```

After executing the configuration file check_sudoers.cf with these lines added, the following audit database is generated:

```
root@my1# ls /var/cfengine/ *.db
/var/cfengine/cf_Audit.db  /var/cfengine/cf_classes.db    /var/cfengine/
cf_LastSeen.db  /var/cfengine/performance.db
root@my1# ls -lh /var/cfengine/reports
total 0
root@my1#
```

If you check, there is a database name cf_Audit.db which is created due to the agent control promise. We can generate reports using the audit database with the help of the cf-report CFEngine utility. Let's see what reports are generated:

```
root@my1.system.com# cf-report /var/cfengine/cf_Audit.db
root@my1.system.com# ls /var/cfengine/reports
cfengine_in.E-sigma  cfengine_in.q  cfengine_out.E-sigma  cfengine_out.q

cfenv-average  cfenv-now  cfenv-stddev  cpu0.E-sigma

cpu0.q  cpu1.E-sigma   cpu1.q  cpu2.E-sigma

cpu2.q  cpu3.E-sigma  cpu3.q  cpu.E-sigma

cpu.q  diskfree.E-sigma  diskfree.q  dns_in.E-sigma

dns_in.q  dns_out.E-sigma
…...
…...

temp2.q   temp3.E-sigma  temp3.q  udp_in.E-sigma

udp_in.q  udp_out.E-sigma  udp_out.q  users.E-sigma
```

```
users.q  webaccess.E-sigma  webaccess.q  weberrors.E-sigma

weberrors.q  www_in.E-sigma  www_in.q  www_out.E-sigma

www_out.q  wwws_in.E-sigma  wwws_in.q  wwws_out.E-sigma

wwws_out.q
```

As you can see from the output, a lot of reports are generated. You may also generate graphs using the `cf-report` utility.

Time for action – finding a file with setuid and setgid

The SUID or SGID bits are special attributes, for a file, provided in Unix or Linux-like operating systems besides the read/write/execute permissions. The SUID attributes 'set' for a file mean that while executing the file, your user would be set as the owner of the file. If the SUID bit is not set, the user has to type `su` and get temporary superuser access to execute the file. This may be a security risk if the SUID bit is set for scripts or commands which have `root` as their owner, because the scripts or commands will be executed with superuser privilege even when the script is being executed with an unprivileged user.

1. Let's write a promises file to find scripts or commands that have the SUID bit set. You may copy the following code snippet to a file `check_SUID.cf`:

```
body common control

{

bundlesequence => { "id_check" };

version => "1.0.0";

}

bundle agent id_check

{

files:

"/sbin/"
```

```
file_select => check_suid,

transformer => "/bin/echo The following file $(this.promiser) has
it's uid set",

depth_search => recurse("inf");



"/usr/bin/"



file_select => check_suid,

transformer => "/bin/echo The following file $(this.promiser) has
its uid set",

depth_search => recurse("inf");

}

body file_select check_suid

{

search_mode => { "4755","4777" };

file_result => "mode";

}

body depth_search recurse(d)

{

depth => "$(d)";

}
```

2. Let's verify the promises using `cf-promises`:

```
root@my1.system.com# cf-promises -f /var/cfengine/inputs/check_
SUID.cf

root@my1.system.com#
```

No output indicates the promises are good to be executed.

3. Let's execute the promises using `cf-agent`:

```
root@my1.system.com# cf-agent -v -f /var/cfengine/inputs/check_
SUID.cf

..

..

Promise handle:

cf3      Promise made by: /sbin/

cf3      .........................................................

cf3

cf3   -> Using literal pathtype for /sbin/

cf3   -> Handling file existence constraints on /sbin/umount.nfs

cf3 Transforming: /bin/echo The following file /sbin/umount.nfs
has its uid set

cf3 The following file /sbin/umount.nfs has its uid set

cf3 Transformer /sbin/umount.nfs => /bin/echo The following file
/sbin/umount.nfs has it's uid set seemed ok

cf3   -> Handling file existence constraints on /sbin/mount.nfs

..

..

cf3      Promise handle:

cf3      Promise made by: /usr/bin/

cf3      .........................................................

cf3

cf3   -> Using literal pathtype for /usr/bin/

cf3   -> Handling file existence constraints on /usr/bin/rsh

cf3 Transforming: /bin/echo The following file /usr/bin/rsh has
it's uid set

cf3 The following file /usr/bin/rsh has its uid set

..

..
```

On execution of the promises file, we see that CFEngine echoes the names of all the files which have their SUID bit set.

What just happened?

In the previous task we wanted to devise a method to get the names of files or scripts which had their SUID bit set. For this we defined a bundlesequence under the common control body having a single bundle names `id_check`. We also defined the version for this file. Now in the `id_check` bundle's body we define the directories under which we want to search for files that have their SUID bit set, using the `files` promise. We define the `file_select` promise to define the criterion for file selection. For defining the criterion we used the `search_mode` promise and gave the file permissions for which we want to do a search. We also defined that CFEngine should echo the name of the file for which the permissions criterion is satisfied. Lastly, we defined the depth of recursion for CFEngine to traverse under the directories that we provided.

Have a go hero – auditing files which are owned by root and have the SUID bit set

In the previous example we saw how to check and get a list of files that have the SUID bit set. We may also want to check for more important files which have the SUID set and are root owned. Write a CFEngine configuration file which may be used for this task.

System state

For CFEngine, the state of a system is defined by policies. These policies define the configuration of operating system elements, the environment available to different users or applications, and the frequency of execution of various tasks. Therefore, CFEngine tries to maintain the state of a system so that it adheres to the set of policies defining the state of that system. Now maintaining a system in a 'secure' state is a two pronged approach; we need to maintain the configuration of the system in a 'secure' state and then again we need to monitor user behavior and make changes to policies so that the system remains secure against all threats. In the previous sections we learned how to maintain or audit the configuration of a system so that the system adheres to the policies defined for its 'secure' state. Now let's see how scanning logs generated by the system or applications helps us monitor user behavior and make changes to the policies on a regular basis so that the system is secure against all threats. There are various system and application generated logs which may be scanned that give us an idea of the threat level, and we may take proactive steps to avoid them. Let's see which log files may be looked at and how the information contained in them may be used to refine our security policies.

The following diagram shows how this may be achieved:

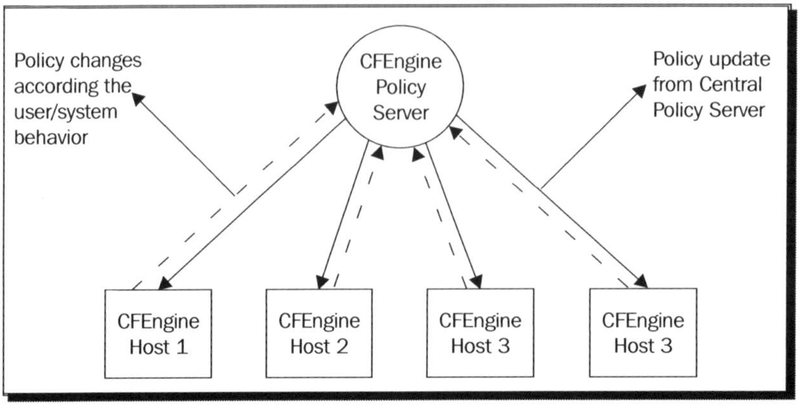

Time for action – auditing Apache logs

1. Let's write a promise file to find out the IP addresses that are trying to access the following restricted URL:

   An Apache log access log entry may appear as follows:

   ```
   192.168.2.23 - - [15/Apr/2010:00:21:23 +0530] "GET /test/styles/
   calendar.css HTTP/1.1" 403
   ```

2. You may copy the following code snippet to the file `apache_log_audit.cf`:

   ```
   body common control

   {

   bundlesequence => { "IP_address" };

   version => "1.0.0";

   }

   bundle agent IP_address

   {

   vars:

   "my_value" string => execresult("/bin/cat /var/log/httpd/access_
   log | grep ' 403 ' | gawk '{print $1}'", "useshell");
   ```

```
reports:

linux::

"$(my_value)"

report_to_file => "/var/cfengine/outputs/apache_forbidden_logs.
txt";

}
```

3. Let's verify the promises file using `cf-promises`:

```
root@my1.system.com# cf-promises -f /var/cfengine/inputs/apache_
log_audit.cf
root@my.system.com#
```

No output indicates that we are good with the promises.

4. Now let's execute the promises using `cf-agent`:

```
root@my1.system.com# cf-agent -f /var/cfengine/inputs/apache_log_
audit.cf
root@my1.system.com#
```

No output indicates that the promises were executed without any errors.

5. Now let's see the report which was was written to the file `/var/cfengine/outputs/apache_forbidden_logs.txt`:

```
root@my1.system.com# cat / var/cfengine/outputs/apache_forbidden_
logs.txt
17.16.0.101

19.167.8.87

191.168.7.172

193.168.8.55

12.168.8.23

12.168.8.55
```

```
129.168.8.55

129.168.8.55
...
root@my.system.com#
```

The contents of the file are IP addresses which were trying to access the restricted URL and got the "403—Forbidden" status code served by the web server.

What just happened?

There may be various other scenarios wherein we need to audit various other log files. One such scenario is when you need to audit the Apache web server logs and try to generate various reports. Let's see how we can get a list of IP addresses that are trying to access URLs which are open only for internal users. A user trying to access the restricted web pages will get a "403—Forbidden" error. All such IP addresses should be blocked with the help of Apache deny/allow directives, firewall rules, or by any other means. A line in Apache access logs appears as follows:

```
192.168.2.23 - - [15/Apr/2010:00:21:23 +0530] "GET /test/styles/
calendar.css HTTP/1.1" 403 -
```

We wanted to get a list of IP addresses that were trying to access pages only accessible to internal users. For this we defined a bundlesequence under the common control body having only one bundle named `IP_address`. We define a variable `my_value` in the `IP_address` bundle agent body. This variable is of type 'string' and stores the result of the command on the left-hand side. Now we write the values stored in the variable `my_value`, which are the IP addresses, to a file named `/var/cfengine/outputs/apache_forbidden_logs.txt`.

Auditing with CFEngine Nova

CFEngine Nova, the enterprise edition CFEngine, takes auditing and reporting to the next level. Firstly, it adds a three year trend summary based on any 'shift-averages'. Secondly, it adds a new 'measurement' promise type in bundles for monitoring agent.

The features mentioned here serve two purposes: you can generate a periodic time series reports or you can scan log files using a generic interface and log the results to custom-defined reports. The data can be extracted with sophisticated methods using the Perl Compatible Regular Expressions library to match text. Let's see how if one of the tasks, reporting the IP address that is trying to access the host over SSH, was to be performed on enterprise CFEngine Nova, we could have used the measurement promises to generate the reports:

```
bundle monitor check_breakin_attempts
{
measurements:
"/var/log/secure"
handle => "ssh_ip_deny",
stream_type => "file",
data_type => "counter",
match_value => scan_log(".*sshd\[.*refused connect from.*]"),
history_type => "log",
action => sample_rate("0");
}
```

Similarly, we may use any of the CFEngine promises given above basis you have Community edition CFEngine or Enterprise edition Nova CFEngine.

While we are discussing security and CFEngine we also need to look at CFEngine's own security principles. A system being used for a system security audit needs to maintain its own secure state so that the reports or data that it provides isn't altered while transmission or during other transactions. Let's take a look at the CFEngine security principles.

CFEngine works on a 'trust' model. This model depends on a trust relationship between the clients and server or between two peers. Now CFEngine adheres to the following security principles:

- The Voluntary Cooperation Model—under this model a host voluntary cooperates with the system. The CFEngine server or the peers cannot force changes to a host's CFEngine policy. Each host reserves its right to *veto* policy decisions at all times.
- It supports the encryption of data being transferred over the network. For data transmission, it used a 128 bit random blowfish encryption key. The challenge response is verified by MD5 hash. The commercial editions of CFEngine use the AES 256 with a 256 bit random key for data transmission and the challenge response is verified by a SHA 256 hash. Let's review the communication that happens between CFEngine client and server:
    - The client attempts to connect to the CFEngine server on port 5308
    - The server examines the IP address of the connecting hosts and checks the access rules specified by `allowconnects`, `allowallconnects`, `denyconnects`

- If the host is allowed to connect the server reads maximum of 2048 bytes to look for a valid hail
- The client sends its host name, user name, and public key to the server
- The server checks whether the public key is from a known server, the client's IP address, or whether the host name has been provided in the list of hosts allowed by the `trustkeysfrom` promise
- If none of these conditions are satisfied, the connection is broken
- If the trust is verified, further checks are performed
- Check whether the user name provided by the client is in the `allowusers` list
- If this fails the connection is broken
- If the user name provided by the client is in the allowusers list, CFEngine further checks the file access permissions
- If `maproot` is not set, only the files or resources owned by the authenticated user name are transmitted
- In the case `ifencrypted` is set, non-encrypted connections are dropped
- The next flowchart explains the CFEngine communication mechanism:

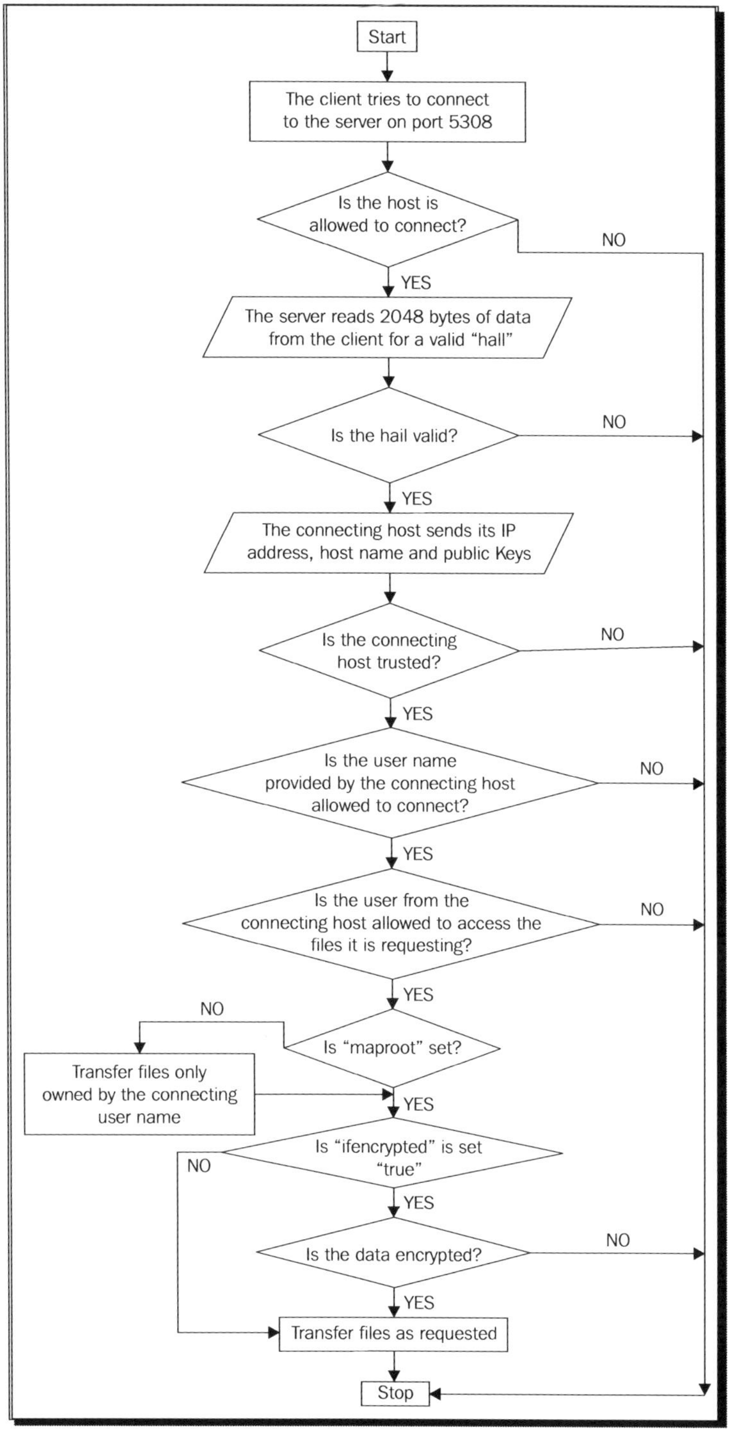
Start
The client tries to connect to the server on port 5308
Is the host is allowed to connect?
NO
YES
The server reads 2048 bytes of data from the client for a valid "hall"
Is the hail valid?
NO
YES
The connecting host sends its IP address, host name and public Keys
Is the connecting host trusted?
NO
YES
Is the user name provided by the connecting host allowed to connect?
NO
YES
Is the user from the connecting host allowed to access the files it is requesting?
NO
YES
NO
Is "maproot" set?
Transfer files only owned by the connecting user name
YES
Is "ifencrypted" is set "true"
NO
YES
Is the data encrypted?
NO
YES
Transfer files as requested
Stop

- CFEngine does not make use of centralized certificate authority for trust relationships, instead it uses the lightweight key based trust model. The CFEngine uses the RSA 2048 public key encryption algorithm.
- The default values for different promises and its attributes are such that they do not grant any access to other hosts.
- You can control when CFEngine drops the incoming connection. For example, you may configure `cf-serverd` to read a fixed number of bytes from the input stream before deciding whether to drop a connection from a remote host. This may act as an additional security measure against DOS attacks. In addition to this you may also control the number of incoming and outgoing connections on the server and clients.
- CFEngine also provides a checksum-based mechanism to copy files from one host to another. This mechanism may be used to establish a distributed monitoring system. Such a system will be based on detecting changes in a checksum with a predefined list of files. Similar hosts may be configured in a group, and each host may monitor for changes in the checksum of files on hosts in its neighborhood. If a change is detected, CFEngine may be configured to either warn of the change or to transmit the correct file with the unaltered checksum. Given next is an example promise file for distributed monitoring. To decide on who the peers are for a host we will use the function `peers` here. Here's a small synopsis of peers:

  Function: `peers`

  - Syntax: `peers(arg0,arg1,arg2) returns type slist`
  - `arg0`: File name of the host list, in the range "?(([a-zA-Z]:\\.*)|(/.*))
  - `arg1`: Comment regex pattern, in the range .*
  - `arg2`: Peer group size, in the range 0,99999999999

  Given next is an example agent body that may be used to set up a distributed checksum-based monitoring system:

```
bundle agent detect_changes
{
vars:
"files_monitor" => { "/etc/passwd","/etc/group","/etc/shadow","/
etc/services","/etc/httpd/conf/httpd.conf","/etc/sysconfig" };
"peer_hosts" slist => peers("/var/cfengine/inputs/list_
peers","#.*",10);

files:
"$(files_monitor)"
changes =>  tripwire,
depth_search => recurse("inf"),
action => WarnOnly;
}
```

```
body changes tripwire
{
hash => "md5";
report_changes => "content";
update_hashes => "false";
}
body action WarnOnly
{
action_policy => "warn";
}

body depth_search recurse(d)

{
depth => "$(d)";
}
```

Let's see how this promise for distributed monitoring works. In the promise we define the bundle agent named `detect_changes`. For this we defined the variable `files_monitor` with `slist` data type. This variable stores the list of files that we need to monitor on each host. We also defined one more variable `peer_hosts` with the data type `slist` that stores host names of the peers. We use the `peers` function to get a list of peers, not including yourself, from the group that we belong to. Next, we defined the promiser `changes` which will detect if there are any changes in the files that are being monitored. We also defined a promiser `action` that will send a warning in case there are any changes detected. As we are running the promises in a warning mode, we don't actually want to update the checksums anywhere as of now. We will be updating the checksums only after we have looked at changes manually. For this we set the value of the attribute `update_hashes` to `false`.

We learned a lot about ways to monitor configuration files and audit log files using CFEngine to detect anomalies.

Pop quiz

1. Which function can be used to get the UID for a named user on a host using CFengine?

   a. `getenv`

   b. `userexists`

   c. `getgid`

   d. None of these

2. Which agent control promise can be used to get a list of compressed files that have been left erroneously by someone in your team under the web document root?
    a. `compressnames`
    b. `zipnames`
    c. `leaf`
    d. `suspiciousnames`
3. Is CFEngine susceptible to buffer overflow attacks?
    a. No
    b. Yes
    c. Depends on how the trust relationships are configured
    d. Can't say
4. Which promise can be used to log all new incoming connections?
    a. `logallconnections`
    b. `syslog`
    c. `allowallconnects`
    d. `serverfacility`

Have a go hero

You have a `sendmail` server on Linux and a log of the e-mails generated, sent, queued, and deferred with their statuses stored in a file `/var/log/maillog`. How can you get the number of e-mails which were deferred from logs?

Hint: You may use the `countlinesmatching` promise.

Summary

In this chapter we learned how to write promises to update the access control files based on incoming SSH requests. In addition to this we also saw how to find a list of files with suspicious names and how to verify important configuration files. We also saw the CFEngine security design principles for remote communication, encryption, access control, CFEngine communication, and so on in detail. In the last section, we learned how to write promises for distributed monitoring where hosts monitor other hosts and warn if they find a change in the files being monitored.

After learning how to audit your systems, let's learn about the logging and reporting promises available in CFEngine in the next chapter.

6
Logging and Reporting with CFEngine

CFEngine has been designed keeping scalability as one of its defining principles. It can do so because it's decentralized. In this distributed architecture each host saves its system state on itself, which means that no data is lost if the network temporarily fails and the disconnection does not impact CFEngine's real-time operations. Once the system state data is stored locally, CFEngine summarizes this data and makes it available for analysis. This helps CFEngine in two ways:

- *Summarized data is available for analysis and you are not presented with raw data which needs processing*
- *Processing of raw data happens on individual hosts which means processing is distributed and hence there is no requirement of high-end machines for running the system*

In this chapter we shall learn about:

- Logging formats
- Reporting in CFEngine
- Monitoring in CFEngine

As we have seen in earlier chapters, CFEngine stores various logs, records, and other information under its "WORKDIR", which defaults to `/var/cfengine`. Let's understand the different formats in which CFEngine may store this data.

1. **Logs in text format**: CFEngine may store the data in text logs. Let's see the various text files and what information CFEngine stores in these files. All the subsequent file names are relative to the CFEngine "WORKDIR":
   - `promise.log`—CFEngine writes an entry to this log containing the details for a fraction of the promises kept after each run. Each entry is written with a time stamp. Here is a sample line from `promise.log`:

     ```
     Sat Oct  2 18:03:21 2010 -> Sat Oct  2 18:03:22 2010:
     Outcome of version (not specified) (agent-0): Promises
     observed to be kept 100%, Promises repaired 0%, Promises not
     repaired 0%
     ```

   - `cf_value.log`—CFEngine logs the business value estimate from the execution of automation promises. Each log entry has a time stamp.
   - `cf3.HOSTNAME.runlog`—CFEngine logs a time-stamped entry whenever it releases a lock after the execution of each individual promise. Here is a sample line from `cf3.HOSTNAME.log`:

     ```
     Thu Sep 30 13:14:17 2010:Lock removed normally :pid=5253:
     lock.test.commands.contain.exec_owner.useshell.._bin_ls_356_
     MD5=89d99be5c8521549f14a0675a1ac6867:
     ```

   - `cfagent.HOSTNAME.log`—CFEngine logs the list of setuid or setgid programs on the system to this file. This log is ambiguously named and is now deprecated.
   - `state/file_hash_event_history`—CFEngine maintains a log of files that have changed since the last review. Changes are determined by the hashing algorithm defined in CFEngine. All the log entries are time-stamped. Here is a sample line from the log:

     ```
     Fri Nov 19 17:57:04 2010,/etc/passwd
     ```

   In addition to the given files the Enterprise version has a number of additional log files which are used to maintain a log of lots of other system data.

2. **Embedded databases**: Apart from logging in text files, CFEngine also logs to embedded databases. These embedded databases may be printed or viewed using `cf-report`. There are various options available for embedded databases; you may choose to use the Berkley DB for example, or Tokyo cabinet. The file extensions for these embedded database files will depend on the option you choose. Let's assume that we are using the Berkley DB and understand all the information CFEngine is logging into these embedded database files.
   - `cf_Audit.db`—CFEngine logs the audit information to this database if auditing is switched on. By default, only minor information about CFEngine runs are recorded. This file should be deleted or truncated on a regular basis as it may grow very large if CFEngine auditing is switched on.

- cf_LastSeen.db—CFEngine logs information regarding the hosts that it contacted, and hosts which contacted it, to this embedded database file. The log entries also contain time stamps.
- cf_classes.db—This is a database of classes defined on the host.
- checksum_digests.db—CFEngine maintains a database of hash values used by CFEngine change management functions.
- performance.db—CFEngine maintains this database for the last, average, and deviation times of jobs executed by cf-agent. Tasks such as file copying are recorded by default. One may define various other checks using measurement_class in the action body of the promise. Let's see the class measurement_class in more detail:

  ```
  measurement_class
                      Type: string
                      Allowed input string: (arbitrary string)
  ```

  This class, if set, will measure and record the performance of the promise. You may set this class as follows:

  ```
  body action measure_performance(x)
  {
  measurement_class => "This $(this.promiser) is a long job";
  }
  ```

By setting this string we have enabled the measurement of execution time for this promise and have also provided an identifier for this performance measurement. The identifier partially identifies the performance measurement data for this promise; the other identifiers are the *promise-type* and *promiser*. The complete identifier may look like the following:

```
ID:promise-type:promiser
```

This identifier should be used to identify promises that you are looking for when you generated HTML reports from *performance.db* using cf-report:

- stats.db—CFEngine maintains a database of external file attributes for change management functionality
- state/cf_lock.db—CFEngine maintains this database of all locks and their expiry times
- state/cf_observations.db—CFEngine maintains this database containing the current state of the observational history of the host as recorded by cf-monitord
- state/cf_state.db—Information regarding all the persistent classes active on the system is stored, in this embedded database, by CFEngine

State information

Most of the system state data refers to the running state of the hosts. The data is generated by `cf-monitord`. Let's understand the data files and the format that it's written in. These files are relative to the "WORKDIR":

- `state/env_data`—This file stores data related to the host's current environment, which is the newly discovered classes and variable values that define the system's state. These values are changed by `cf-monitord`. The new values are compared with old values to check for anomalies.
- `state/all_classes`—This file contains all the classes defined during the last Cfengine run.
- `state/cf-*`—These files refer to cached data.

Time for action – generating custom reports

Let's write a promises file to generate a custom report of logged-in users, incoming or outgoing SSH connections, and incoming or outgoing FTP connections for the host:

1. The data that we are looking for may be generated using the `showstate` CFEngine promise. You may copy the following code snippet to a file named `system_state.cf`:

```
body common control
{
bundlesequence => { "systemstate" };
}
body agent systemstate
{
reports:
"linux"
showstate => { "users","ssh_in","ssh_out","ftp_in","ftp_out" };

}
```

2. Let's verify the promises with `cf-promises`:

```
root@my1# cf-promises -f /var/cfengine/inputs/system_state.cf
root@my1#
```

No output indicates the promises file is good to be executed.

3. Let's execute the promises file using `cf-agent`:

```
root@my.system.com# cf-agent -f /var/cfengine/inputs/system_state.
cf
root@my.system.com#
```

No error output indicates that the promises were executed successfully.

The reports for various services that we wanted to see are generated under `/var/cfengine/state/` folder. Let's see the contents of a few such reports:

```
root@my1[/var/cfengine/state]# cat cf_outgoing.www
tcp      267      0 172.16.3.178:54506        137.226.34.229:80          CLOSE_WAIT
tcp        1      0 172.16.3.178:51155        137.226.34.227:80          CLOSE_WAIT
tcp      332      0 172.16.3.178:59566        130.225.254.116:80         CLOSE_WAIT
tcp        0      0 172.16.3.178:55562        96.17.182.8:80             ESTABLISHED
tcp        1      0 172.16.3.178:60494        134.160.38.1:80            CLOSE_WAIT
tcp      322      0 172.16.3.178:33617        193.1.193.64:80            CLOSE_WAIT
root@my1[/var/cfengine/state]#
```

```
root@my1[/var/cfengine/state]# cat cf_incoming.ssh
tcp        0      0 172.16.3.178:22           192.168.2.57:55400         ESTABLISHED
root@my1[/var/cfengine/state]#
```

What just happened?

In the given promises file, we defined a bundlesequence under the common control body with a single bundle named `systemstate`. Next, we defined the body for the bundle `systemstate` wherein we use the `showstate` CFEngine promise. We provided the `showstate` promise with a list of services. We also defined that the state of the services should be reported to the file `/var/cfengine/outputs/my_host_state`. Let's learn about the `showstate` promise in more detail:

- **showstate**
  - Type: slist
  - Allowed input range: (arbitrary string)

This promise is used to generate status reports for the list of services provided to the standard output. A few of these services are as follows:

- Users logged in (`users`)
- Privileged system processes (`rootprocs`)
- Non-privileged processes (`otherprocs`)
- Free disk on partition (`diskfree`)
- Loadavg (`% kernel load utilization`)
- Incoming netbios name lookups (`netbiosns_in`)
- Outgoing netbios name lookups (`netbiosns_out`)

- Incoming CFEngine connections (`cfengin_in`)
- Outgoing CFEngine connections (`cfengine_out`)
- Web server history (`webaccess`)
- Web server errors (`weberrors`)
- New syslog entries (`syslog`)
- New log entries (`messages`)
- All %CPU utilization (`cpu`)
- Incoming DNS requests (`dns_in`)
- Outgoing DNS requests (`dns_out`)
- Incoming FTP connections (`ftp_in`)
- Outgoing FTP connections (`ftp_out`)

Pop quiz

1. Why is switching `full auditing` on for long durations on CFEngine not recommended?
   a. The audit logs may not be used to generate reports
   b. It utilizes more CPU, memory, and disk space
   c. It serves no purpose
   d. It makes a large number of connections to CFEngine server and slows it down

Summary

We learned a lot about CFEngine logging and reporting mechanisms. We covered the following topics:

- The two different formats: *files* and *database*, in which CFEngine stores information regarding system state data, remote hosts information, information on file changes, and audit data
- The various files or databases and the information they maintain
- How to generate custom reports
- How to generate reports providing the state information of various services

With this we have covered almost all aspects of CFEngine and we can start writing bigger work flows to execute more complex tasks, as we will in the next chapter.

7
Workflows

Let's take a break and review our progress

- Initially, we had no configuration management tool and we managed our systems using shell or Perl scripts, running them on a predefined frequency.
- We then came across CFEngine, that promised to maintain the state of a system as per defined policies.
- We used CFEngine to perform tasks on individual systems, get updates on policies from a centralized system and report changes to a centralized system.

CFEngine is a framework which allows users to build complex work flows involving multiple hosts, in addition to performing these tasks. The CFEngine framework may be used to design a self-healing system which maintains the state of hosts, monitors them, and repairs the system's state in case an anomaly is discovered. It provides a 'promise' language which clearly defines the desired state of a host, and CFEngine tries to maintain this state. In other words, it is a bottom-up methodology rather than a top-down methodology.

In this chapter we shall:

- Write menu driven policies
- Write content driven policies
- Write CFEngine templates
- Maintain knowledge maps
- Learn how CFEngine can help with compliance
- Learn how CFEngine can be used to design a self-healing system

We automated a lot of tasks using community edition CFEngine. After this, we should also feel confident that by proper use of the 'promise' language we can automate almost any kind of task. If you still do not feel confident, I'd suggest you go back a few pages and read chapters 1 to 5 and try to solve whatever issues that you feel CFEngine may not help you with.

Menu driven configuration

As the name suggests, a menu driven configuration presents a list of options to hosts in your environment to choose from. So you can group a number of promises in a bundle, give the bundle a name, and present a list of bundles to the hosts in your environment to choose from. There are various ways to present such menu to your host, a few of them are listed next:

1. One way is to embed bundles in a master-bundle by the use of the `methods` promise. For those who may have forgotten—`methods` promises in the agent control body are compound promises that refer to a whole bundle of promises. Let's see how we can create menus using the `methods` promise with an example:

```
body common control
{
bundlesequence => { "default", "menu_test" };
}
bundle agent menu_test
{
methods:
Apache::           # Menu for servers running Apache web server

"method2" usebundle => php_apache;

Jboss::             #Menu for servers running Jboss server
"method2" usebundle  => java_def;
"method2" usebundle  => jboss'account;
"method2" usebundle  => jboss_server;

any:: # Menu items for all application servers
"method1" usebundle => Webanalytics;
"

}
bundle agent php_apache()
{
commands:
"/usr/bin/php -q /home/user/my_scripts.php";
}
```

```
bundle agent Webanalytics
{
commands:
"/usr/local/awstats.pl --updateall"
}
```

In this example we used an agent `methods` promise. The `methods` promises refer to a bundle of promises. They are written in a form which is ready for future development. We may say that they act as identifiers which refer to a collection of lower level objects that may be affected by the promise bundle. Any string can be used as an identifier because it is for future use, and we used `method1` and `method2` here as the identifiers. Methods may be parameterized. Methods are used for referring to repeatedly used bundles of promises and for iterating over parameters.

In the previous promises file we first defined a bundlesequence with two bundles named `default` and `main`. Now for the `menu_test` bundle we define a menu using the `methods` promise. We list the bundles that we want to combine into a menu, in order. So, for an 'Apache' menu the hosts see a PHP menu, and for a 'Jboss' menu the hosts see a bundle of promises for Java and Jboss. Lastly, for the `any` menu we present the `webanalytics` option for all hosts. After this we defined the bundle agents `php_apache` and `Webanalytics`. The first bundle agent, `php_apache`, executes a PHP script `my_scripts.php`, while the other bundle agent, `Webanalyitcs`, starts the compilation of web server logs with `awstats`. Similarly, you may define the other bundles `j_def`, `jboss_acount`, and `jboss_server`. In most of the cases, the ordering for the execution of the menu options will be preserved, but this may not be guaranteed at all points due to various constraints in CFEngine. However, you will see that ordering is not so important in the grand scheme of things, in many cases. Having said that, there are ways to define strict ordering.

2. The other approach is to use the bundlesequence as a menu. You can define a master bundle list and an order using bundlesequence and we may 'choose' promise bundles by commenting the ones not needed in the list. For instance, the following bundlesequence presents the PHP menu as an option to the host:

```
body common control
{
bundlesequence => { "default",
                      "web_analyticity",
                      "php_apache",
                      "java_def", "jboss_account", "jboss_server",
#                     "Ubuntu_install",
#                      "Fedora_install",
#                      "MySQL_install",
#                      "Mailserver",
```

```
#                           "FreeBSD_iinstall",
#                           "ftp_server",
                            "changemanagement"};
}
```

In this example, we have a list of bundles that may be executed by CFEngine and we present a few of them as menu options to a host by commenting the ones which are not needed. Another advantage of using a bundlesequence is the 'ordering' of the bundles; you may define a strict order for execution of bundles. On the other hand, the disadvantage is that it is a bit tough to implement in a complex and dynamic environment. Each host gets what is given to it, which seems to be pretty strict for many complex networks.

How to select from menus

We defined menus here, but how do hosts select them? As we saw earlier, CFEngine is based on mutual cooperation and hence each host makes its own choice. We define a menu for a specific class or group of machines, and all the hosts that fall into that specific class or group are presented the menu defined for that class or group. The specific classes or groups need to be defined in a separate global configuration file or may be defined in this file itself. For instance, in the following example the hosts choose the menu on the basis of application:

```
body common control
{
bundlesequence => { "default", "menu_list" };
version => '1.1.1';
}
bundle agent menu_list
{
methods:

Apache::
"menu2" usebundle => php_apache;
"menu2" usebundle => webanalytics;

MySQL::
"menu2" usebundle => MySQL_install
"menu2" usebundle => db_backup

Jboss::
"menu2" usebundle => java_def;
"menu2" usebundle => jboss_account;
"menu2" usebundle => jboss_server;
```

```
any::
"menu1" usebundle => backup;

}
```

Now the menu may be presented to hosts in various contexts. The context is user defined and may be based on various environment variables. The system chooses the menu defined for it.

Now CFEngine is flexible enough to allow us to introduce nested menus and dependencies. This helps us in defining the hierarchy and simplifying the view of the system. For example, you may define a menu 'backup' which is dependent on 'backup_webservers' and 'backup_dbservers'.

Content driven configuration

A content driven policy is defined with the help of semicolon separated fields in a text file. Each line in the file is parsed and a specific type of promise is made, depending on which type the content driven policy selects. A file defining an application content driven policy may be similar to the following:

```
Apache;stop;fix;linux
Sendmail;start;warn;linux
MySQL;stop;warn;DB
```

Now these lines in the text file are parsed into corresponding CFEngine lists. So for `application_list.txt` there will be a `cdp_application.cf` which actually converts the fields into relevant promises and executes them.

> This is a feature of enterprise **CFEngine Nova**.

CFEngine templates

In our day-to-day life managing systems, we come across a lot of tasks that are repetitive and generic. For example, you may want to copy the last day's access logs from all the web servers to a centralized server for web analytics. Now on all the web servers only the name of the access log may change, whereas the process of finding the exact log file to be copied and copying the log file remains the same. Tasks such as these may be written in a generic template that can be used on any systems. Given next is a sample generic template for such a task.

Time for action – distributing a MySQL configuration file using template expansion

1. Let's write a configuration file for distributing MySQL configuration files to all the hosts from the master policy distribution server. The configuration file needs to be placed at `/etc/my.cnf` on all hosts. The following lines may be copied to a configuration file named `mysql_params.cf`:

```
body common control

{

bundlesequence => { "db_config_template" };

version => "1.0.1";

inputs => { "cfengine_stdlib.cf" };

}

bundle agent db_config_template

{

methods:

MySQL::



"DBserver" usebundle => get_template("/etc/my.cnf") ;

vars:


"socket" string => "/tmp/mysql.sock";


"key_buffer_size" string => "14M";


"max_allowed_packet" string => "2M";
```

```
"table_open_cache" string => "512";


}



##Generic template defining the 'get_template bundle'.



bundle agent get_template(template_config)

{

vars:

"template_files" string => "/var/cfengine/masterfiles";

"templates" string => lastnode("$(template_config)","/");

"policy_server" string => "172.16.3.113";

files:

"$(template_config).temp"

copy_from => remote_cp("$(template_files)/$(templates).temp",
"$(policy_server)");



"$(template_config)"

create => "true",

edit_line => expand_template("$(template_config).temp"),

action => if_elapsed("60");

}
```

2. Let's try executing the file. But before that, let's see the contents of the template `my.cnf.temp` on the policy distribution server, and the contents of the file `/etc/my.cnf` on the host, and the following:

   - Contents of the file template `my.cnf.temp`:

     ```
     root@my.system.com# cat /var/cfengine/masterfiles/my.cnf.
     temp
     socket     = ${db_config_template.socket}

     key_buffer_size = ${db_config_template.key_buffer_size}

     max_allowed_packet = ${db_config_template.max_allowed_
     packet}

     table_open_cache = ${db_config_template.table_open_cache}

     root@my.system.com#
     ```

   - Contents of the file `/etc/my.cnf` on the client host:

     ```
     root@my1.system.com# cat /etc/my.cnf
     …. . .
     …. . .
     [client]

     #password = your_password

     port      = 3306

     socket    = /tmp/mysql.sock


     # The MySQL server

     [mysqld]

     port      = 3306

     …. . . .
     …. . . .
     root@my1.system.com#
     ```

   Now let's execute the configuration file using `cf-agent`:

   ```
   root@my1.system.com# cf-agent -v -f /var/cfengine/inputs/mysql_
   params.cf
   ```

```
........
cf3>       BUNDLE get_template( {'/etc/my.cnf'} )

cf3>       * * * * * * * * * * * * * * * * * * * * * * * * * * *

cf3>

cf3> Initiate variable convergence...

cf3>     ? Augment scope get_template with template_config (s)

cf3>  -> Connect to 172.16.3.113 = 172.16.3.113 on port 5308

cf3>  -> Matched IP 172.16.3.113 to key MD5=aba77e2d0baf5ab33a464e
85cb5d37ac

cf3>  -> Going to secondary storage for key

cf3> ....................[.h.a.i.l.]............................

cf3> Strong authentication of server=172.16.3.113 connection
confirmed

.....
.....
cf3> Performance(Copy(172.16.3.113:/var/cfengine/masterfiles/
my.cnf.temp > /etc/my.cnf.temp)): time=0.0001 secs, av=0.0007 +/-
0.0026

cf3> Existing connection just became free...

cf3>  -> Handling file existence constraints on /etc/my.cnf.temp

cf3>

cf3>     ........................................................

cf3>     Promise handle:

cf3>     Promise made by: /etc/my.cnf

cf3>     ........................................................

cf3>
```

```
cf3>  -> Using literal pathtype for /etc/my.cnf

cf3>  -> No mode was set, choose plain file default 600

cf3>  -> Created file /etc/my.cnf, mode = 600

cf3>  -> Handling file edits in edit_line bundle expand_template

cf3>     Promise handle:

cf3>     Promise made by: /etc/my.cnf.temp

cf3>     .........................................................

cf3>

cf3>  -> Inserting the promised line "[mysqld]" into /etc/my.cnf
after locator

cf3>  -> Inserting the promised line "socket          = /tmp/mysql.
sock" into /etc/my.cnf after locator

cf3>  -> Inserting the promised line "key_buffer_size = 14M" into
/etc/my.cnf after locator

cf3>  -> Inserting the promised line "max_allowed_packet = 2M"
into /etc/my.cnf after locator

cf3>  -> Inserting the promised line "table_open_cache = 512" into
/etc/my.cnf after locator

cf3>  -> Inserting the promised line "" into /etc/my.cnf after
locator

cf3>      ??  Private class context

…...
```

Let's see the contents of the file `/etc/my.cnf` after the execution of all the promises:

```
root@my1.system.com# cat /etc/my.cnf
…...
…...
[client]
#password = your_password
```

```
port       = 3306
socket     = /tmp/mysql.sock
# The MySQL server
[mysqld]
…......
…......
port       = 3306
socket     = /tmp/mysql.sock
key_buffer_size = 14M
max_allowed_packet = 2M
table_open_cache = 512
root@my1.system.com#
```

In the output, we can see that the variables and its values were appended to the file `/etc/my.cnf`.

What just happened?

In this example we created a template to distribute a MySQL configuration file on all hosts. This is a very generic template that can be saved in a library and invoked from within a promise. In the previous promise file we defined a bundlesequence with only one bundle named `db_config_template`. While defining the bundle we defined a `methods` promise `DBServer`, which makes a call for the bundle `get_template(template_config)`. In addition to this, we also defined a class `MySQL` to ensure that promises are executed only if the hosts are among the `MySQL` class of servers. This class needs to be defined separately in a global configuration file and we are just quoting the class here. Under this class we defined a list of `mysql` variables and the values that need to be set for these variables. Now we define this bundle `get_template(template_config)` as a template so that its definition is generic and should take the file name provided while defining `Dbserver` as the argument. So if you define `Dbserver` as follows, the `get_template` bundle will be executed for `/etc/my.cnf`:

```
"DBserver" usebundle => get_template("/etc/my.cnf")") ;
```

If you want any other file to be altered, you may define it as follows:

```
"WebServer" usebundle => get_template("/etc/httpd/conf/httpd.conf") ;
```

For this method the `get_template` bundle will be executed for `/etc/httpd/conf/httpd.conf`.

Additionally, we have defined a template file `my.cnf.temp` that lists the scalars to be expanded.

Next, we defined the bundle `get_template()`.

- We defined two variables. The first one is `template_files`, which stores the path for the template directory. The second one is `templates`, which uses the special function `lastnode` and gets the name of the file from the `get_template()` bundle's argument.
- Next, we defined a `files` promise which has two files defined within, the temporary file and the final destination file that needs to be changed.
- Then we define a `copy_from` promise which tells CFEngine to copy the template from the path defined by `template_files` and writes it to the temporary file.
- For the destination file that needs to be changes we use the `edit_line` promise to expand the contents of the temporary file and add it to the destination file.

In this template we came across a new special function, `lastnode`, and two new promises, `expand_scalars` and `insert_type`; let's see why they are used in some more detail:

- Function **lastnode**
    - Syntax: `lastnode(arg0,arg1)`
    - `arg0`: Input string, in the table .*
    - `arg1`: Link separator, for example / in the range `.*`

  The function extracts the last of a string separated by the link separator.
- **expand_scalars**
    - Type: Menu option
    - Allowed input range: True, false, yes, no, on, off
    - Default value: False

  This promise expands any unexpanded variable.
- **insert_type**
    - Type: Menu option
    - Allowed input range: Literal, string, file, `preserve_block`
    - Default value: Literal

  This constraint defines the type of object that the promiser refers to.

Knowledge management

Maintaining a good knowledge base is a challenge for a lot of IT organizations. Organizations waste a lot of time *reinventing the wheel*. Every organization can have a bunch of brilliant associates who perform a specific set of tasks brilliantly, but then they do not know about each other's role. This is a significant risk. In a collaborative environment each associate should impart his or her learning in a manner such that it's available to others. Documenting changes, maintaining a wiki that has all past issues and resolutions documented, writing generic and reusable code, and writing generic policies are a few aspects that help improve the productivity and success of an organization. This is called knowledge management.

CFEngine provides another such tool for knowledge management, known as `cf-know`, in the form of topic maps. The aim of providing this feature is not to let everyone know everything but to help improve the process and productivity. Whether you are part of an IT enabled services domain, product development domain, or any other domain, knowledge of what happened in the past and what were the takeaways helps you to respond to changes in a better way. You feel more in control of the situation. CFEngine also takes care of the basic challenge of writing the documentation. To all engineers, documentation is one thing that seems to be a waste of time as they are more adept at solving technical issues than at creative writing. CFEngine tries to make documentation a part of configuration. To implement this philosophy, CFEngine expects the user to write correct annotations while writing the promises. Let's look at an example promise file with a few annotations and then we can delve deeper:

```
files:

"/var/cfengine/inputs/repo-policy"

handle => "update ⊠policy",

comment => "Update the cfengine input files from the policy server
repository",

depends_on => { "server_updates" },
perms => system("600"),

copy _from => remote_cp("$(master ⊠_location)","$(policy _server)"),

depth ⊠search => recurse("inf"),

file _select => input _files,

action => immediate;
```

If you look closely at this promise file, we provided a `handle`, `depends_on`, and a `comment`. These annotations are used internally by CFEngine to provide meaningful error messages with context and to compute dependencies that reveal the existence of process chains. Another aspect that CFEngine requires from the user is 'standardization', in context with knowledge base. So, while writing promises, one should try to use the following syntax:

```
comment =>
handle =>
depends_on =>
..
{promises}
..
```

To ensure that the topic maps are always updated with relevant policy information you may force it using the `require_comments` common control promise. When the `require_comments` promise is set to True, `cf-promises` will alert the user on promises that do not have comments. Let's look at an example:

```
body common control
{

bundlesequence => { "example" } ;

require_comments => "true";

}

bundle agent example

{

vars:

"test" string => "prompt for comments";

commands:

"echo $test";

}
```

Let's copy the this content to the file `alert-comments.cf` and try to verify it using `cf-promises`:

```
root@my.system.com# cf-promises -f /var/cfengine/inputs/alert-
comments.cf
!! Un-commented promise found, but comments have been required by
policy

Promise (version not specified) belongs to bundle 'example' in file
'./alert-comments.cf' near line 11
```

In this output we saw that CFEngine prompted the user on promises that do not have a comment. This may used as a method to request a user to put proper comments.

A topic represents a 'subject' which could be anything that you may want to document or discuss. Topics can be further classified as topic-types, which is helpful in separating objects that are not related and collating objects which are related. Once a topic has been classified, it can point point to a number of references called occurrences. So **occurrences** give you the locations where information for this particular topic exists. Now CFEngine allows one to define any kind of association between topics which act as cross-reference types. So let's say we have two topics, 'topic-x' and 'topic-y'; now we can define a number of associations between these two topic types. For instance:

topic-x "is an explanation of" topic-y

topic-x "resolves the problem with" topic-y

We can safely classify the topic maps into the following containers:

1. **Topics**: These represent a subject
2. **Types**: This is the container to classify topics with same names but with different contexts
3. **Occurrences**: These are specific information resources for a topic
4. **Occurrences Types**: This defines how a specific occurrence is related to a topic

There are few knowledge control promises which should help us to create topic maps and a knowledge base. Lets look at few of them below:

- **build_directory**
  - Type: String
  - Allowed input range: .*
  - Default value: Current working directory

The `build_directory` knowledge control promise is used to define the directory in which to generate the output files. The directory can be specified as in the following example:

```
body knowledge control
{
build_directory => "/var/cfengine/knowledge_base";
}
```

- **manual_source_directory**
    - Type: String
    - Allowed input range: "?(([a-zA-Z]:\\.*)|(/.*))

This knowledge control promise is used to define the path to the directory where the raw text about manual topics is found. The path can be defined as follows:

```
body knowledge control
{
  manual_source_directory => "/var/cfengine/manual";
}
```

- **query_engine**
    - Type: String
    - Allowed input type: (arbitrary string)

This knowledge control promise is used to define the dynamic web page, which is used to accept and drive queries in a browser. When displaying topics in the HTML format, it is possible to make a dynamic web query by embedding CFEngine in the web page as a system call and then passing the argument with the query. This is possible because while displaying topics in the HTML format, `cf-know` will render each topic as a link to the URL provided for `query_string` and pass a new topic as the argument to it. The engine can be specified as follows:

```
body knowledge control
{
query_engine => "http://my.webserver.com/query.php"
}
```

In addition to these knowledge control promises, CFEngine also provides a few promise bundles for the knowledge management engine. Let's look at a few of them in more detail.

Topics promises in knowledge—As we just saw, topics represent a subject. A topic may be associated with another topic or another topic may be associated with it. Let's see how a topic may be defined:

```
bundle knowledge example
{
topics:
"MySQL"
comment => "An RDBMS",
association => a("is a database","MySQL","LAMP stack");

}
```

In this example, we defined the context of the topic and also its association. Let's see the two promises `association` and `comment` in more detail:

- **association** (compound body)
  - Type: Ext body

  The above bundle supports a few promises as given later.

- **forward_relationship**
  - Type: String
  - Allowed input range: (arbitrary string)

  The promise defines a forward association between the promiser topic and the associates. The forward association may be defined as follows:

```
body association test
{
forward_relationship => "is a manual for";
}
```

- **backward_relationship**
  - Type: String
  - Allowed input range: (arbitrary string)

  This promise is used to define the backward association, that is, from associates to promiser topic. The forward association may be defined as follows:

```
body association test
{
backward_relationship => "is a topic for the manual";
}
```

- **comment**
  - Type: string
  - Allowed input range: (arbitrary string)

  The `comment` promise is used to add a note about the real intention of the promises that one is going to write. The comments additionally appear in error reports and error messages. A comment can be added as follows:

  ```
  comment => "installing a package"
  ```

Occurrences promise in knowledge—occurrences are pointers to documents or resources about a topic. An occurrence may be a string or a link to an external document. An occurrence promise defines that a particular information resource has information about one or more topics. A generic occurrence definition can be as follows:

```
occurrences:
topic::
"A URL or a string"
represents => { "Sub Topc 1", "Sub Topic 2", "Sub Topic 3"..},
representation => "a URL or a string";
```

In this occurrence definition, we came across two promises, `represents` and `representation`; let's look at the syntax for both the promises in detail:

- **represents**
  - Type: slist
  - Allowed input range: (arbitrary string)

  The `represents` promise defines a list of subtopics that explain the information type represented by the occurrence. Here's an example of its usage:

  ```
  occurrences:
  Secure_Code_practice::
  "Guidelines for writing secure code"
  represents => { "Guidelines" },
  representation => "literal";
  ```

- **representation**
  - Type: Menu option
  - Allowed input range: literal, url, db, file, web, image, portal

  This promise defines how to interpret the promise string.

Inferences promise in knowledge—the inference promises are used to define patterns that have some kind of association with the knowledge promised by a topic. There are a few promises to define the promise type. Let's look at the syntax for these promises:

- **follow_topics**
  - Type: String
  - Allowed input range: (arbitrary string)

  The `follow_topics` promise is used to define patterns for a topic so that it can also use the knowledge promised by topics matching the pattern defined.

- **Infer** (compound body)
  - Type: Ext body
- **pre_assoc_pattern**
  - Type: String
  - Allowed input range: (arbitrary string)

  This promise is used to define the name of a forward association between promises topics and associates.

- **post_assoc_pattern**
  - Type: String
  - Allowed input range: (arbitrary string)

  This promise is used to define the name of an inverse association from associates to the promiser topic.

- **Inference**
  - Type: String
  - Allowed input range: (arbitrary string)

  This promise is used to define patterns that match associations which infer an association between topics. So for instance, if association 'X' is associated to Topic 'A', and association 'Y' is associated to Topic 'B', and associations 'X' and 'Y' match the above pattern, then Topic 'A' is somehow related to Topic 'B'.

Armed with the knowledge of all knowledge promises and bundles, let's write a promise file to create our topic maps.

Time for action – topic map for services

1. Let's create a topic map for the LAMP (Linux, Apache, MySQL, PHP) for hosts in your network. You may copy the following code snippet to the file `services_map.cf`:

```
body common control
   {
   any::
   bundlesequence  =>  { "services_map" };
   }

body knowledge control
{
build_directory => ".";
id_prefix => "lamp";
query_output => "text";
query_engine => "none";
sql_database => "maps";
sql_owner => "root";
sql_type => "mysql";
sql_passwd => "secret";
}

bundle knowledge services_map
{
vars:
"linux_distros" slist => { "suse", "ubuntu", "fedora", "redhat",
  "debian" };
"WebServer_hosts" slist => { "Hosts running Apache",
  "PHP configuration", "Apache Configuration" };
"Database_hosts"  slist => { "Hosts running MySQL",
  "MySQL configuration" };

topics:
   "operating system";
…..
   "webmaster";
   "Apache";
   "MySQL";
   "PHP";

   comment => "List of topics";
  operating_system::
   "linux";

  distro::
```

```
    "$(linux_distros)"
        association => a("is distro of","linux","has distro");
  WebServer_hosts::
    "my.webserver.com"
association => a("Apache","Web Server for Application X",
  "Connects to MySQL DB 1");
   "my1.webserver.com"
…...
  webmaster::
    "admin"
        association => a("Web server configuration","Database
Server configuration","Managed by");

occurrences:
  Apache::
     "http://www.apache.org"
            represents => { "website" },
            representation => "url",
            comment => "Web site for Apache reference";

  MySQL::
  …....
  PHP::
  …....
webmaster::
     "webmaster@system.com"
            represents => { "email address" },
            representation => "literal";
}

body association a(fwd,name,bwd)
{
forward_relationship => "$(fwd)";
backward_relationship => "$(bwd)";
associates => { $(name) };
}
```

2. Let's verify the promise file with the help of `cf-promises`:

   root@my.system.com# cf-promises -f /var/cfengine/inputs/ services_map.cf

   root@my.system.com

   No output justifies the promises file.

3. Next, we need to populate the database for the promises. You need to execute the following queries on the MySQL instance, details for which you have provided in the `services_map.cf` file:

```
Mysql> CREATE DATABASE lamp_topic_map;

mysql> CREATE TABLE topics(topic_name varchar(256),topic_
comment varchar(1024),CREATE TABLE associations(from_name
varchar(256),from_type varchar(256),from_assoc varchar(256),to_
assoc varchar(256),to_type varchar(256),to_name varchar(256));

mysql>
```

4. Let's create a knowledge map with the promises file using `cf-know`:

```
root@my.system.com# cf-know -f / var/cfengine/inputs/ services_
map.cf -s

root@my.system.com#
```

No error means the topic maps were successfully created.

5. Let's see the ontology for the topics and associations. The command `cf-know` creates a file named `ontology.html` under the defined build directory. You may open this file on your favorite browser. Given next is a screenshot of what the map we just created will look like:

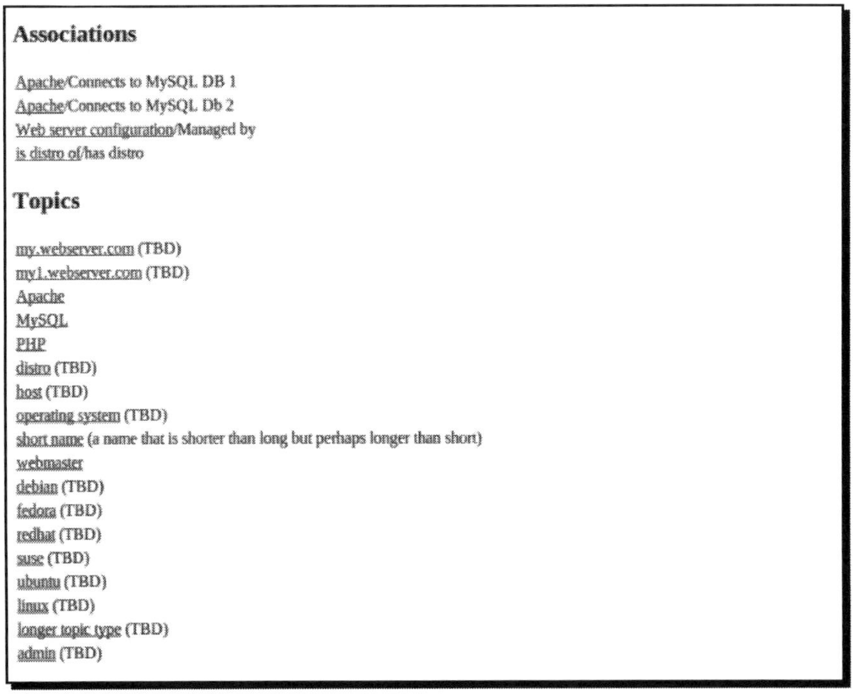

Let's see a sample topic map if we use the CFEngine web interface, which can be enabled by changing the value of `query_output` to `html`.

> The next diagram is not related to the previous promise file `services_cf`. It is a sample topic map taken from the official CFEngine documentation.

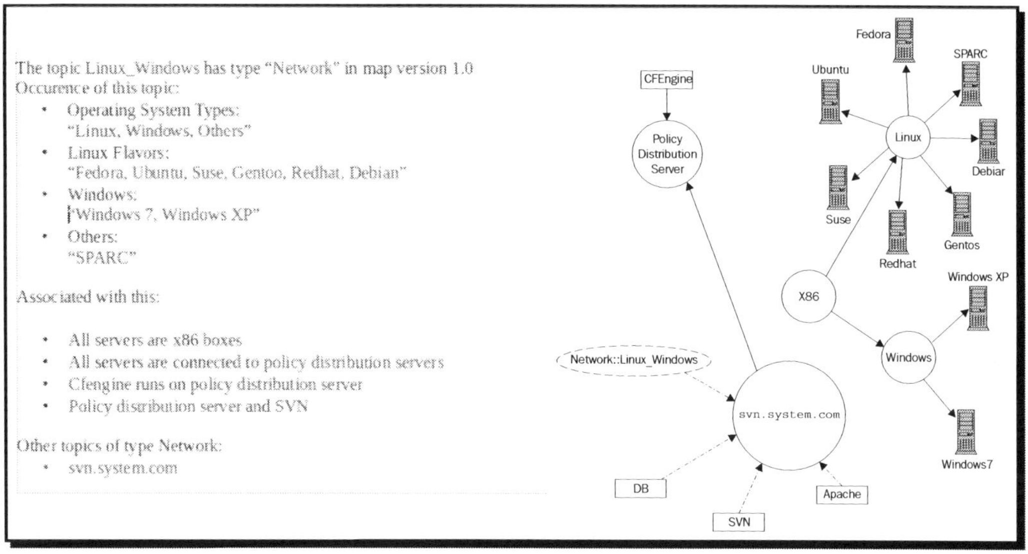

6. Once we have created the promises file and corresponding database, we may query the database for specific topics. Here is an example:

```
root@my.system.com# cf-know -f / var/cfengine/inputs/ services_
map.cf -t WebServers
```

What just happened?

Let's see what we just did. In the promises file `services_map.cf`, under the common control body, we defined a class `any` that has a bundlesequence defined with a single bundle named `services_map`. We defined the build directory, query engine, query output, and database details for the knowledge control body. Next, we defined each topic and their associations. After this we defined occurrences for each topic and what they represent, whether a text document or an external link. Next we defined how the associations work between the topics and its associates, which is a forward relationship or backward relationship. Data for topic maps is stored in a database which may either be MySQL or PostgreSQL. Here we have used MySQL. After creating the database and table we may populate data by running `cf-know` with the `-s` switch and provide the promises file name as an argument. We also saw how we can query the knowledge base for a specific topic. For running a knowledge base you need to have:

1. Apache web server.
2. Active Server Page technology to use a wrapper for CFEngine—PHP for example.
3. A backend SQL database for PHP. It can be either MySQL or PostgreSQL. In the previous example we used MySQL.

Compliance

Another very important domain for an organization is compliance. Different organizations tend to follow different compliance standards. Here we'll see one compliance standard in detail and the same methodology may be followed for other standards. One of the important standards today is PCI, also called **PCI DSS** (**Payment Card Industry Data Security Standard**) which is a comprehensive set of requirements for payment count data security. It is a set of 12 high level requirements designed to protect the user's credit card payment data. Let's see how CFEngine Nova may help us with PCI compliance. PCI DSS was designed to mitigate the increasing data theft threat. It provides a check list of points which need to be complied to before a compliance certificate is awarded. CFEngine can help organizations to align systems so that they comply with the organization's security policy based on the points suggested by the PCI standard. It can also help organizations audit these systems and processes on a regular basis and generate compliance reports. In addition to this there are a few PCI requirements which may be achieved only through a OEM security software—CFEngine can easily integrate with these and ensure successful execution of the checks performed by the security software, and hence take the complete ownership of compliance. Given next are the six basic control objectives, with a number of points under each objective, as defined by the PCI standard:

1. Protect cardholder data.
2. Implement strong access control measures.

3. Build and maintain a secure network.
4. Maintain a vulnerability management program.
5. Regularly monitor and test networks.
6. Maintain an information security policy.

If we take a look at these requirements, points 2, 3, 5, and 6 can be handled by CFEngine very well and we have already seen this in previous chapters. For control objective 1, which is protecting the cardholder's data, we need to manage files and databases that contain sensitive data. CFEngine can check that a log of all the changes being made to a file is maintained. It can also run scheduled jobs to check the sanity of databases and tables. Apart from this, CFEngine can also ensure that the certificates used for encrypting sensitive data during transfer are changed and they expire on time. Control objective 4, which is maintaining a vulnerability management program, emphasizes using a regularly updated anti-virus software on all systems commonly affected by malware, and also developing and maintaining secure systems and applications. To achieve this control objective CFEngine can ensure that the correct software, applications, and patches are installed on all machines in addition to verifying that appropriate vulnerability assessment scripts have been run successfully before a software or a patch is deployed onto production machines.

CFEngine, in addition to the previous points, maintains the status of compliance so that an appropriate action may be taken in case any of the points required by the compliance standard is not adhered to. Given next is a schematic representation of how a PCI standard compliant security policy works:

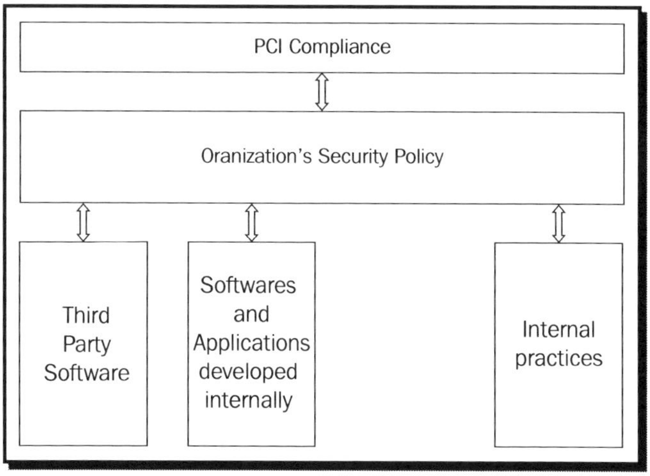

Let's also see the reports that CFEngine can generate in context with compliance. Here is a generic report generated by CFEngine:

Start check	End check	Policy version	% scheduled promises kept	% scheduled promises repaired	% scheduled promises ignored
Sun Apr 19 12:45:02 2009	Sun Apr 19 12:45:04 2009:	(not specified) (agent-1)	88%	12%	0%
Sun Apr 19 12:45:02 2009	Sun Apr 19 12:45:02 2009:	(not specified) (agent-0)	100%	0%	0%
Sun Apr 19 12:35:02 2009	Sun Apr 19 12:35:04 2009:	(not specified) (agent-1)	88%	12%	0%
Sun Apr 19 12:35:02 2009	Sun Apr 19 12:35:02 2009:	(not specified) (agent-0)	100%	0%	0%
Sun Apr 19 12:25:02 2009	Sun Apr 19 12:25:03 2009:	(not specified) (agent-1)	88%	12%	0%
Sun Apr 19 12:25:01 2009	Sun Apr 19 12:25:02 2009:	(not specified) (agent-0)	100%	0%	0%
Sun Apr 19 12:15:03 2009	Sun Apr 19 12:15:04 2009:	(not specified) (agent-1)	88%	12%	0%
Sun Apr 19 12:15:02 2009	Sun Apr 19 12:15:03 2009:	(not specified) (agent-0)	98%	2%	0%
Sun Apr 19 12:06:07 2009	Sun Apr 19 12:06:08 2009:	(not specified) (agent-0)	98%	2%	0%
Sun Apr 19 12:01:30 2009	Sun Apr 19 12:05:56 2009:	(not specified) (agent-0)	79%	21%	0%

The given report snapshot has been taken from the official CFEngine documentation.

Observing the previous report, if any of the promises is able to achieve only 50 percent compliance we may review that and make appropriate changes.

CFEngine and ITIL

ITIL (**Information Technology Infrastructure Library**) is a set of guidelines and practices for **Information Technology Services Management** (**ITSM**), and IT operations.

In 2007, ITIL V3 was out extending ITIL V2. ITIL V3 is aimed at providing the best practices for the entire service life cycle. The five stages of a service life cycle, as defined by ITIL V3, are as follows:

1. ITIL Service Strategy
2. ITIL Service Design
3. ITIL Service Transition

4. ITIL Service Operation
5. ITIL Continual Service Improvement

CFEngine can help you implement all these practices. The names for these practices may be different in CFEngine but the objectives remain the same. Let's analyze the life cycle's stages in more detail.

The first stage of a service life cycle as defined by ITIL V3 is Service Strategy, which is to provide guidance to an organization on investments in services. This guidance is based on service value definition, service assets, market analysis, and so on. Now you may define the services that need to be formalized under CFEngine based on these key topics.

The second stage of service cycle as defined by ITIL V3 is Service Design, which provides best practices guidelines for design of IT services and processes. The processes under this category are:

1. Service Catalog Management.
2. Service Level Management.
3. Risk Management.
4. Capacity Management.
5. Availability Management.
6. IT Service Continuity Management.
7. Information Security Management.
8. Compliance Management.
9. IT Architecture Management.
10. Supplier Management.

We have already seen that CFEngine can take care of Service Level Management, Availability Management, IT Service Continuity Management, Information Security Management, and Compliance Management. Service Catalog management is implemented by CFEngine in the form of menu-driven policies. Capacity Management is implemented by CFEngine through the monitoring and reporting of the performance for various promise executions. IT Architecture management is taken care of by the Knowledge Management promises in CFEngine.

The third stage of service life cycle management is Service Transition, which defines best practices for the following processes:

1. Service Asset and Configuration Management.
2. Service Validation and Testing.
3. Evaluation.

4. Release Management.
5. Change Management.
6. Knowledge Management.

We already know that CFEngine provides promises and controls for Knowledge Management. Service Asset and Configuration Management are things for which CFEngine has been written for; we have already seen that it can install and configure systems without any manual intervention. Change Management and Release Management are again processes handled by CFEngine under Configuration Management. For Service Validation testing and evaluation CFEngine can easily integrate with third-party tools or execute custom written scripts. One such scenario discussed previously is validation of anti virus patches on all machines.

The fourth stage of service life cycle management as defined by CFEngine is Service Operation. Under this category the ITIL V3 defines the best practices for achieving the delivery of agreed levels of services, both for the end users and the customers. It also sets the guidelines for monitoring of issues to ensure service reliability. The main functions under this category are:

1. Event Management.
2. Incident Management.
3. Problem Management.
4. Request Fulfillment.
5. Access Management.

The first three functions, which are Event Management, Incident Management and Problem Management, are a feature of CFEngine in the form of self-healing promises and repair. CFEngine ensures that the desired state of a machine is maintained at all times. In the case a machine comes up with a fault, CFEngine acknowledges it and takes corrective action as it has been told to maintain the state of the machine.

The fifth and the final stage in service life cycle management as defined by ITIL is Continual Service Improvement. This aims to improve process effectiveness, cost effectiveness, and the efficiency of IT processes. The objective is to improve the service quality with business in perspective. For Continual Service Improvement one must clearly define what needs to be measured and what needs to be controlled. This also involves reviewing the processes on a regular interval. Under this category, best practices for the following functions are defined:

1. Continual Service Improvement.
2. Service Level Management.
3. Service Measurement and Reporting.

The Service Measurement and Reporting functions of ITIL V3 are supported by CFEngine through the measurement and reporter control promises and bundles. Service Level Management is another function which is supported by CFEngine through the reporter control promises and bundles. The next flowchart shows a generic process flow under the ITIL V3 framework. The shaded boxes represent the functions that can be easily automated using CFEngine:

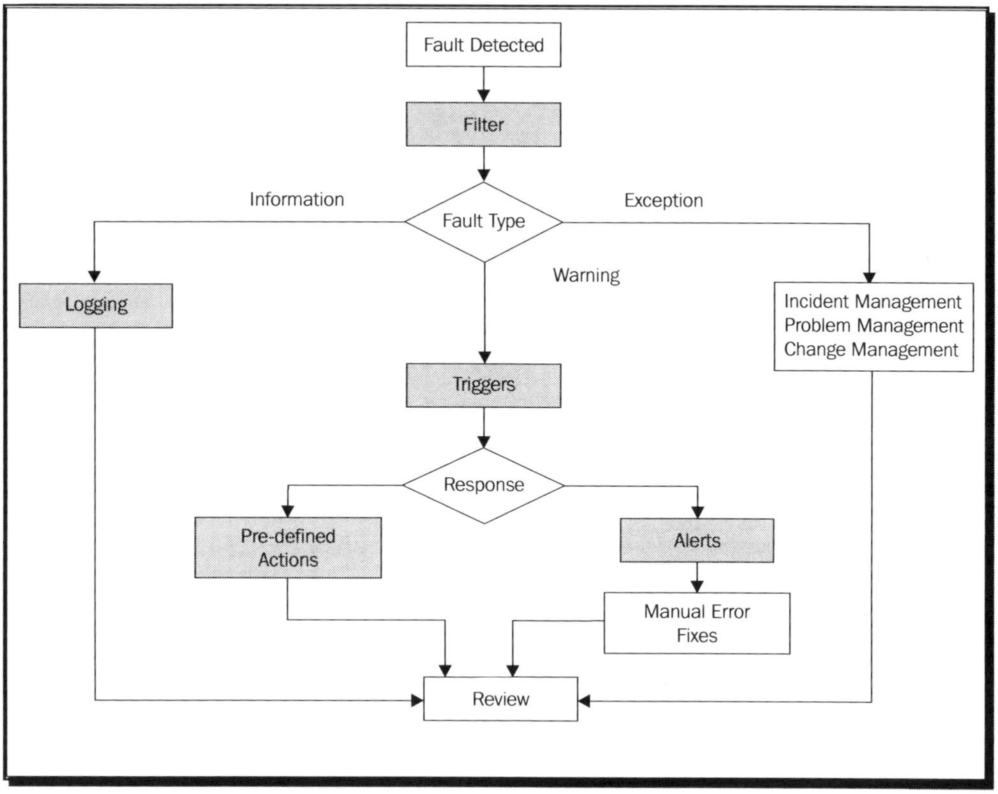

Database management

We learned how to install MySQL using CFEngine. There are other database management tasks which need to be completed on a regular basis. Let's see how types of CFEngine Nova helps with managing a database. CFEngine supports three types of databases:

1. LDAP—The Light Weight Directory Access Protocol
2. SQL—Structured Query Language
3. Registry—Microsoft registry

The following database promises are available under the agent bundle:

- **database_server** (compound body)
  - Type: Ext body
  - The next promises define a complete `database_server` body
- **db_server_owner**
  - Type: String
  - Allowed input range: (arbitrary string)

  This promise defines the user for the database connection. The user can be specified as follows:

  ```
  body database_server mysqldb
  {
  db_server_owner => "Bruce";
  }
  ```
- **db_server_password**
  - Type: String
  - Allowed input range: (arbitrary string)

  This promise is used to supply the password for the database connection.
- **db_server_host**
  - Type: String
  - Allowed input range: (arbitrary string)

  This promise is used to specify the host name or IP address for the database connection. If no host name or IP address is specified it means that the connection is to be used for a connection to localhost.
- **db_server_type**
  - Type: Menu option
  - Allowed input range: postgres, mysql

  This promise is used to define the SQL database whether it is MySQL or PostgresSQL.

- **db_server_connection_db**
  - Type: String
  - Allowed input range: (arbitrary string)

  This promise is used to specify the name of an existing database to connect to for creating or managing databases and tables.

- **database_operation**
  - Type: Menu option
  - Allowed input range: create, delete, drop, cache, verify, restore

  This promise is used to define a database operation involving tables or a database.

- **database_columns**
  - Type: slist
  - Allowed input range: .*

  This promise is used to define columns of a table in a database. The column definitions may be defined as follows:

```
#Populating Apache access logs to a DB
"Webserver/access_logs"
database_operation => "create";
database_type => "sql",
database_columns => {
                                        "IP Address", floatint, 256,
                                        "Time",varchar,256,
                                         "Request_URI", varchar, 256
                          ..
               ..

},
database_server => mysql_db_server;
```

- **database_rows**
  - Type: slist
  - Allowed input range: .*

  The `database_rows` promise is used to specify a list of row values to be populated to a table.

- **database_type**
  - Type: (menu option)
  - Allowed input range: sql, ms_registry
  - Default value: none

  The `database_type` promise is used to specify the type of database being used.

Pop quiz

1. How can you pass information or arguments to cf-agent or cf-runagent ?
   a. With the help of the `- arg` switch.
   b. With the help of the `-n` switch.
   c. Writing a class for the information and using the `-D` switch.
   d. No information can be supplied while running `cf-agent` or `cf-runagent`; all information should be written in the promises files.

Have a go hero

Write down a promises file to create a topic map defining the hierarchy of your team and which group, under this hierarchy, has access to which servers.

CFEngine Nova—an introduction

Here I'll take the opportunity to introduce the commercial or enterprise version of CFEngine, known as **CFEngine Nova**. Here are a few features of CFEngine Nova:

- PCI compliance
- Easy integration with third parties
- Asset management
- Database management
- Change management
- Virtualization management
- LDAP integration

As I said earlier, most of these tasks may be done with the smart use of 'promise' language. Then there are a few tasks that are more complex and which may need a huge amount of work—for example: compliance, integrating with third parties, asset management, change management, and so on. This is where the commercial edition may help a lot as it has pre-defined policies to manage these.

Summary

In this chapter we learned about:

- Writing menu driven policies and how to choose from the available menus.
- Writing content driven policies and creating generic CFEngine templates.
- CFEngine's knowledge management feature and how to create topic maps under a knowledge base.
- How CFEngine Nova is a complete framework that can handle your organization's security policy and complies to a standard. We saw how CFEngine may help us with PCI compliance.
- How CFEngine can help us to follow the best practices or guidelines recommended by ITIL V3 to improve the quality of service.
- The inbuilt database management promises.

With the knowledge gained in this chapter, let's move to more granular aspects of CFEngine and learn a few special functions and variables provided with CFEngine that could be very handy.

8

Advanced Functions and Variables

CFEngine provides a number of functions to perform small important tasks, apart from the number of promises and bundles. These special functions, if used judiciously, may help in reducing the number promises you write and also in increasing the performance of CFEngine. Finding the right function amongst the huge number of functions is a daunting task in itself. This chapter provides a list of functions based on their usage to make your tasks easier.

In this chapter we will learn about:

- The various special functions and variables provided by CFEngine
- The syntax for various special functions provided with CFEngine
- The syntax for various special variables provided with CFEngine

CFEngine special functions

CFEngine provides a number of native special functions that may be used to define arrays, lists, get environment values, string comparisons, and various other tasks which one may encounter on a daily basis. These functions have their own syntax and usage. Let's see a few of them:

- **getindices**
    - Usage: `getindices(arg0)`
    - arg0: CFEngine array identifier, in the range [a-zA-Z0-9_$()\[\].]+

  This function returns a list of keys to the array whose ID is the argument and assigns them to a variable. The next example shows how this can be used while writing the promises file.

- **canonify**
  - Usage: canonify(arg0)
  - arg0: String containing non-identifier characters, in the range .*

  This function is used to convert an arbitrary string into a legal class name.

Let's use these special functions in an example wherein we need to change system configuration parameters using the system configuration file `/etc/sysctl.conf` on hosts.

Time for action – setting system variables

1. Let's write a configuration file with which we want to reset the system variables in the system configuration file. For Red Hat based systems this file is `/etc/sysctl.conf`. The following lines may be copied to the file `system_set_vars.cf`:

```
bundle agent set_variables

{

vars:



  "sys_config[net.ipv4.tcp_syncookies]" string => "1";

  "sys_config[net.ipv4.icmp_echo_ignore_broadcasts]" string =>
"1";

 "sys_config[net.ipv4.tcp_fin_timeout]" string => "45";;

"sys_config[net.ipv4.tcp_keepalive_time]" string => "3600";



files:



  "/etc/sysctl.conf"
```

```
        create => "true",

      edit_line => set_variable_values("set_variables.sys_config");

}

bundle edit_line set_variable_values(v)

{

vars:

  "index" slist => getindices("$(v)");

  "cindex[$(index)]" string => canonify("$(index)");

field_edits:

  "$(index)\s*=.*"

      edit_field => col("=","2","$($(v)[$(index)])","set"),

        classes => if_ok("not_$(cindex[$(index)])");

insert_lines:

  "$(index)=$($(v)[$(index)])",
```

```
      ifvarclass => "!not_$(cindex[$(index)])";

}


body edit_field col(split,col,newval,method)


{

field_separator    => "$(split)";

select_field       => "$(col)";

value_separator    => ",";

field_value        => "$(newval)";

field_operation    => "$(method)";

extend_fields      => "true";

allow_blank_fields => "true";

}



body classes if_ok(x)

{

promise_repaired => { "$(x)" };

promise_kept => { "$(x)" };

}
```

2. Before executing the configuration file, let's check the content of the file `/etc/sysctl.cf`, as seen in the following screenshot:

```
root@my1[/var/cfengine/inputs]# cat /etc/sysctl.conf
# Kernel sysctl configuration file for Red Hat Linux
#
# For binary values, 0 is disabled, 1 is enabled.  See sysctl(8) and
# sysctl.conf(5) for more details.

# Controls IP packet forwarding
net.ipv4.ip_forward = 0

# Controls source route verification
net.ipv4.conf.default.rp_filter = 1

# Do not accept source routing
net.ipv4.conf.default.accept_source_route = 0

# Controls the System Request debugging functionality of the kernel
kernel.sysrq = 0

# Controls whether core dumps will append the PID to the core filename
# Useful for debugging multi-threaded applications
kernel.core_uses_pid = 1

# Controls the use of TCP syncookies
net.ipv4.tcp_syncookies = 1

# Controls the maximum size of a message, in bytes
kernel.msgmnb = 65536

# Controls the default maxmimum size of a mesage queue
kernel.msgmax = 65536

# Controls the maximum shared segment size, in bytes
kernel.shmmax = 4294967295

# Controls the maximum number of shared memory segments, in pages
kernel.shmall = 268435456
root@my1[/var/cfengine/inputs]#
```

Let's execute the configuration file and check if we get the desired results:

```
root@my1[/var/cfengine/inputs]# cf-agent -v -f ./system_set_vars.
cf

cf3> Cfengine - autonomous configuration engine - commence self-
diagnostic prelude

…..

…..

cf3>  -> Verifying the syntax of the inputs...
```

```
cf3>  -> Caching the state of validation

cf3>   > Parsing file ./system_set_vars.cf
cf3>    files in bundle set_variables (1)

cf3>     .....................................................

cf3>     Promise handle:

cf3>     Promise made by: /etc/sysctl.conf

cf3>     .....................................................

cf3>  -> Using literal pathtype for /etc/sysctl.conf

cf3>  -> File "/etc/sysctl.conf" exists as promised

cf3>  -> Handling file existence constraints on /etc/sysctl.conf

cf3>  -> Handling file edits in edit_line bundle set_variable_
values

cf3>       * * * * * * * * * * * * * * * * * * * * * * * * * * *

cf3>       BUNDLE set_variable_values( {'set_variables.sys_
config'} )

cf3>       * * * * * * * * * * * * * * * * * * * * * * * * * * *

cf3>

cf3> Initiate variable convergence...

cf3>     ? Augment scope set_variable_values with v (s)

…....
cf3>     Promise handle:

cf3>     Promise made by: index
```

```
cf3>    ..........................................................

cf3>    Promise handle:

cf3>    Promise made by: cindex[net.ipv4.tcp_fin_timeout]

cf3>    ..........................................................

cf3>      field_edits in bundle set_variable_values

cf3>    ..........................................................

cf3>    Promise handle:

cf3>    Promise made by: net.ipv4.tcp_fin_timeout\s*=.*

cf3>    ..........................................................

cf3>    Promise handle:

cf3>    Promise made by: net.ipv4.tcp_fin_timeout=45

cf3>  -> Inserting the promised line "net.ipv4.tcp_fin_timeout=45"
into /etc/sysctl.conf after locator

cf3>

cf3>    ..........................................................

cf3>    Promise handle:

cf3>    Promise made by: net.ipv4.tcp_keepalive_time=3600

cf3>    ..........................................................

cf3>  -> Inserting the promised line "net.ipv4.tcp_keepalive_
time=3600" into /etc/sysctl.conf after locator
…....
cf3>  -> Writing last-seen observations
```

```
cf3>  -> Keyring is empty

cf3>  -> No lock purging scheduled


root@my1[/var/cfengine/inputs]#
```

Let's check the contents of the file `/etc/sysctl.conf` again:

```
root@my1[/var/cfengine/inputs]# cat /etc/sysctl.conf
# Kernel sysctl configuration file for Red Hat Linux
#
# For binary values, 0 is disabled, 1 is enabled.  See sysctl(8) and
# sysctl.conf(5) for more details.

# Controls IP packet forwarding
net.ipv4.ip_forward = 0

# Controls source route verification
net.ipv4.conf.default.rp_filter = 1

# Do not accept source routing
net.ipv4.conf.default.accept_source_route = 0

# Controls the System Request debugging functionality of the kernel
kernel.sysrq = 0

# Controls whether core dumps will append the PID to the core filename
# Useful for debugging multi-threaded applications
kernel.core_uses_pid = 1

# Controls the use of TCP syncookies
net.ipv4.tcp_syncookies = 1

# Controls the maximum size of a message, in bytes
kernel.msgmnb = 65536

# Controls the default maxmimum size of a mesage queue
kernel.msgmax = 65536

# Controls the maximum shared segment size, in bytes
kernel.shmmax = 4294967295

# Controls the maximum number of shared memory segments, in pages
kernel.shmall = 268435456
net.ipv4.tcp_fin_timeout=45
net.ipv4.tcp_keepalive_time=3600
net.ipv4.icmp_echo_ignore_broadcasts=1
root@my1[/var/cfengine/inputs]#
```

If we observe the last few lines of the file, we see that the required variables have been set to the desired values.

What just happened?

In the previous example we wanted to add a few configurations to the system configuration file /etc/sysctl.conf. For this we defined a bundlesequence named set_variables. Under the definition of this bundle agent we defined the values of of the system configuration variables that we need to add or change. Here we use associative arrays to define the variables, and the array identifier is named sys_config. After this we defined the file to which these variables and their corresponding values are added. For this, we used an edit_line bundle which defines the scope of the variable and its values which need to be edited.

Let's analyze the bundle agent edit_line in detail to understand how the array is expanded. While defining the bundle agent edit_line we used a function getindices. This is used to get a list of keys to the array whose identifier is the argument and assign to a variable. It returns a slist. In the previous example, the getindices function assigns a list of keys to the array to the variable index. We used the canonify function in the next step to make all arbitrary strings assigned to the variable index, legal class names. To edit a parameter value in /etc/sysctl.conf we first need to locate the line, and for this we need to match a line similar to parameter_name = value; for this we defined the regular expression **$(index)\s*=.*** that matches lines in the file with each of the keys assigned to the variable index. Therefore, in our case this will try to look for the three variables we have defined.

Once CFEngine has got the lines that match the variables it needs to replace the values currently assigned to the variables with the new values. For this we split the matched line parameter_name = parameter_value on the identifier =. When we do this we get two columns: parameter_name and parameter_value. We chose the second column, parameter_value, and replace the existing value with the new values specified in the CFEngine configuration file.

It may be possible that all the parameters we are trying to define now are not previously defined and hence there may be parameters which may not match any of the lines present in the file. In such a case we need to insert this parameter and and its value to the file. To verify that there are parameters which do not match a line we defined a class if_ok, and if it is set we define another local class, insert_lines, which appends the parameter and the parameter value to the file. So here we take care of both the requirements which are setting a new value of a parameter which is already defined in the file, and appending the parameter name and its value if they are not already defined.

Let's look at a few more functions and their usage with examples.

Functions that work on or with regular expressions

Regular expressions, also referred to as a **regex**, are flexible means to match strings of text, characters, patterns, or patterns of text. CFEngine provides various special functions that work on or with regular expressions. Let's look at the usage of one such special function, `regarray`.

Time for action – getting a list of servers that are up and running on the network

1. Let's write a promises file to check which hosts on the network are up and running. You may copy the following lines to a text file. Here we will use the file `servers_responding.cf`:

```
body common control

{


bundlesequence  => { "up_servers"  };

version => "1.0.1";
}


bundle agent up_servers


{


vars:


"servers_host_names" slist => { "192.168.2.12","192.168.2.13","192
.168.2.14" };


"servers_up" int =>
  selectservers("@(servers_host_names)","22",
  "","","100","servers_up_running");
```

```
classes:

  "servers_reachable" expression =>
    isgreaterthan("$(servers_up)","0");

  "servers_reachable_details" expression =>
    regarray("servers_up","$(host)|$(fqhost)");

reports:

  servers_reachable::
    "Number of active servers $(servers_up)"
    action => always;
}

body action always

{

ifelapsed => "0";

}
```

2. Let's verify the promises file with the help of `cf-promises`:

   root@mysystem.com# cf-promises -f ./servers_responding.cf

   root@mysystem.com#

   Having errors justifies the promises that we have written.

3. Let's execute the promises file using `cf-agent` and check how many hosts are up:

   root@mysystem.com

   # cf-agent -v -f ./servers_responding.cf

   ..

   ..

   cf3 Initiate variable convergence...

```
cf3 Set cfengine port number to 22 = 22

cf3  -> Connect to X1.mysystem.com = X1.mysystem.com on port 22

cf3 LastSaw host X1.mysystem.com now

cf3 Host X1.mysystem.com is alive

cf3 Set cfengine port number to 22 = 22

cf3  -> Connect to X2.mysystem.com = X2.mysystem.com on port 22

cf3 LastSaw host X2.mysystem.com now

cf3 Host X2.mysystem.com is alive

cf3 Set cfengine port number to 22 = 22

cf3  -> Connect to X3.mysystem.com = X3.mysystem.com on port 22

cf3 LastSaw host X3.mysystem.com now

cf3 Host X3.mysystem.com is alive

cf3 Set cfengine port number to 22 = 22

cf3  -> Connect to X4.mysystem.com = X4.mysystem.com on port 22

cf3 LastSaw host X4.mysystem.com now

cf3 Host X4.mysystem.com is alive

..
..
cf3     Promise handle:
```

```
cf3     Promise made by: Number of active servers 3

..
..
```

This output verifies that all the systems provided in the list are up and running.

What just happened?

We defined a bundlesequence `up_servers` under the common control body. Under the definition of the bundle agent `up_servers` we defined a list containing the host names of the servers which need to be checked with the help of a `slist` variable `servers_host_names`. Next we defined the hosts list, port number, query string, the response string, number of bytes to be read, and the name of the array results for the servers to be checked using the `selectservers` special function. We supplied a list of host names that need to be checked to the function `selectservers` when we used `@servers_host_names`. Please note that argument two and argument three, which are the query string to be sent and the regex to match in the reply string respectively, are empty. No query string is sent and any reply from the client is deemed fit. You may actually supply a query string to be sent to the client host and a regex to be matched in the response from the client host. After this we defined two classes, namely `servers_reachable` and `servers_reachable_details`. The first class returns true if the response from the remote servers is greater than `0`. The second class gives the host name or the fully qualified domain name for the servers which are up. Under the reports class we define the total number of servers that are up and running. Let's see the functions `selectservers` and `regarray` in detail:

- **selectservers**
  - Usage: selectservers(arg0,arg1,arg2,arg3,arg4,arg5)
  - arg0: The identifier of a list of CFEngine list of hosts or addresses to contact, in the range @[(][a-zA-Z0-9]+[)]
  - arg1: The port number, in the range 0,99999999999
  - arg2: A query string, in the range 0,99999999999
  - arg3: A regular expression to match success, in the range .*
  - arg4: Maximum bytes to read from the server, in the range 0,99999999999
  - arg5: Name of the array of results, in the range [a-zA-Z0-9_$()\[\].]+

  This function is used to select TCP servers that respond correctly to a query, return their number, and set array of names.

- **regarray**
  - Usage: regarray(arg0,arg1)
  - arg0: CFEngine array identifier, in the range [a-zA-Z0-9_$()\[\].]+
  - arg1: Regular expression, in the range .*

This function returns the class `true` if the regular expression specified by `arg1` matches an item in the associative array with `id=arg2`. The next example shows how this can be used while writing the promises file:

```
body common control
{
bundlesequence => { "test" };
version => "1.0.0";
}
bundle agent test
{
vars:
"array[0]" string => "value1";
"array[1]" string => "value2";
"array[2]" string => "value3";
"array[3]" string => "test4";
classes:
"OK" expression => regarray("array","val*")
reports:
OK::
"Found in list";
!OK::
"Not found in list";
}
```

Functions that return string

Under various circumstances you may want to use functions with return type string. CFEngine provides a number of functions that return string values such as `join`, `execresult`, `canonify`, and so on. Let's look at the usage of one such special function, `join`.

Time for action – concatenating individual objects using a given conjunction

1. Let's write a promises file to concatenate individual objects or strings using a given conjunction. You may copy the following code snippet to a file named `object_concat.cf`:

```
body common control
{
bundlesequence => { "concat_object" };
version => "1.0.1";

}
bundle agent concat_object
{
vars:
"values" slist => { "1","2","3","4","5" };
"values_joined" string =>  join( " < ","values");

reports:
linux::
"The concatenated string is $(values_joined)";

}
```

2. Let's verify the promises file using `cf-promises`:

```
root@mysystem.com# cf-promises -f ./object_concat.cf
root@mysystem.com#
```

No output justifies that the promises file is correct.

3. Now let's execute the promises file and check the results:

```
root@mysystem.com# cf-agent -v -f ./object_concat.cf
..
..
cf3 Verifying SQL table promises is only available with Cfengine
Nova or above


cf3


cf3     .......................................................
```

```
cf3     Promise handle:

cf3     Promise made by: Concatenated 1 < 2 < 3 < 4 < 5

cf3     ..............................................

cf3

cf3 Reporting about this...

cf3 R: Concatenated  1 < 2 < 3 < 4 < 5
..
..
root@mysystem.com#
```

The promises file was executed successfully and we got the required concatenated output.

What just happened?

We defined the bundlesequence `concat_object` under the common control body. Next we defined the bundle agent `concat_object` by first defining the list of objects and the list is named as `values`. After this we defined the variable `values_joined`, which uses the special function `join` to concatenate the objects provided in the list with the help of a conjunction that is provided to the function `join` as an argument. Let's look at the function `join` in detail:

- **join**
  - Usage: join(arg0,arg1)
  - arg0: join conjunction or glue-string, in the range .*
  - arg1: CFEngine array identifier, in the range [a-zA-Z0-9_$()\[\].]+

Functions that fill arrays

CFEngine provides a number of functions which fill arrays such as `readstringarray`, `readrealarray`, `getfields`, `readintarray`, and `regextract`. The return values of these functions depend on the number of items processed. Let's look at the usage of one such function, `readstringarray`.

Time for action – configuring Apache virtual hosts from a list of domains in a file

1. We need to write a promises file so that name base virtual hosts are created automatically once we provide a domain. You may copy the following code snippet to a file named `Vhost_config.cf`:

```
body common control

{

bundlesequence => { "vhost_config" };

version => "1.0.0";

}

bundle agent vhost_config

{

vars:

"host_list" int => readstringarray("vhost_array", "/tmp/virtual_
hosts_list", "#.*", ":", "100", "10000");



"index" slist => getindices("vhost_array");

files:

"/etc/httpd/conf/httpd.conf"

create => "true",

edit_line => Insert_vhost("$(index)");



}

bundle edit_line Insert_vhost(h)
```

```
{
vars:
insert_lines:
"
<VirtualHost *:80>      # Start of Virtual host configuration for
$(h)
    DocumentRoot /usr/local/apache/htdocs/$(h)
    ServerName $(h)
    ErrorLog logs/$(h)-error_log
   CustomLog logs/$(h)-access_log common
</VirtualHost>    # End of Virtual host configuration for $(h)
";
}
```

2. Let's try to verify the promises file using `cf-promises`:

   ```
   root@mysystem.com# cf-promise -f ./Vhost_config.cf
   root@mysystem.com#
   ```

   No error output shows that there are no issues with the promises file.

3. Let's try to execute the promises using `cf-agent`:

   Before that, let's see the contents of the file `/etc/httpd/conf/httpd.conf`:

   ```
   root@mysystem.com# cat /etc/httpd/conf/httpd.conf
   ...
   ...
   NameVirtualHost *:80
   #
   # NOTE: NameVirtualHost cannot be used without a port specifier
   # (e.g. :80) if mod_ssl is being used, due to the nature of the
   # SSL protocol.
   ```

```
#
# VirtualHost example:
# Almost any Apache directive may go into a VirtualHost container.
# The first VirtualHost section is used for requests without a
known
# server name.
#
#<VirtualHost *:80>
#     ServerAdmin webmaster@dummy-host.example.com
#     DocumentRoot /www/docs/dummy-host.example.com
#     ServerName dummy-host.example.com
#     ErrorLog logs/dummy-host.example.com-error_log
#     CustomLog logs/dummy-host.example.com-access_log common
y #</VirtualHost>
root@mysystem.com#
```

Let's also see the contents of the file `/tmp/virtual_hosts_list`:

```
root@mysystem.com# cat /tmp/virtual_hosts_list
abc.com:Domain 1

ghi.com:Domain 2

def.com: Domain 3
```

This file lists the domain names for which the virtual hosts need to be configured. Now let's run `cf-agent` and verify whether we get the desired results:

```
root@mysystem.com# cf-agent -f ./Vhost_config.cf
root@mysystem.com#
```

No error output shows that the promises were successfully executed. Let's see whether the required lines were added to the file or not:

```
root@mysystem.com# cat /etc/httpd/conf/httpd.conf
….
…
NameVirtualHost *:80
#
# NOTE: NameVirtualHost cannot be used without a port specifier
# (e.g. :80) if mod_ssl is being used, due to the nature of the
```

```
# SSL protocol.
#
# VirtualHost example:
# Almost any Apache directive may go into a VirtualHost container.
# The first VirtualHost section is used for requests without a
known
# server name.
#<VirtualHost *:80>
#    ServerAdmin webmaster@dummy-host.example.com
#    DocumentRoot /www/docs/dummy-host.example.com
#    ServerName dummy-host.example.com
#    ErrorLog logs/dummy-host.example.com-error_log
#    CustomLog logs/dummy-host.example.com-access_log common
y #</VirtualHost>

<VirtualHost *:80> # Start of Virtual host configuration for def.
com

    DocumentRoot /usr/local/apache/htdocs/def.com

    ServerName def.com

    ErrorLog logs/def.com-error_log

   CustomLog logs/def.com-access_log common

</VirtualHost>    # End of Virtual host configuration for def.com



<VirtualHost *:80> # Start of Virtual host configuration for abc.
com

    DocumentRoot /usr/local/apache/htdocs/abc.com

    ServerName abc.com
```

```
    ErrorLog logs/abc.com-error_log

   CustomLog logs/abc.com-access_log common

</VirtualHost>    # End of Virtual host configuration for abc.com

<VirtualHost *:80> # Start of Virtual host configuration for ghi.
com

    DocumentRoot /usr/local/apache/htdocs/ghi.com

    ServerName ghi.com

    ErrorLog logs/ghi.com-error_log

   CustomLog logs/ghi.com-access_log common

</VirtualHost>    # End of Virtual host configuration for ghi.com
```

This output shows that the required lines were successfully added to the requested file.

What just happened?

For creating the virtual hosts in Apache we defined a bundlesequence with a single bundle named `vhost_config`. Next in the definition of the bundle agent `vhost_config` we defined a variable `host_list` which is assigned an array of fully qualified domain names from a file `/tmp/vhost_hosts_list`. For assigning the array we used the function `readstringarray`, which sets the array identifier as `vhost_array`. The array is the name of the domains for which we want to create a virtual host. Next, we assigned the list of keys of the array to the variable `index` using the function `getindices`. After this we defined the file to which the VirtualHost lines need to be added. We specified that if the file does not exist, create it, and we also defined an `edit_line` promise. Next we defined the bundle `edit_line` wherein we instruct CFEngine to insert the lines necessary for creating a working VirtualHost entry with the domain names as an argument. The arguments are the keys of the array which are assigned to the variable `index`. Let's look at the function readstringarray that we used here in some more detail:

- **readstringarray**
    - Usage: readstringarray(arg0,arg1,arg2,arg3,arg4,arg5)
    - arg0: Array identifier to populate, in the range [a-zA-Z0-9 $()—""["].]+
    - arg1: File name to read, in the range "?(([a-zA-Z]:"".*)—(/.*))
    - arg2: Regex matching comments, in the range .*
    - arg3: Regex to split data, in the range .*
    - arg4: Maximum number of entries to read, in the range 0,99999999999
    - arg5: Maximum bytes to read, in the range 0,99999999999

  This function reads an array of strings from a file and assigns the dimensions to a variable.

CFEngine special variables

CFEngine also provides a number of special variables that may be used in various contexts. Let's see how these special variables may help us in writing promises:

1. Variable context **edit**—The **edit** context is used to edit promises while they are being executed. For example, the variable `$edit.filename` points to the file name of the file specified by the `files` promiser and currently making the **edit** promise. Here is an example:

    ```
    bundle agent file_edit
    {
    files
    "/home/clark/samplefile"
    edit_line => "edit";
    }
    bundle edit_line test
    {
    classes:
    "successful" expression => regline(".*mark.*","$(edit.filename)");
    reports
    successful::
    "File matched $(edit.filename)";
    }
    ```

2. Variable context **match**—Whenever CFEngine matches a string while executing a promise or a function, the values are assigned to a special variable context `$(match.n)`. As we have already seen, matching a string is needed in many places; for example, editing or replacing a pattern, searching for a file, and so on. Let's look at an example to understand how CFEngine special variables help us:

```
bundle agent match_string
{
files:
"/home/clark/samplefile_1"
create => "true";
edit_line => testedit("second backref: $(match.2)")
}
```

Now in these promise files, here are the values stored in `$(match.n)`:

```
"$(match.0)"     -    '/home/clark/samplefile'
'$(match.1)"     -     ''
"$(match.2)"     -     'test'
```

3. Variable context **this**—The context this is used to get information about a promise during its execution. It provides a context for variables wherever it is needed. There are two contexts where this can be used:

   - `$(this.handle)`—this variable is used to refer to the handle of the currently executed promises. For example, referring to a prefix in log messages which gives the origin of the log message. In CFEngine Nova and higher, every promise has a default handle which is based on the filename and line number. You may specify your own handle for better reference.
   - `$(this.promiser)`—this variable is used to refer to the current value of the promiser itself. For example, during pattern matching or searching for files that match multiple objects, the variable `$(this.promise)` refers to the currently identified file that makes the promise.

Here is an example to understand this better:

```
bundle agent find_world_writable_files
{
files:
"home"
files_select => world_writable_files,
transformer =>  "/bin/echo DETECTED $(this.promiser)",
depth_search => recurse("inf");

"/etc/*"
file_select => world_writable_files,
transformer =>  "/bin/echo DETECTED $(this.promiser)",
depth_search => recurse("inf");

}
body file_select world_writable_files
{
search_mode => { "o+w" };
file_result => "mode";
}
```

4. The variables defined by cf-monitord are placed in this **monitoring** context. You may want to monitor a lot of variables on a system and CFEngine provides a number of predefined variables for this. Let's see a few of the available variables:

   - **mon.value_diskfree**

     This variable stores the free disk on '/' partition.

   - **mon.value_loadavg**

     This variable stores the *percentage kernel load utilization*. This value is collected by cf-monitord every 2.5 minutes.

   - **mon.value_cpu**

     This variable stores the *percentage CPU utilization* for all CPUs available on the host. We may also store the value of individual CPUs. For example, for CPU0 the variable mon.value_cpu0 may be used.

> All CFEngine special variables have two more monitoring variables along with them which provide the average values and the deviations. For example, mon.value_cpu0 has two more variables, mon.avg_cpu0 and mon.dev_cpu0 along with it, which may be used individually while writing promises. A more generic rule may be if there is a monitoring variable mon.value_<parameter_name>, then it will also have mon.avg_<parameter_name> and mon.dev_<parameter_name>.

5. Variable context **sys**—CFEngine provides predefined variables which store various system values. These system variables can be directly called within a promise to derive a system specific values. Let's see a few of these system variables:

   - **sys.arch**

     This variable stores the kernel's short architecture.

   - **sys.cdate**

     This variable stores the system date in canonical form. The date is stored as follows:

     ```
     #cdate = Thu_Apr__15_12_36_54_2010
     ```

   - **sys.interface**

     This variable stores the name of the default system interface on the host.

   - **sys.ipv4**

     This variable stores all four octets of the ipv4 address of the primary interface. If the host has only one interface then 'sys.ipv4' stores all the octets of the ipv4 address of this interface. In the case the host has multiple interfaces, the variable stores all the octets of the ipv4 address of the first interface in the list.

- **sys.ipv4[interface_name]**

  This variable stores the complete ipv4 address of the interface named as an associative index array. For example, let's suppose the interface name is *eth0* and the IPV4 address is *192.168.2.12*, then:

  ```
  ipv4_1[eth0] = 192
  ipv4_2[eth0] = 192.168
  ipv4_3[eth0] = 192.168.2
  ipv4[eth0] = 192.168.2.12
  ```

Let's see how we can use the various special variables provided by CFEngine.

Variable context mon

As we have just seen, monitoring variables discovered by `cf-monitord` are placed in this context. These monitoring variables are rapidly changing. The values of these variables are connected from `cf-monitord` every 2.5 minutes, in general. These variables may be used to capture a number of system parameters. Let's see how we can capture these system parameters.

Time for action – logging information in case the system's load average is above the threshold

1. Let's write a CFEngine configuration file that logs system and process information if the load average of the system is above the threshold.

2. We need to log the following values in case the system's load average breaches the threshold:

   - The number of processes running with user `root`
   - The number of processes running with non-privileged users
   - The percentage CPU utilization
   - The current load average of the system

   For this you may copy the the following lines to a file named `load_alert.cf`:

   ```
   body common control
   {
   bundlesequence => { "load_alert" };
   version => "1.0.0";
   }
   ```

```
bundle agent load_alert
{
vars:
"threshold" int => "1"
classes:
"loadavg_high" expression => isgreaterthan("$(mon.value_loadavg)",
  "$(threshold)");
reports:
loadavg_high::
"1. The current load average of the system is $(mon.value_loadavg)
2. The current number of processes running with user root are
$(mon.value_rootprocs)
3. The current number of processes running with non-privileged
users are $(mon.value_otherprocs)_
4. The current CPU utilization is $(mon.value_cpu)",
report_to_file => "/var/log/load_alert.log";
!loadavg_high::
"Load average is below the threshold, nothing to do";
}
```

3. Let's try to execute the configuration file and see what report we get:

```
root@myl[/var/cfengine/inputs]# cf-agent -v -f ./load_alert.cf
cf3> Cfengine - autonomous configuration engine - commence self-
diagnostic prelude
…..
…..
cf3>    reports in bundle load_alert (1)



cf3>     ...................................................


cf3>     Promise handle:


cf3>     Promise made by: 1. The current load average of the
system is 2


2. The current number of processes running with user root are 80


3. The current number of processes running with non-privileged
users are 30
```

```
4. The current CPU utilization is 0

cf3> Report: 1. The current load average of the system is 2

2. The current number of processes running with user root are 80

3. The current number of processes running with non-privileged
users are 30

4. The current CPU utilization is 0

…....
…....
cf3> Outcome of version 1.0.0 (agent-0): Promises observed to be
kept 0%, Promises repaired 100%, Promises not repaired 0%

cf3> Estimated system complexity as touched objects = 0, for 5
promises

cf3>  -> Writing last-seen observations

cf3>  -> Keyring is empty

cf3>  -> No lock purging scheduled

root@my1[/var/cfengine/inputs]#
```

We saw the output of the execution of promises. Let's now see the log file to which the values are written:

```
root@myl[/var/cfengine/inputs]# cat /var/log/load_alert.log
…...
…...
1. The current load average of the system is 4

2. The current number of processes running with user root are 80

3. The current number of processes running with non-privileged
users are 30
```

```
4. The current CPU utilization is 0

.....
.....
root@my1[/var/cfengine/inputs]#
```

What just happened?

We wanted to compare the current load average of the system to a threshold load average of "1" and log a few system resource utilization values in case the threshold is breached. For this we defined a bundle `load_alert` under which we defined a variable `threshold` and assigned a value of "1" to it. Next, we defined a class `loadavg_high`, which is defined if the current load average of the system is greater than "1". This comparison is done by the function `isgreaterthan`. If the class is defined, we log the other parameters to a log file `/var/log/load_alert.log`. In case the class is not set, when the system load average is below "1", we need not do anything. Let's see the syntax of the function `isgreaterthan` which we just used:

- **isgreaterthan**
  - Usage: isgreaterthan (arg0,arg1)
  - arg0: Larger string or value, in the range .*
  - arg1: Smaller string or value, in the range .*

  The function returns a class `true` if `arg1` is numerically greater than `arg2`. If the values for `arg1` and `arg2` are not numeric then the values are compared similar to `strcmp`.

While trying to make changes to configuration files, you may always want to disable a few functionalities or a few parameters. On a Linux or Unix based operating systems you may always do this by commenting the specific modules or parameters in the configuration files. Let's see an example of how this can be done.

Variable context match

The variable is used to match a string. The values are assigned to a special variable `$(match.n)` each time CFEngine matches a string. Let's see how it can be used for pattern replacement while editing a file.

Time for action – comment matching lines

1. Let's look another example for replacing patterns. In the next example, we need to search for lines in a file and comment them out. The following lines may be copied in a file named `commenting_lines.cf`:

```
body common control
{
bundlesequence => { "commenting" };
version => "1.0.0";
}
bundle agent commenting
{
files:
"/home/clark/samplefile"
create => "true",
edit_line => myedit;
}
bundle edit_line myedit
{
vars:
"lines_match" slist => { "The.*","configuration.*" };
replace_patterns:
"^($(lines_match))$"
replace_with => comment("#    ");
}
body replace_with comment(k)
{
replace_value => "$(k) $(match.1)";
occurrences => "all";

}
```

2. Let's try to verify the promises file with `cf-promises`:

```
root@my.system.com# cf-promises -f ./commenting_lines.cf
root@my.system.com#
```

No output means we are good with promises.

3. Let's try executing the promises file with `cf-agent`. Before this, let's check the contents of the sample file:

```
root@my.system.com# cat /home/clark/samplefile
The.
The
```

```
configuration
configuration.*
clark
Apache
root@my.system.com#
```

Now let's execute the promises file using `cf-agent`:

```
root@my.system.com# cf-agent -f ./commenting_lines.cf
root@my.system.com#
```

No output means that the promises were executed successfully. Let's check the contents of the file:

```
root@my.system.com# cat /home/clark/samplefile
#     The.
#     The
#     configuration
#     configuration.*
clark
Apache
```

This output for the file verifies that the promises were executed successfully and the required lines were commented.

What just happened?

We needed to comment all the lines starting with "The" and "configuration". For this we defined a bundlesequence with only one bundle, named `commenting`. We described the file that needs to be edited under the bundle agent `commenting`. We defined an `edit_line` promise `myedit`. We defined the body for the `edit_line` promise wherein we define an `slist` variable `lines_match` and assign a list of regular expressions which need to be matched. After this we defined a class `replace_patterns`, which defines that the lines matching the regular expressions assigned to the slist variable `lines_match` should be prefixed with `#`.

Have a go hero – doing more with the thing

Write a promises file list all the users in the Active Directory. The user's information is stored in a LDAP directory. We just need to get the list of users by querying the LDAP directory server.

Hint: You may use the `ldaplist` function.

Pop quiz

1. When will the special function classify return true?
    a. When a class has been defined previously
    b. When a promise can be classified into a previously defined category
    c. When the canonicalization of the argument is a currently defined class
    d. When a regular expression provided as an argument matches a currently defined class
2. Which special function may be used to get a list of hosts which may have contacted the current host's CFEngine?
    a. hostrange
    b. hostsseen
    c. hostinnetgroup
    d. irange
3. In CFEngine, how can you check whether a command given was executed successfully?
    a. Function `execresult` gives the exit status
    b. `cf-agent` does not throw and error after executing the promise
    c. Function `returnszero` gives the exit status
    d. `cf-promises` does not throw and error when we try to verify the promises file before execution

Summary

In this chapter we familiarized ourselves with the CFEngine built-in special functions and variables. We learned about:

- The syntax for various functions that were categorized on the basis of what output they provide
- What the special variables store and how we may use this while writing the promises file
- Writing tasks with the use of native special functions and variables so that promise execution is quicker
- What a context for a variable is and what all context variables are available with CFEngine

We learned about a number of special functions and variables provided by CFEngine. Now we need to follow a few best practices while writing the configurations and while using the promises so that the configurations are self explanatory, generic, extensible, and easily understandable by others. Let's see a few such best practices that may be followed while writing the configuration files in *Chapter 9, CFEngine Best Practices*.

9
CFEngine Best Practices

We have been writing promises to achieve various objectives in the last eight chapters. When we are working in teams, there may be various administrators who might write CFEngine promises to automate tasks. To ensure that the promises are written methodically, can be easily deciphered by other members of the team, are crisp, and optimally written, there are various suggestions—these suggestions or recommendations form the best practices for writing CFEngine promises.

In this chapter, we will learn about:

- A few basic considerations while writing the CFEngine promises
- General do's and don'ts while writing policy files
- Version control for the policy files
- Delegating responsibility

Each organization has its own security policy, device nomenclature, and compliance standards to follow. These policies form the basis of how we manage the hosts and networks. You may refer to the CFEngine forum and the mailing list for specific recommendations by the CFEngine community at the following URLs:

- `https://cfengine.com/forum/`
- `https://cfengine.org/pipermail/help-cfengine/`

Let's look at a few generic recommendations which may be used "as is" across networks while writing promises and recommendations for writing promises.

Basic considerations while writing CFEngine promises

In order to maintain consistency while handling a large number of configuration files, defining bundles or methods, defining variables, or classes, and following a self descriptive bundle naming mechanism, the following recommendations should be considered:

- CFEngine policy files management: As we come across a huge number of small and big tasks that need to be automated, we use the CFEngine promises file to automate them. This results in a good number of `.cf` files under the CFEngine work directory. Managing these files may become a daunting task as the number of files grows. Therefore, we should always try to put a hierarchy of files in place. The files should be arranged in a hierarchy which is easy to traverse for a casual user. For example, you may create folders basis the services and write files affecting the service to the folder. In a scenario where you manage a multi location data center, you may create location specific parent folders, break them to service specific folders, and write the files affecting the services to these folders. In addition to providing a better policy management, this also helps in efficient updating of files, as fewer files need to be checked. In addition to this, the convention which should be followed while naming the policy files should easily identify the task for which the policy file has been written. The following screenshot shows one such simple hierarchy:

```
root@my1[/var/cfengine/inputs]# ls */*|more
application-configs/access_logs_copy_template.cf
application-configs/apache_log_audit.cf
application-configs/apache_stats.cf
application-configs/apache-unhash.cf
application-configs/commenting_lines.cf
application-configs/installjailkit.cf
application-configs/MySQL_template.cf
application-configs/rotate-logs.cf
application-configs/Vhost_config.cf
application-configs/web_blacklist.cf
application-configs/webmonitor.cf
host-configs/housekeeping.cf
host-configs/load-report.cf
host-configs/network-interface-configure.cf
host-configs/nfs-exports.cf
host-configs/OSinstall.cf
host-configs/portcheck.cf
host-configs/self-heal.cf
host-configs/servers_responding.cf
host-configs/ssh_deny.cf
```

- **Naming convention for CFEngine bundles**: Choosing a relevant name for a bundle is another aspect which makes identifying the task easier for which the promise bundle has been written. The name of the promise bundle should be such that it easily identifies the context, service, and the subject heading. For example, one of the policy file we used in *Chapter 2, Configuring Systems with CFEngine* was `network-interface-configure.cf` which clearly defines the task that this file is going to perform, which is configuring the network interface. Similarly, another promises file we used was `addusergroup.cf`, which clearly specifies that the promises file can be used for adding user and group on a host.
- **When to make a bundle**: CFEngine bundles help to isolate subtasks which contribute to a bigger task or work flow. It is very important to decide when and which promises need to be put in a single bundle. The following rules of thumb may be followed:
    - Promises for tasks or services that do not need to be switched on or off independently should be put in a single bundle.
    - Promises for tasks that contextually perform the same task or contribute to a similar task.
    - Promises for tasks that need to be verified before all the promises in another bundle should be put in different bundles.
    - If you want to reuse the promises with different parameters—they should be put in a separate bundle.
    - In addition to these rules, we should aim for keeping the number of bundles to a minimum. If we use the concept of bundles judiciously, then we can actually bring in a lot of clarity, and this also helps in knowledge management.
- **Use of a parameterized bundle or method**: If there is a sequence of tasks that need to be executed for a list of promisers, then use a bundle. For example, if you want to execute task1, task2, task3, and more, for a list of promisers, then use a bundle to define the list of promisers and a separate bundle to define the tasks that need to be performed for each of the promisers. Here is an example:

```
bundle agent check_permissions
{
  vars:
    "list_users" string => { "clark","peter","bruce" };
  methods:
    "any" usebundle => check_homedir_permissions("$(list_users)");
}
bundle agent check_homedir_permissions (user)
{
  files:
```

```
    "/home/$user/"
    comment => "Checking permissions for user's home directory";
    create => "true";
    perms => m("0755");
  }
```

- **Defining variables and classes**: The variables should be defined as close as possible to where they are used. If the variable is specific to a bundle, then it should be defined in the bundle primarily. If the variable stores a generic or global data, then it should be defined in a common bundle. For example, a variable defining a well known Unix or Windows path should be defined under the common bundle, as it will be accessed globally. Please note that CFEngine variables are accessible globally through their fully qualified name, which is of the format `$(bundle.variable)` or `@(bundle.variable)`.
- Classes that need to be accessed in multiple bundles should be defined in the common bundle which has a global scope.
- Variables that need to be accessed by multiple bundles should be defined under the common bundle.
- Variables should be defined in the current bundle in the following scenarios:
    - If it is not needed outside the current bundle
    - If they are used for iteration
    - If they are being used for a specific task being defined by the bundle

General do's and don'ts while writing policies

There are number of things that should be done and should not be done when you are managing your entire infrastructure using CFEngine. Given next are a few recommendations for things that you should and should not do. Although these recommendations are generic, it may vary from organization to organization.

- Always verify that a change in the policy is working as per your expectation.
- In previous chapters, we have already seen that CFEngine can work as a centralized job scheduler. For this, create relevant time classes which may then be used for job scheduling. This way, it is easier to track jobs which are running and you may use all your groups and user-defined classes to define which hosts run what programs. In addition to this, you get an improved control and security provided by CFEngine. Finally, CFEngine can provide collated and summarized outputs from multiple tasks for reporting and monitoring purposes.

- One should never embed simple shell commands with CFEngine commands promises. For example, one should never embed the `rm` command into CFEngine policy files. This is because shell commands cannot be managed by CFEngine and thus, the security provided by CFEngine does not apply to these commands. Additionally, shell commands start a new process which may put additional load on the system resources. Therefore, always try to use the CFEngine's native promises, functions, and variables to achieve your objective.
- The preceding recommendations also apply for custom written scripts which you may want to embed to a CFEngine policy file. Again, try to achieve the objective using the native promises, functions, and tools provided by CFEngine.
- CFEngine has an adaptive locking mechanism for system protection which should be used wherever possible. For example, setting the `ifelapsed` time to `0` means the system tries to execute the promises for an infinite duration, and this is not what is expected. This may put additional load on system resources, block other promises from execution, and put the system in an undesired state for a long time.
- One of the major resource hogging operations is searching for a file or files across the disk. However, if you have to do it, try combining operations in a single promise. This way, the resources are used optimally.
- Changes to a policy are an ongoing process and depend on the ever-changing needs of the infrastructure. We should always try to break down large and high-impact changes into small and low impact changes. Always try to make many small changes rather than fewer large changes. This is because large changes have more interdependencies and hence, have a higher probability of a failure. Smaller changes can be easily isolated and fault detection is easier. Moreover, CFEngine is unaffected by the number of changes.
- Always try to document the promises by adding a comment that is helpful in knowledge management or by maintaining separate documentation. If the promise depends on another promise to be run, then use the `depends_on` promisee. Here is an example:

```
bundle agent example_for_documentation
{
  files:
    "/home/user/test"
    handle => "change_owner",
    comment => "Changing ownership of the folder",
    create => "true",
    owners => { "$(user)" };

    "/home/user/test/example.php"
    depends_on => { "change_owner" },
    comment => "Changing permissions for the file",
```

```
    create => "true",
    perms => m("644");
}
```

- Use the CFEngine language while defining promises. This is the best way to utilize all the features provided by CFEngine.
- If you want to make the same promises for multiple objects use lists, then this is how it is done:

```
bundle agent example
{
  vars:
    "users_list" => { "clark","peter","bruce" };
  classes:

    "exists" expression =>
      fileexists("/home/$(users_list)/mailbox");
  reports:
  exists::
  "File exists";
}
```

- CFEngine provides a number of predefined templates in the file named `cfengine_stdlib.cf`. These are generic and may be included anywhere. One just needs to include the file named `cfengine_stdlib.cf` under the common bundle. This helps in standardizing policies and the other CFEngine users can understand it easily. The following is a sample predefined template in `cfengine_stdlib.cf`:

```
body edit_field quoted_var(newval,method)

{

  field_separator => "\"";

  select_field    => "2";

  value_separator  => " ";

  field_value     => "$(newval)";

  field_operation => "$(method)";

  extend_fields => "false";

  allow_blank_fields => "true";

}
```

Now the preceding template has been taken from `cfengine_stdlib.cf` and can be quoted directly anywhere in the policy file. We just need to include the `cfengine_stdlib.cf` file.

- There are a number of system variables provided by CFEngine that may store values for various system resources. This is done in CFEngine through a `sys` variable context. These variables are operating system and user dependent. Therefore, the same set of promises may be run on hosts with different operating systems and hence, the policies are more portable. Here is an example:

```
bundle agent example_sys_variable_usage
{
  files:
    "$(sys.resolv)"
    comment => "Adding name servers to the system resolver file",
    create => "true",
    edit_line => nameservers,
    edit_defaults => "test";
}
bundle edit_line nameservers
{
  insert_lines:
    "Generated by Network Manager" location => start;
    "nameserver  121.121.121.121";
    "nameserver  123.123.123.123";
}
```

- We should always use variables as pointers to paths and servers. We should avoid coding paths and the name of resources directly in the policy files. Instead, we should use the global variable as a pointer to the resource. For example, instead of coding the path for the default CFEngine working directory `/var/cfengine` everywhere, we should use the `$(sys.workdir)` variable as follows:

```
bundle agent example_variables
{
  vars:
    "repo_files_location" string  =>
      "$(sys.workdir)/repo-policy-file";
}
```

Policy changes

Policy changes should always be taken seriously and a lot of thought should go into making policy changes. We need to understand that policy changes are a necessity due to the ever-changing requirements of the infrastructure and hence, it should be planned well and should be made as simple as possible. In order to ensure proper change management, the following recommendations may be considered:

- Always try to break big policy changes into smaller, isolated, and doable changes or tasks.
- Prepare a schedule for the start and completion of each task.
- The role of all the team members should be clearly defined.
- Before starting with the changes, ensure that all necessary software, components, scripts, and additional hardware, if needed, are handy.
- All new items for the policy release should be easily identifiable. This helps in quicker fault detection.
- The changes should always be documented either by putting comments or by maintaining a separate documentation.
- Always test the policy changes in a test environment if it is available.
- If possible, we should again verify the policy changes on a selected low impact group of servers. This is recommended to iron out issues related to communications on WAN.

Version control for policy files

It is recommended to add a version version number to each policy file. Although CFEngine does not provide a native version control system, one may use other version control systems, such as subversion, for this. We can add a version number to a policy file in the following way:

```
body common control
{
  version => "1.0.0";
}
```

This version number is quoted in all messages from CFEngine. When CFEngine saves the current version of a file which it is modifying or replacing, the file is given a new extension and is saved in the same directory. If one does not want this, but want to maintain a separate repository for these files, then one may specify the repository location as follows:

```
body agent control
{
  default_repository => "/var/cfengine/repo-policy";
}
```

When we specify the repository location, the files are copied to this location before it is modified or replaced. The name that is given to these files reflects their complete path with "/" or "\" replaced by an underscore. Once you have the version number for all files, you may perform a rollback of policies by simply providing the version number. CFEngine's change management is not based on transactions, it is based on convergence to a known system end-state.

Delegation of responsibility

As more and more systems and applications are added to the network, we need to delegate the responsibility of managing a specific group of servers to specific teams. This means different groups will be writing promises for various tasks for a group of servers allocated to them. This may lead to a lot of confusion as there is no control mechanism which may decide who can write policy rules for which issue. CFEngine currently does not provide such a mechanism. Still, CFEngine proposes the following solution:

- Delegate the responsibility for different issues to different teams and then:
    - Each of these teams should maintain the version control for their own policy files.
    - An intermediate agent should be responsible for checking these policy files, conflicts, irregularities, and merging these rules the main CFEngine repository. The agent should also ensure that members of one team should not be able to write rules for issues that are the responsibility of other teams.
    - Once the policy files are successfully merged to the main repository after the verification, they can then be published for all hosts.
    - In addition to this, the policies should be periodically reviewed.

The preceding mechanism is a simple control mechanism which may involve a team or software as an intermediate agent. In this mechanism, the verifying agent is most important and owns the complete responsibility of managing the policy files from different resources and avoiding conflicts. The following diagram shows the complete flow just discussed:

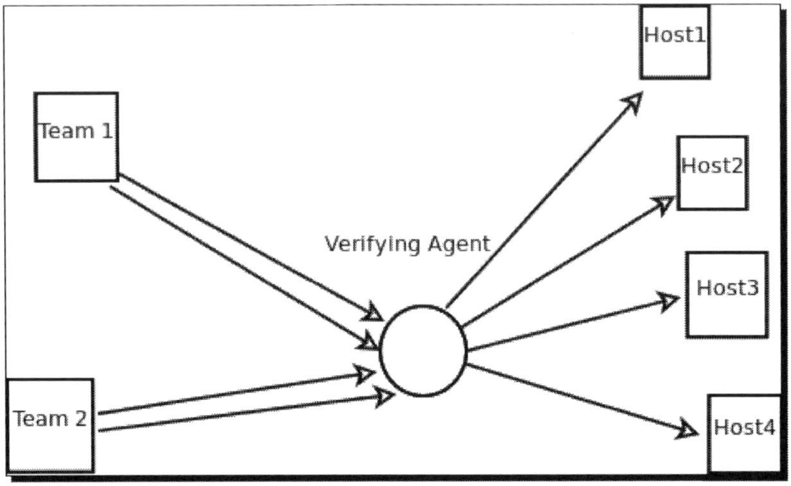

Pop quiz

1. Name the theory on which the repair and rollback mechanism for CFEngine is based.
   a. Baseline and recipe
   b. Promise theory
   c. The law of least commons
   d. Theory of convergence to end state

2. You have a variable defined as `bundle.variable`; if we refer to this as `@(bundle.variable)` somewhere else, it refers to:
   a. Individual values of the list variable are requested
   b. Variables from the list having `@` at their start are requested
   c. The complete list
   d. Variables from the list having `@` anywhere

Summary

In this chapter, we learned about:

- Under what conditions a new bundle should be added to the policy file and what tasks should be clubbed in a bundle
- The generic criterion on the basis of which new classes, variables, and so on should be defined and where they should be defined
- A generic list of do's and don'ts
- The importance of version control, rollback mechanism, delegation of responsibility, and planning the policy changes

A
CFEngine Cloud Pack—Orion

Cloud computing offers various operating system and application platforms as a service. It is a new consumption and delivery model for IT services based on Internet protocols. It typically involves provisioning of dynamically scalable and often virtualized resources. Management of a cloud infrastructure is done using web-based tools or applications which can be accessed by a user through a web browser. CFEngine, capable of installing, maintaining, and repairing systems, has come out with an excellent product for managing cloud instances, named **Orion Cloud Pack**. *The* **CFEngine Orion Cloud Pack** *has been specifically written to work with* **Amazon Elastic Compute Cloud** *(***Amazon EC2***). The software enables you to configure server instances running services in a reproducible and maintainable way.*

The Orion Cloud Pack is not a tool that will help you with scaling the compute cloud; it will only help you to speedily install multiple consistent Amazon instances. The beauty of the software is that you can use it with any other non-cloud systems which run the recommended base operating systems.

Below are the prerequisites for installing the Orion Cloud Pack.

- An Amazon web services account.
- A running **Amazon Machine Instance** (**AMI**). It is a preconfigured OS image which is available on demand. You may create your own images using the tools provided by Amazon web services.
- A running CFEngine server. This may be an Enterprise CFEngine server or a Community Edition CFEngine server. The Orion Cloud Pack comes free with the CFEngine Enterprise Server. If you are using a Community Edition CFEngine server, the Orion Cloud Pack can be used for a free trial for 30 days.
- A CFEngine Orion Cloud Pack.

Here are the steps for configuring the Orion Cloud Pack on a running Amazon Machine Instance:

1. Copy the CFEngine Orion Cloud Pack onto your running EC2 instance and unpack the files in `/var/cfengine/`.
2. You may want to edit the master file `promises.cf`. The default promises construct a PHP enabled server. You also need to specify the IP address for the master policy server. This can be done as follows:

   ```
   root@my.aws.system.com# echo "<IP-address>" > /var/cfengine/
   policy_server.dat
   ```

   You will also need to fill in the IP address for the `policy_server` variable in `update.cf` and `promises.cf`.
3. You can start the CFEngine agent by executing the following command:

   ```
   root@my.aws.system.com# cf-agent -f /var/cfengine/masterfiles/
   failsafe.cf
   ```

4. Now you have a running CFEngine instance.

The Orion Cloud Pack's contents

Once you unpack the Orion Cloud Pack you will see a number of files which may be categorized in three categories as follows:

1. **Essential files**:
   - `promises.cf`—Main configuration file
   - `update.cf`—Update configuration
   - `failsafe.cf`—Failsafe configuration
   - `cfengine_stdlib.cf`—Standard CFEngine library file
2. **Maintenance examples**:
   - `change_mgt.cf`—Implement security tripwire on files or directories
   - `ensure_ownership.cf`—Home directory ownership and permission maintenance
   - `fix_broken_software`—Package installation and permission correction
   - `garbage_collection.cf`—Log rotation and removal
   - `harden_xinetd.cf`—Disable `xinetd` services specified
   - `iptables.cf`—Secure system with `sysctl.conf` and `iptables`
   - `name_resolution.cf`—Edit `/etc/resolv.conf` with the required DNS servers

3. **System setup examples**:
    - c_cpp_env.cf—Set up C programming environment
    - db_mysql.cf—Install and run MySQL
    - db_postgresql—Install and run PostgreSQL
    - db_sqllite.cf—Install and run SQLlite
    - jboss_server.cf—Prepare JAVA environment and run JBOSS
    - nagios.cf—Set up a nagios monitoring node
    - nginx_perlcgi.cf—Set up a nginx webserver perlCGI
    - nginx_phpcgi.cf—Set up nginx webserver phpCGI
    - ntp.cf—Set up NTP server and clients
    - perl_env.cf—PERL programming language installation
    - php_webserver.cf—Set up a PHP web server
    - python_env.cf—Python programming installation
    - ruby_env.cf—Set up a Ruby on Rails environment
    - sshd_conf.cf—Ensure that your sshd configuration is correct
    - tomcat_server.cf—Set up a tomcat server
    - varnish.cf—Set up a Varnish web accelerator

The Orion Cloud Pack hacks

In the Orion Cloud Pack all bundles are listed in a single bundlesequence, making it simpler to choose the desired services by commenting or uncommenting the bundles. Additionally, you can also create newer bundles by combining available bundles. For this we can create a single agent bundle and call other bundles as method promises. For instance, you may want to have different groups of servers supporting different platforms. For example, you may want a group of servers as web servers and another group of servers as database servers. Let's see an example of how this can be done:

```
body common control
{
bundlesequence => { "WebServer","DBServers" };
}
bundle agent WebServer
{
methods:

web_servers::
```

```
"nginx_servers" usebundle => nginx_phpcgi;
app_servers::
"Tomcat_servers" usebundle => tomcat_server;
}

bundle agent DBServers
{
methods:

Db_mys_severs::
"mysql_servers" usebundle => db_mysql;

DB_postgre_servers::
"postgres_servers" usebundle => db_postgresql;
}
```

If you observe carefully, this approach gives greater control over the execution of bundles.

Advantages of running Orion Cloud Pack on CFEngine Nova

If you are using the enterprise edition of CFEngine Nova, the Orion Cloud Pack comes bundled for free, and here are a few of the advantages of using the Cloud Pack with the enterprise edition CFEngine:

1. Your organization's compliance policy gets automatically integrated with every new instance once you start using the Cloud Pack, and hence compliance reporting for a huge number of virtual instances becomes a lot easier.
2. CFEngine Nova's enhanced monitoring and reporting features are available for all new virtual instances that are created using the Cloud Pack without any further configuration or third party software.
3. CFEngine's knowledge management features are automatically configured for all instances using the Cloud Pack.
4. CFEngine Nova's database promises can be used by instances configured using the Cloud Pack without any further configurations.

B

Important Control Promises

In continuation of the knowledge gained in Chapter 3, System Audit with CFEngine let's see a few more common control promises.

Common control promises

- **ignore_missing_bundles**
  - Type: Menu option
  - Allowed input range: true, false, yes, no, on, off
  - Default value: false

  This control parameter tells CFEngine to continue even if a few bundles mentioned in the *bundlesequence* do not exist. The default value is false so that parsing undefined bundles cause a fatal error and you are able to review the promises.

- **version**
  - Type: String
  - Allowed input range: (arbitrary string)

The version control parameter is used to specify a scalar version string for the configuration. This version string is used in error messages and reports. This string should not contain `:` because this has special meaning in the context of knowledge management. The usage is as follows:

```
body common control
{
version => "3.15.18";
}
```

- **lastseenexpireafter**
    - Type: int
    - Allowed input range: 0-99999999999
    - Default value: One week

This control parameter defines the number of minutes after which the last-seen entries are purged. Here is an example where we specify the `lastseenexpireafter` time as `72` minutes.

```
body common control
{
lastseenexpireafter => "72";
}
```

The information regarding the peers which were last seen is stored in db file `cf_Lastseen.db`.

- **domain**
    - Type: String
    - Allowed input range: .*

The `domain` control parameter is used to specify a domain to the host. The data type is string and there is no default value as an arbitrary string may be assigned to a host. Here is how the domain `my1.system.com` that we have been using in the previous two chapters may be assigned to the host:

```
body common control
{
domain =>  "my1.system.com";
}
```

- **require_comments**
    - Type: Menu option
    - Allowed input range: true, false, yes, no, on, off
    - Default value: false

When this control parameter is set, CFEngine reports on promises that do not have comments. This can be used to set a quality assurance measure for policy makers so that the promises they write have proper comments. You may set this parameter as follows:

```
body common control
{
require_comments => "true";
}
```

Agent control promises

- **abortclasses**
    - Type: slist
    - Allowed input range: .*

The `abortclasses` promise lists classes which, if defined, lead to the termination of `cf-agent`. You can define it as follows:

```
body agent control
{
abortclasses => { "exit_the_program", "terminate"};
}
```

- **abortbundleclasses**
    - Type: slist
    - Allowed input range: .*

The `abortbundleclass` promise lists classes which, if defined, lead to the termination of the current bundle.

- **addclasses**
    - Type: slist
    - Allowed input range: .*

The `addclasses` promise lists a series of classes which are to be defined always in the correct context. It is used to add global literal classes.

```
any::
   addclasses => { "web_server" };

dbserver::
{
addclasses => { "MySQL_db", "Oracle_db" };
```

```
}
```

- **agentaccess**
    - Type: slist
    - Allowed input range: .*

The `agentaccess` promise is used to list the name of users who are allowed to run `cf-agent`. The next example allows the users `clark`, `peter`, and `bruce` to execute the current configuration with `cf-agent`:

```
agentaccess => { "clark", "peter", "bruce" };
```

- **agentfacility**
    - Type: Menu option
    - Allowed input range:

```
LOG_USER, LOG_DAEMON, LOG_LOCAL0,
LOG_LOCAL1, LOG_LOCAL2, LOG_LOCAL3,
LOG_LOCAL4, LOG_LOCAL5, LOG_LOCAL6,
LOG_LOCAL7
```

`agentfacility` is used to set the agent's *syslog* facility. It also sets the *syslog* level. This is not available on Microsoft Windows as it uses event logs. The syntax is as follows:

```
agentfacility => "LOG_LOCAL3"
```

- **auditing**
    - Type: Menu option
    - Allowed input range: true, false, yes, no, on, off
    - Default value: false

The auditing promise is used to enable or disable the CFEngine auditing promises in the current configuration. If this is enabled, all details regarding the verification of the current promise are recorded in the audit database. This database may be inspected using `cf-report`. The following example shows how to enable it:

```
body agent control
{
auditing => "On";
}
```

- **binarypaddingchar**
  - Type: string
  - Allowed input range: (arbitrary string)
  - Default value: space (ASC=32)

This agent control promise is used to pad unequal replacements during binary editing. CFEngine will not allow replacements that are larger in size than the original but shorter strings can be padded out to the same length. The following example shows how to use this:

```
body agent control
{
binarypaddingchar => "@";
}
```

- **checksum_alert_time**
  - Type: int
  - Allowed input range: 0-60 minutes
  - Default value: 10 minutes

This promise defines the persistence time for the `checksum_alert` classes. The following example shows how to set this duration:

```
body agent control
{
checksum_alert_time => "20";
}
```

- **max_children**
  - Type: int
  - Allowed input range: 0-9999999999
  - Default value: 1 concurrent agent promise

For the run agent this represents the maximum number of background child processes when parallelizing connection to servers. The default value is only one concurrent process. This can be specified as follows:

```
body agent control
{
max_children => "3";
}
```

- **mountfilesystems**
  - Type: Menu option
  - Allowed input range: true, false, yes, no, on, off
  - Default value: false

If this promise is set to 'true' CFEngine issues the generic command to mount the file systems defined in the file system table. This can be enabled as follows:

```
body agent control
{
mountfilesystems => "true";
}
```

- **default_repository**
  - Type: string
  - Allowed input range: "?(([a-zA-Z]:\\.*)|(/.*))

The `default_repository` is used to specify the location where versions of files altered by CFEngine are stored. The location may be specified as follows:

```
body agent control
{
default_repository => "/var/cfengine/repo"
}
```

This directory may be backed up to keep a track of CFEngine file changes.

- **secureinput**
  - Type: Menu option
  - Allowed input range: true, false, yes, no, on off
  - Default value: false

If this promise is set, CFEngine will not accept an input file which is not owned by a privileged user. This can be enabled as follows:

```
body agent control
{
secureinput => "true";
}
```

- **syslog**
    - Type: Menu option
    - Allowed input range: true, false, yes, no, on, off
    - Default value: false

The `syslog` control promise may be used to switch `syslog` logging on or off. If this is set the `syslog` outputs logs at the inform level. This can be switched on as follows:

```
body agent test
{
syslog => "true";
}
```

- **default_timeout**
    - Type: int
    - Allowed input range: 0-9999999999
    - Default value: 10 seconds

This control parameter is used to define the maximum time in seconds that a network connection should attempt to connect. The value can be set as follows:

```
body agent control
{
default_timeout => "30";
}
```

- **timezone**
    - Type: slist
    - Allowed input range: (arbitrary string)

This control promise is used to specify a list of time zones with which the system must comply. The time zones may be listed as follows:

```
body agent control
{
timezone => { "GMT", "EST" };
}
```

- **skipidentify**
    - Type: Menu option
    - Allowed input range: true, false, yes, no, on, off
    - Default value: false

Often, a host may not have a proper DNS resolution, which may break the execution of promises. This control promise allows CFEngine to ignore the missing DNS credentials for a host. The agent can be told to skip the error in DNS resolution for a host as follows:

```
body agent control
{
skipidentify => "true";
}
```

- **track_value**
    - Type: Menu option
    - Allowed input range: true, false, yes, no, on off
    - Default value: off

This control parameter is used for tracking the promise valuation. If this is set to true, it generates a log in `$WORKDIR/state/cf_value.log` of the estimated `business value` of automation. The format of the file is:

```
date, sum_value_kept, sum_value_repaired, sum_value_notkept
```

This control parameter may be set as follows:

```
body agent control
{
track_value => "true";
}
```

Server Control promises

- **dynamicaddresses**
  - Type: slist
  - Allowed input range: (arbitrary string)

The `dynamicaddresses` server control promise is used for specifying a list of IP addresses or host names for which the host name or IP address binding is expected to change. The list can be specified as follows:

```
body server control
{
dynamicaddresses => { "dhcp.mysystem.*" };
}
```

- **logallconnections**
  - Type: Menu option
  - Allowed input range: true, false, yes, no, on, off
  - Default value: false

If this server control promise is set to 'yes', then the CFEngine server logs all new connection to `syslog`. This facility may be enabled as follows:

```
body server control
{
logallconnections => "true";
}
```

- **logencryptedtransfers**
  - Type: Menu option
  - Allowed input range: true, false, yes, no, on, off
  - Default value: false

If this is set to true, then the server logs all encrypted transfer of files. Files that are being transferred in an encrypted format are usually the ones that have sensitive information. This can be set to true as follows:

```
body server control
{
logencryptedtransfers => "true";
```

C
Important Functions and Variables

With the knowledge gained in Chapter 7, Workflows, let's move to more granular aspects of CFEngine and learn a few special functions and variables that could be very handy.

- **generate_manual**
  - Type: Menu option
  - Allowed input range: yes, no, true, false, on, off
  - Default value: false

  This knowledge control promise, if enabled, generates `texinfo` manual pages. The promise can be enabled as follows:

```
body knowledge control
{
generate_manual => "true";
}
```

- **graph_directory**
  - Type: string
  - Allowed input range: "?(([a-zA-Z]:\\.*)|(/.*))

  The knowledge control promise `graph_directory` is used to define the path to the directory where rendered `.png` files will be created. The path may be defined as follows:

```
body knowledge control
{
graph_directory => "/var/cfengine/graphs";
}
```

- **graph_output**
  - Type: Menu option
  - Allowed input range: true, false, yes, no, on, off

This knowledge control promise is used to enable the `.png` visualization of a topic map. It requires GraphViz libraries. The generation of visualizations can be enabled as follows:

```
body knowledge control
{
graph_output => "true";
}
```

- **html_banner**
  - Type: string
  - Allowed input range: (arbitrary string)

This knowledge control promise is used to define HTML code for a banner to be added to the rendered HTML after the header. This can be added as follows:

```
body knowledge control
{
html_banner => "<img src=\"http://my.webserver.com/images/banner.
png\">";
}
```

- **html_footer**
  - Type: string
  - Allowed input range: (arbitrary string)

This knowledge control promise is used to define the HTML code for a page footer which is to be added to the rendered HTML before the end body tag. This can be added as follows:

```
body knowledge control
{
html_footer => "<div id=\"footer\">">Cfengine Topic Map<\div>
}
```

- **id_prefix**
  - Type: string
  - Allowed input range: .*

The `id_prefix` knowledge control promise is used to define the identifier prefix used to label topic maps. This is helpful in disambiguating identifiers when merging the topic maps, especially in Linear Topic Map format. This prefix can be provided as follows:

```
body knowledge control
{
id_prefix => "Redhat";
}
```

- **query_output**
  - Type: Menu option
  - Allowed input range: HTML, text

The `query_output` knowledge control promise is used to define the format for the generated output. This can be defined as follows:

```
body knowledge control
{
query_output => "html";
}
```

- **sql_type**
  - Type: Menu option
  - Allowed input range: mysql, postgres

The `sql_type` knowledge control promise is used to define the database type which can be used. This can be defined as follows:

```
body knowledge control
{
sql_type => "mysql";
}
```

- **sql_database**
  - Type: string
  - Allowed input range: (arbitrary string)

This knowledge control promise is used to define the database that is to be used for topic maps. The database may be defined as follows:

```
body knowledge control
{
sql_database => "topic_map_db";
}
```

- **sql_owner**
    - Type: string
    - Allowed input range: (arbitrary string)

The `sql_owner` knowledge control promise is used to define the user id for the database defined by the `sql_database` promise. The user id can be specified as follows:

```
body knowledge control
{
sql_owner => "clark";
}
```

- **sql_passwd**
    - Type: string
    - Allowed input range: (arbitrary string)

This knowledge control promise is used for specifying the password for accessing the SQL database. This can be specified as follows:

```
body knowledge control
{
sql_passwd => "secret";
}
```

- **sql_server**
    - Type: string
    - Allowed input range: (arbitrary string)

This knowledge control promise is used to define the name or IP address for the database server. By default CFEngine tries to connect to the localhost. This can be specified as follows:

```
body knowledge control
{
sql_server => "192.168.2.200";
}
```

- **sql_connection_db**
    - Type: string
    - Allowed input range: (arbitrary string)

The above knowledge control promise is used to define the name of an existing database to connect to for creating other databases. This database can be defined as shown below

```
body knowledge control
{
sql_connection_db => "mysql";
}
```

- **style_sheet**
    - Type: string
    - Allowed input range: (arbitrary string)

The knowledge control promise `style_sheet` is used to define the name of the style sheet to be used in rendering HTML output. The name of the style sheet may be defined as follows:

```
body knowledge control
{
style_sheet => "http://my.webserver.com/css/stylesheet.css"
}
```

- **view_projections**
    - Type: Menu option
    - Allowed input range: true, false, yes, no, on, off

This knowledge control promise is used to enable or disable view-projection analysis in graph generation. If this is enabled, CFEngine computes additional representation for dependencies between CFEngine promises. This can be enabled as follows:

```
body knowledge control
{
view_projections => "true";
}
```

- **associates**
    - Type: slist
    - Allowed input range: (arbitrary string)

This promise is used to define a list of associated topics by this forward relationship. The associates may be defined as follows:

```
body association test(topic1, topic2, topic3)
{
associates => { "topic1", "topic2", "topic3"};
}
```

- **web_root**
  - Type: string
  - Allowed input range: (arbitrary string)

  This promise is used to define the base URL for the occurrence when rendered as a web URL.

- **path_root**
  - Type: string
  - Allowed input range: (arbitrary string)

  This promise is used to define the base path for the occurrence when the occurrence is defined in a file system.

D
Functions by Usage

Let's learn about some important functions based on their usage.

Functions for capturing the environment

- **getenv**
  - Usage: gentenv(arg0,arg1)
  - arg0 : Name of the environment variable, in the range [a-zA-Z0-9_$()\[\].]+
  - arg1 : Maximum number of characters to read, in the range 0-99999999999

  This special function returns a string. It returns the environment variable named `arg1` and truncated by `arg2` characters. The string is truncated to the number of characters to avoid returning an unexpectedly large value.

Functions that read files

- **getfields**
  - Usage: getfields(arg0,arg1,arg2,arg3)
  - arg0: Regular expression to match line, in the range .*
  - arg1: Filename to read, in the range "?(([a-zA-Z]:\\.*)|(/.*))
  - arg2: Regular expressions to split fields, in the range .*
  - arg3: Return array name, in the range .*

- **peers**
  - Usage: peers(arg0,arg1,arg2)
  - arg0: File name of host list, in the range "?(([a-zA-Z]:\\.*)|(/.*))
  - arg1: Comment regex pattern, in the range .*
  - arg2: Peer group size, in the range 0-99999999999

  This function is used to get a list of peers, not including yourself, from the partition to which we belong. It returns a list of host names after reading the host names from a file, which may be considered peers of the current host. The file contains a fully qualified host name per line which is broken into peer group sized groups as specified by `arg2`.

- **peerleader**
  - Usage: peerleader(arg0,arg1,arg2)
  - arg0: File name of host list, in the range "?(([a-zA-Z]:\\.*)|(/.*))
  - arg1: Comment regex pattern, in the range .*
  - arg2: Peer group size, in the range 0-99999999999

  This function is used to get the `peerleader` of the partition to which we belong. It returns the name of the host that may be considered the leader of a group of peers of the current host. The host names are again read from a file which has a fully qualified domain name for each host per line. CFEngine then breaks the list into smaller groups based on the `groupsize` specified by `arg2`. The first host in each group is considered as the `peerleader`.

- **peerleaders**
  - Usage: peerleaders(arg0,arg1,arg2)
  - arg0: File name of host list, in the range "?(([a-zA-Z]:\\.*)|(/.*))
  - arg1: Comment regex pattern, in the range .*
  - arg2: Peer group size, in the range 0-99999999999

  This function returns a list of peer leaders from the named partitioning. The following example explains how peers are discovered and grouped:

```
bundle agent my_peers
{
vars:
"group"  slist => peers("/opt/list_hosts","#.*",6);
"leader" string => peerleader("/opt/list_hosts","#.*",6);
"leaders" string => peerleaders("/opt/list_hosts","#.*",6);

report:
```

```
linux::
"mypeer $(group)";
"mypeerleader $(leader)";
"all leaders $(leaders)";
}
```

- **readfile**
  - Usage: readfile(arg0,arg1)
  - arg0: File name, in the range "?(([a-zA-Z]:\\.*)|(/.*))
  - arg1: Maximum number of bytes to be read, in the range 0-99999999999

This function reads the number of bytes specified by `arg1` from the file specified by `arg0` and assigns them to a variable. The next example shows how the function may be used:

```
bundle agent example
vars:
'strip_data'
string => readfile( "/home/clark/test", "15");
```

- **readintlist**
  - Usage: readintlist(arg0,arg1,arg2,arg3,arg4)
  - arg0: File name to be read, in the range "?(([a-zA-Z]:\\.*)|(/.*))
  - arg1: Regex for matching comments, in the range .*
  - arg2: Regex to split data, in the range .*
  - arg3: Maximum number of entries to be read, in the range 0-99999999999
  - arg4: Maximum bytes to read, in the range 0-99999999999

This function is used to read and assign a list of variables from a file containing a list of integers separated by a delimiter.

- **readintarray**
  - Usage: readintarray(arg0,arg1,arg2,arg3,arg4,arg5)
  - arg0: Array identifier to populate, in the range [a-zA-Z0-9_$()\ [\].]+
  - arg1: File name to read, in the range "?(([a-zA-Z]:\\.*)|(/.*))
  - arg2: Regex matching comments in the range .*
  - arg3: Regex to split data, in the range .*
  - arg4: Maximum number of entries to read, in the range 0-99999999999
  - arg5: Maximum bytes to read, in the range 0-99999999999

This function is used to read an array of integers from a file and assign it to variable.

- **readstringlist**
  - Usage: readstringlist(arg0,arg1,arg2,arg3,arg4)
  - arg0: File name to read, in the range "?(([a-zA-Z]:\\.*)|(/.*))
  - arg1: Regex matching comments, in the range .*
  - arg2: Regex to split data, in the range .*
  - arg3: Maximum number of entries to read, in the range 0-99999999999
  - arg4: Maximum bytes to read, in the range 0-99999999999

  This function is used to read from a file of separated strings and assign them to a list variable.

- **regline**
  - Usage: regline(arg0,arg1)
  - arg0: Regular expression, in the range .*
  - arg1: Name of the file to search, in the range .*

  This function returns a class. It returns 'true' if the regular expression specified in arg0 matches a line in the file specified by arg1. The regular expression should match an entire line for the function to return a 'true'.

Functions that look at attributes of the file

- **accessedbefore**
  - Usage: accessedbefore(arg0,arg1)
  - arg0: Newer file name, in the range "?(([a-zA-Z]:\\.*)|(/.*))
  - arg1: Older file name, in the range "?(([a-zA-Z]:\\.*)|(/.*))

  This function returns the class 'true' if access time of the file specified by `arg1` is newer than the access time of the file specified by `arg2`.

- **changedbefore**
  - Usage: changedbefore(arg0,arg1)
  - arg0: Newer file name, in the range "?(([a-zA-Z]:\\.*)|(/.*))
  - arg1: Older file name, in the range "?(([a-zA-Z]:\\.*)|(/.*))

  This function returns the class 'true' if the file specified by `arg1` was changed before the file specified by `arg2`.

- **isdir**
  - Usage: isdir(arg0)
  - arg0: Name of the file object, in the range "?(([a-zA-Z]:\\.*)|(/.*))

This function returns the class 'true' if the object specified by `arg0` is a directory.

- **isplain**
  - Usage: isplain(arg0)
  - arg0: Name of the file object, in the range, "?(([a-zA-Z]:\\.*)|(/.*))

This function returns the class 'true' if the object specified by `arg0` is a regular or plain file.

Functions that read classes

- **classify**
  - Usage: classify(arg0)
  - arg0: Input string, in the range .*

This function returns the class 'true' if the canonicalization of the argument is a currently defined class.

- **classmatch**
  - Usage: classmatch(arg0)
  - arg0: Regular expression, in the range .*

This function returns the class 'true' if the regular expression matches any currently defined classes.

Functions that read from the network

- **readtcp**
  - Usage: readtcp(arg0,arg1,arg2,arg3)
  - arg0: Host name or IP address of the server socket, in the range .*
  - arg1: Port number, in the range 0-99999999999
  - arg2: Protocol query string, in the range .*
  - arg3: Maximum number of bytes to read, in the range 0-99999999999

This function is used to connect to a TCP port, send a string and assign the result to a variable.

Functions that compare variables

- **islessthan**
  - Usage: islessthan(arg0,arg1)
  - arg0: String or value, in the range .*
  - arg1: String or value, in the range .*

  The function returns the class 'true' if `arg1` is numerically less than `arg2`. If the values for `arg1` and `arg2` are not numeric then the values are compared in a manner similar to `strcmp`.

- **isvariable**
  - Usage: isvariable(arg0)
  - arg0: Variable identifier, in the range [a-zA-Z0-9_$()\[\].]+

  This function returns the class 'true' if the variable specified by `arg0` is defined.

Functions that read data from remote CFEngine

- **remoteclassesmatching**
  - Usage: remoteclassesmatching(arg0,arg1,arg2,arg3)
  - arg0: Regular expression, in the range .*
  - arg1: Server host name or IP address, in the range .*
  - arg2: Use encryption, in the range yes, no, true, false, on, off
  - arg3: Return class prefix, in the range [a-zA-Z0-9_$()\[\].]+

  This special function is used to read persistent classes matching a regular expression (`arg0`) from a remote CFEngine server (`arg1`) and add them to the local context with the prefix (`arg3`).

- **remotescalar**
  - Usage: remotescalar(arg0,arg1,arg2)
  - arg0: Variable identifier, in the range [a-zA-Z0-9_$()\[\].]+
  - arg1: Host name of IP address of the remote server, in the range .*
  - arg2: Use encryption. The values may be true, false, yes, no, on, off

  This function is used to read a scalar value from a remote CFEngine server.

Function that read strings

- **regextract**
    - Usage: regextract(arg0,arg1,arg2)
    - arg0: Regular expression, in the range .*
    - arg1: Match string, in the range .*
    - arg2: Identifier for back-references, in the range [a-zA-Z0-9_$()\[\].]+

  This function returns the class 'true' if the regular expression in `arg1` matches the string in `arg2` and sets a non-empty array of back-references names `arg3`.

- **translatepath**
    - Usage: translatepath(arg0)
    - arg0: Unix style path, in the range [a-zA-Z0-9_$()\[\].]+

  This function takes a UNIX style path string as argument with slashes as path separators and translates it to the native format for path separators on the host. So `translatepath("/x/y/z")` will yield `/x/y/z` on a Unix platform, but `\x\y\z` on Microsoft Windows.

- **hash**
    - Usage: hash(arg0,arg1)
    - arg0: Input text, in the range .*
    - arg1: Hash or digest algorithm. This could be any of the following md5, sha1, sha256, sha512, sha384, crypt

  This function returns a hash of `arg0` of the type `arg1` and assigns it to a variable.

Functions that read LDAP data

- **ldaparray**
    - Usage: (arg0,arg1,arg2,arg3,arg4,arg5)
    - arg0: URI, in the range .*
    - arg1: Distinguished name, in the range .*
    - arg2: Filter, in the range .*

- arg3: Record name, in the range .*
- arg4: Search scope policy; this can have any one of the following values - subtree, one level, base
- arg5: Security level. This can have any one of the following values none, SSL, SASL.

This function is used to retrieve a record with all elements and populates an associative array with the entries. It returns a class which is 'true' if there was a match and 'false' if nothing was retrieved. The following example shows how this function may be used while writing a promises file:

```
bundle agent example
{
classes:
"user_data_ldap" =>
   ldaparray("user_array","ldap://ldap.mysystem.com","dc=mysystemL
LC,dc=com",
     "(uid=clark)","subtree","none")
}
```

- **ldaplist**
  - Usage: ldaplist(arg0,arg1,arg2,arg3,arg4,arg5)
  - arg0: URI, in the range .*
  - arg1: Distinguished name, in the range .*
  - arg2: Filter, in the range .*
  - arg3: Record name, in the range .*
  - arg4: Search scope policy; this can have any one of the following values - subtree, one level, base
  - arg5: Security level; this can have any one of the following values none, SSL, SASL

This function is used to retrieve a single field from all matching LDAP records identified by the search parameters. The following example shows how this can be used while writing a promises file:

```
bundle agent example
{
vars:
"ldap_single_field"  =>
  ldaplist("ldap://ldap.mysystem.com","dc=mysystemLLC,dc=com",
    "sn=User","uid","subtree","none")
};
```

- **ldapvalue**
  - Usage: ldapvalue(arg0,arg1,arg2,arg3,arg4,arg5)
  - arg0: URI, in the range .*
  - arg1: Distinguished name, in the range .*
  - arg2: Filter, in the range .*
  - arg3: Record name, in the range .*
  - arg4: Search scope policy; this can have any one of the following values subtree, one level, base
  - arg5: Security level; this can have any one of the following values - none, SSL, SASL

This function retrieves a single field from the first LDAP record which matches the search parameters specified. The following example shows how this function may be used while writing a promises file:

```
bundle agent example
{
vars:
"first" string =>
  ldapvalue("ldap://ldap.my.system.com","dc=mysystemLLC,dc=com",
    "sn=group","gid","subtree"."none");
}
```

- **regldap**
  - Usage: regldap(arg0,arg1,arg2.arg3,arg4,arg5,arg6)
  - arg0: URI, in the range .*
  - arg1: Distinguished name, in the range .*
  - arg2: Filter, in the range .*
  - arg3: Record name, in the range .*
  - arg4: Search scope policy; this can have any one of the following values - subtree, one level, base
  - arg5: Regex to match results, in the range .*
  - arg6: Security level; this can have any one of the following values - none, SSL, SASL

This function returns 'true' if the regular expression as specified by `arg6` matches a value item in LDAP search. The following example shows how this can be used while writing a promise:

```
classes:
"ldap_match" =>

  regldap("ldap.mysystem.com","dc=mysystemLLC,dc=com",

    "sn=Group","gid","subtree","clark.*","none");
```

E

Pop quiz Answers

Chapter 1, Getting Started with CFEngine

- Name the core theory on which CFEngine is based.
  - **Answer**: Promise Theory
- Which file is read by `cf-agent` when run without an argument, by default?
  - **Answer**: cf-promises
- Name three promise types we came across in this chapter.
  - **Answer**: control, reports. classes
- Which directory serves as the work space for CFEngine, by default?
  - **Answer**: `/var/cfengine`

Chapter 2, Configuring Systems with CFEngine

- How can you ensure that cf-serverd always binds only to the IP 192.168.2.3 after restart or a reboot?
  - **Answer**: Use `bindtointerface` attribute as shown here

```
     bundle agent example
{
bindtointerface => "192.168.2.3";
}
```

- How can you ensure that whenever the CFEngine agent process runs it sets the default Java home to `/usr/local/jdk-1.6.0_23`?
    - **Answer**: Use the `environment` attribute as shown here

```
bundle agent example
{
environment => { "JAVA_HOME=/usr/local/jdk-1.6.0_23" };
}
```

- How can you schedule a promise to be executed at 1500 Hrs on the fifteenth day of a month if and only if the fifteenth day is a Sunday?
    - **Answer**: Use the `and` class for the common bundle promise, as shown here

```
bundle agent example
{
classes:
"myscript" and => { "Day15", "Sunday", "Hr1500"};
}
```

Chapter 3, System Audit with CFEngine

- We wrote a promise for rotating files in one of the sections above. Now, if we want to rotate the files basis size which other constraint should be used?
    - **Answer**: The `search_size` constraint for the `file_select` promise should be used
- Which promise constraint may be used for checking if any of the attributes of a file are changed?
    - **Answer**: `report_changes => "all"`
- We added a few IP addresses to the web server blacklist and now we want to remove a few of them because we don't consider them suspicious—which `edit_line` promise will you use?
    - **Answer**: `delete_select`
- We rotated a log files in one of the sections above. If we want to create a compressed backup of the log files which file promise can be used?
    - **Answer**: transformer

Chapter 4, Scheduling Tasks with CFEngine

- Given below is an example using multiple lists for iteration. Will this work?

  Please provide reasons for the success and failure.

```
bundle agent example
{
vars:
"stats" slist =>  { "value", "av", "dev" };
"inout" slist => { "in", "out" };
"monvars" slist => {"rootprocs",
                    "otherprocs",
                    "diskfree",
                    "loadavg",
                    "smtp_$(inout)",
                    "www_$(inout)",
                    "wwws_$(inout)";
reorts:
cf3::
"mon.$(stats)_$(monvars) is $(mon.$(stats)_$(monvars))";
}
```

  - **Answer**: No, it will not work because we have made multiple attempts to define the variables

- In the time class given below for a configuration file, when will cf-agent execute the file when there is no `splaytime` defined and cf-agent executes every 5 minutes. The time class is:

```
MorningShift or => { "Hr08", "Hr09", "Hr10", "Hr11", "Hr12",
"Hr13" };
```

  - **Answer**: Every five minutes starting from 0805 hrs to 1205 hrs

Chapter 5, Security Audit with CFEngine

- Which of the following functions may be used to get the UID for a named user on a host using CFEngine?
  - **Answer**: None of these

- Which of the below agent control promises may be used to get a list of compressed files that have been left by mistake by some one in your team under the web document root?
    - **Answer**: suspiciousnames
- Is CFEngine susceptible to buffer overflow attacks?
    - **Answer**: Depends on how the trust relationships are configured.
- Which promise may be used for logging all new incoming connections?
    - **Answer**: logallconnections

Chapter 6, Logging and Reporting with CFEngine

- Why is switching `full auditing` on for long durations on CFEngine not recommended?
    - **Answer**: It utilizes more CPU, memory, and disk space

Chapter 7, Workflows

- How can you pass information or arguments to cf-agent or cf-runagent?
    - **Answer**: No information can be supplied while running cf-agent or cf-runagent, all information should be written in the promise files.

Chapter 8, Advanced Functions and Variables

- When will the special function classify return true?
    - **Answer**: When the canonicalization of the argument is a currently defined class
- Which special function may be used to get a list of hosts that may have contacted the current host's CFEngine?
    - **Answer**: `hostsseen`
- In CFEngine, how can you check whether a command given was executed successfully?
    - **Answer**: **Function** `returnszero` **gives the exit status**

Chapter 9, CFEngine Best Practices

- Name the theory on which the repair and rollback mechanism for CFEngine is based.
    - **Answer**: Promise Theory
- You have a variable defined as `bundle.variable`, if we refer this as `@(bundle.variable)` somewhere else, it refers to?
    - **Answer**: Individual values of the list variable are requested

Index

Symbols

A

B

C

D

E

F

G

L

M

N

O

P

Q

R

Thank you for buying

CFEngine 3 Beginner's Guide

About Packt Publishing

Packt, pronounced 'packed', published its first book "*Mastering phpMyAdmin for Effective MySQL Management*" in April 2004 and subsequently continued to specialize in publishing highly focused books on specific technologies and solutions.

Our books and publications share the experiences of your fellow IT professionals in adapting and customizing today's systems, applications, and frameworks. Our solution based books give you the knowledge and power to customize the software and technologies you're using to get the job done. Packt books are more specific and less general than the IT books you have seen in the past. Our unique business model allows us to bring you more focused information, giving you more of what you need to know, and less of what you don't.

Packt is a modern, yet unique publishing company, which focuses on producing quality, cutting-edge books for communities of developers, administrators, and newbies alike. For more information, please visit our website: `www.packtpub.com`.

About Packt Open Source

In 2010, Packt launched two new brands, Packt Open Source and Packt Enterprise, in order to continue its focus on specialization. This book is part of the Packt Open Source brand, home to books published on software built around Open Source licences, and offering information to anybody from advanced developers to budding web designers. The Open Source brand also runs Packt's Open Source Royalty Scheme, by which Packt gives a royalty to each Open Source project about whose software a book is sold.

Writing for Packt

We welcome all inquiries from people who are interested in authoring. Book proposals should be sent to author@packtpub.com. If your book idea is still at an early stage and you would like to discuss it first before writing a formal book proposal, contact us; one of our commissioning editors will get in touch with you.

We're not just looking for published authors; if you have strong technical skills but no writing experience, our experienced editors can help you develop a writing career, or simply get some additional reward for your expertise.

[PACKT] open source
community experience distilled
PUBLISHING

Linux Shell Scripting Cookbook

ISBN: 978-1-84951-376-0   Paperback: 360 pages

Solve real-world shell scripting problems with over 110 simple but incredibly effective recipes

1. Master the art of crafting one-liner command sequence to perform tasks such as text processing, digging data from files, and lot more
2. Practical problem solving techniques adherent to the latest Linux platform
3. Packed with easy-to-follow examples to exercise all the features of the Linux shell scripting language

---

Moodle Administration

ISBN: 978-1-847195-62-3   Paperback: 376 pages

An administrator's guide to configuring, securing, customizing, and extending Moodle

1. A complete guide for planning, installing, optimizing, customizing, and configuring Moodle
2. Secure, back up, and restore your VLE
3. Extending and networking Moodle
4. Detailed walkthroughs and expert advice on best practices

Please check **www.PacktPub.com** for information on our titles

[PACKT] open source
PUBLISHING
community experience distilled

Mastering phpMyAdmin 3.3.x for Effective MySQL Management

ISBN: 978-1-84951-354-8 Paperback: 412 pages

A complete guide to get started with phpMyAdmin 3.3 and master its features

1. The best introduction to phpMyAdmin available
2. Written by the project leader of phpMyAdmin, and improved over several editions
3. A step-by-step tutorial for manipulating data with phpMyAdmin
4. Learn to do things with your MySQL database and phpMyAdmin that you didn't know were possible!

MySQL for Python

ISBN: 978-1-849510-18-9 Paperback: 440 pages

Integrate the flexibility of Python and the power of MySQL to boost the productivity of your applications

1. Implement the outstanding features of Python's MySQL library to their full potential
2. See how to make MySQL take the processing burden from your programs
3. Learn how to employ Python with MySQL to power your websites and desktop applications
4. Apply your knowledge of MySQL and Python to real-world problems instead of hypothetical scenarios

Please check **www.PacktPub.com** for information on our titles